O9-BUD-939

The Transfer of Care

The Transfer of Care

PSYCHIATRIC DEINSTITUTIONALIZATION AND ITS AFTERMATH

PHIL BROWN

DEPARTMENT OF SOCIOLOGY
BROWN UNIVERSITY

Routledge & Kegan Paul
London, Boston, Melbourne and Henley

First published in 1985
by Routledge & Kegan Paul plc

14 Leicester Square, London WC2H 7PH, England

9 Park Street, Boston, Mass. 02108, USA

464 St Kilda Road, Melbourne,
Victoria 3004, Australia and

Broadway House, Newtown Road,
Henley-on-Thames, Oxon RG9 1EN, England

Set in Times, 10 on 12 pt
by Electronic Village, Richmond, Surrey
and printed in Great Britain
by T.J. Press (Padstow) Ltd, Padstow, Cornwall

Library of Congress Cataloging in Publication Data

Brown, Phil,

The transfer of care.
Bibliography: p.
Includes indexes.
1. Mentally ill—Care and treatment—United States.
2. Mental health services—United States.
3. Mental health policy—United States.
I. Title [DNLM:
1. Deinstitutionalization—trends—United States
2. Health Policy—trends—United States
3. Mental Health Services—trends—United States
4. Mental Health Services—United States. WM 30 B878]
RA790.6.B78 1984 362.2'0973 84-9797

British Library CIP data also available

ISBN 0-7100-9900-2

Contents

Tables and Figures

Acknowledgments

I am very grateful to several friends for their aid in this book. Joseph P. Morrissey read preliminary outlines and two drafts of this book. He gave extensively of his knowledge in the many areas covered here. In conversations and written comments, Joe's interest and involvement in this book were central to its final outcome. Joe pushed me to think more analytically and theoretically on a number of issues. His prodding helped me to pursue trends which I might otherwise have underemphasized. Irving K. Zola also read and commented on the entire manuscript. His knack for drawing out the broader significance of many points was always welcome and helpful. Irv's specific comments were amplified by his long-term encouragement and support for the issues addressed herein. Carol Baker, my editor at Routledge & Kegan Paul, also read two drafts, and was involved at so many stages in the conceptualization of this book. Carol provided the right mixture of input of style, content, and guidance through the book's development. I thank these friends and colleagues very much.

Paul P. Freddolino contributed his expertise in the area of mental patients' rights in his reading of the chapter on that subject.

Judy Quattrucci and Debra Konicki patiently typed many drafts of the book, allowing me to revise as much as I wanted to.

Ronnie Littenberg, my wife, has been my most long-term reader and critic. Ronnie's reading of part of this book follows upon her reading of much of what led up to it. She has always put her utmost into thoughtful, deep analysis of this material, and into the most supportive encouragement I could ask for. Michael Zachary Littenberg-Brown, my son, has lived through the duration of the writing of this book. Michael was born one week after final arrangements for the book's contract were made. During his infant sleeping periods I began to outline and write. As he progressed into toddlerhood I revised incessantly. The new excitement and joy of Michael's life has imprinted itself upon this book's own birth. In deep respect and love, I dedicate this book to Ronnie and Michael.

PART I

The Crisis in Mental Health Care and the Formation of a National Mental Health Policy

CHAPTER 1

Current Problems and General Progress in Mental Health Care

Mental health planners and providers have usually considered current trends in psychiatric services to be a path of continuing progress from a backward, dehumanizing past to a progressive, humanistic present. Good intentions, a belief in the progress of knowledge and practice, and a lack of clear vision of the pitfalls continue to hinder professionals' awareness of the mental health care system. Caught in the middle of the system's workings and trying to function within so many constraints, providers and planners are unlikely to develop an accurate picture of the system's problems and limitations. To protect themselves and prevent burnout, they may emphasize the positive aspects of policy, even if those positive aspects are more likely goals than actual outcomes.

To the general observer, however, the psychiatric system looks very different. She or he is likely to perceive public mental health care as a continual failure which eats up large portions of state and federal spending, while resulting in a growing corps of urban bag people and increase in ex-patient criminal activity. The average citizen may be bothered by homeless psychotics in bus stations and fear that community residences will reduce property values and threaten the safety of their children.

Neither the relatively optimistic views of the professional nor the exaggerated anxiety of the public are accurate, though certainly each has some truth for the believer. Moving away from these caricatures we can turn to the general crisis in mental health services to describe the crisis and offer an analysis of its causes. As one of the major elements of social spending and one of the most problematic social issues, mental health care requires a comprehensive analysis.

In recent years, mental health policy and treatment have been criticized from many sides. Criticism has come from within the mental health fields, from various parts of state and federal governments, from patients and ex-patients, civil liberties organizations, lay mental health groups, trade unions, media, academia, the public interest bar, and the judicial bench.

Within the mental health field, studies of specific problems, such as lack of coordination between facilities, reimbursement problems, or underfunding usually examine a single agency or small segment of the psychiatric system. While the accumulation of such studies accounts for substantial criticism, there are no comprehensive critiques. Government reports have been very important in detailing problems, even if they don't examine their fundamental causes. Most notable are various studies by the Congress's General Accounting Office (GAO), an investigation by the Inspector-General of the Department of Health, Education, and Welfare (now the Department of Health and Human Services), reports of Congressional committees, studies produced under contract to the National Institute of Mental Health (NIMH), and the voluminous reports of the President's Commission on Mental Health (PCMH).

Civil liberties groups, public interest lawyers, consumer interest groups, and mental patients' rights organizations have contributed a major element of criticism. They range from the Nader-sponsored report on NIMH (Chu & Trotter, 1974) to compendia of legal rights and advocacy material (Friedman, 1979) to a wealth of literature by patient and ex-patient activists (e.g. Chamberlin, 1978). In academia, criticism has been voiced by psychiatric sociology as well as by clinical and community psychology. As will be argued in this book, this array of popular forces has played a significant role in the critique and reform of mental health policy, though this has not usually been recognized by mental health professionals.

Lay mental health groups, trade unions of mental health workers, and the media have also contributed to the growing understanding that there are many deficiencies in the system. They do this in somewhat opposite fashion: Mental Health Associations (MHAs) tend to share the moderated criticism offered by mental health professionals, while some unions and the media often focus on the more alarming aspects of psychiatric policy, such as violent crimes by ex-patients. As will be discussed later, not all unions act this way, at least not all the time, and they do have many legitimate complaints about the outcome of public mental health directions.

Let us turn to a brief overview of the general critique of mental health policy and practices. Community Mental Health Centers (CMHCs), designed to be a thoroughly new and innovative program, have been criticized for delivering insufficient care to discharged chronic hospital patients, for failure to coordinate services with nearby state hospitals. State hospitals, which were supposed to have been improved while being gradually phased out, remained expensive, inefficient, and in poor condition and their phase-out was not adequately planned. The many new community facilities, which were to provide community-based services to psychiatric patients, have been found to be in short supply. And among those community facilities which proliferated, most are nursing homes which have been targeted for not providing conditions sufficiently advanced over the old state hospital back wards.

Various mental health agencies and facilities failed to coordinate their activities with one another, and state and federal mental health officials were criticized for not providing that coordination. Federal officials were faulted for not carrying out a nationally unified plan; state mental health departments were faulted for not adequately transforming their institutional networks into community networks.

Mental health providers were found to have slighted certain populations very much in need: children, the elderly, racial minorities, the poor in general, rural citizens, and those with physical disabilities. Too little emphasis was placed on preventive mental health programs, a largely unproven strategy, but one which 1950s and 1960s planners felt to be valuable. There has been inadequate protection of hospital workers' jobs and of the jobs and businesses of small communities dependent on hospitals which were phased out. The rights of patients have not been being given sufficient safeguards or positive action. Cultural and political critiques have charged that the mental health system uncritically accepts prevailing class, gender, race, and professionalist social structures. Obviously not all the critics agree on the details or extent of the criticism. Certainly they do not share consensus on the causes of the problems. Indeed, this divergence makes for a more difficult task of comprehensive analysis.

The flaws in mental health services should not be allowed to mask the progress in psychiatric care. Great changes have occurred in the psychiatric landscape in the post-World War II era. Mostly this happened in the 1950s with the expansion of milieu-type therapy and other active approaches, with the advent of psychoactive drugs, and with humanitarian orientations to patient life. The 1955 peak of 559,000 state hospital inpatients fell to approximately 137,810 in 1980. A person diagnosed psychotic in a state hospital in 1950 would stay there for an average of twenty years, a neurotic for nine years. In 1975, the duration of inpatient treatment for psychotics averaged nine months, while the outpatient treatment for neurotics averaged five months. By 1980, state hospital average length of stay was slightly over six months. In facilities which treat the majority of inpatients — general hospitals — average length of stay is only 11.6 days (Kiesler and Sibulkin, 1982). Outpatient treatment was rare in the immediate postwar years, but has risen 1000 per cent to the point where five times as many new psychiatric admissions are to outpatient services as to inpatient ones (Redlich and Kellert, 1978; Kiesler, 1982c). State hospitals in 1977 accounted for 9 per cent, rather than the 1955 figure of 49 per cent of all psychiatric episodes. (An episode is a period of treatment in any service during the reporting year which is begun by an admission or transfer, and terminated by a discontinuation or transfer. Episodes are counted even if the patient has been treated in the service at a prior time in the same year, and thus represents a duplicated count.) Community mental health centers, a new phenomenon of the mid-1960s, handle nearly one-third of all episodes (Witkin, 1980). Looking at only inpatient episodes, we see important changes in the location of mental health care. State hospitals and private asylums in 1979 accounted for only 25 per cent of the nation's 3,012,500 inpatient episodes. General hospitals (with and without psychiatric units), however, accounted for 60 per cent of total episodes. Looking only at general hospitals without psychiatric units, we find those facilities alone care for 40 per cent of all inpatient episodes; these have become the largest site of inpatient treatment. NIMH's claim that inpatient admissions remained stable from 1965 to 1979 err, since those data exclude general hospitals without psychiatric units.

These changes in practice were both a cause and a result of major alterations in psychiatric and psychological ideologies. Rather than warehousing and forgetting about patients, mental health professionals and planners sought less total institutional settings, developed rehabilitation programs, and introduced preventive mental health education. These changes were part of what has often been called the 'third mental health revolution' due to the deep critique of past practices and promulgation of drastically new methods. (Pinel's eighteenth-century reforms are considered to be the first revolution, followed by the second revolution of Freudian psychoanalysis). The critique of custodialism was very significant in the 1950s and 1960s, particularly through scholarly books such as Greenblatt et al.'s *From Custodial to Therapeutic Patient Care in Mental Hospitals* (1955) and Goffman's *Asylums* (1961), and through popular exposés such as Albert Deutsch's *The Shame of the States* (1948) and Mike Gorman's *Every Other Bed* (1956). Maltreatment of patients through overcrowding, inadequate living space, poor food, and physical abuse was shown to be prevalent in all state hospitals. Even in highly reputed private facilities, such as those studied by Stanton and Schwartz (1954), dehumanization and depersonalization of patients were antagonistic to therapy and rehabilitation. The critique of custodialism was accompanied by attempts to lessen the stigma of mental illness. This was done partly by education, but mainly by the expansion of types and numbers of facilities (e.g., outpatient care, day treatment, halfway houses, community mental health centers) so that treatment was seen as far more varied than primary long-term warehousing in state asylums.

After World War II and the fight against the inhumanity of fascism, it was hard for many people to tolerate the state hospitals as they were. And memories of poverty in the Depression may have enabled people to sympathize with the plight of locked up mental patients. If this appears to assume too much public awareness, it was an awareness that the mental health lobby believed in. Certainly there was some increase in public support for psychiatric services. More importantly, mental health lobby members convinced professional colleagues and government officials that such support existed. Additionally, professionals and government officials learned many lessons from wartime military mental health services; for instance, milieu therapy, brief treatment, and rapid training of caregivers. And, as in World War I, large numbers of psychiatrically impaired soldiers fueled a fear of excessive prevalence of mental illness. These lessons provided the necessary background for a major reorganization of mental health services.

As World War II ended, the 'mental health lobby' coalesced. Legislators, governors, mental health professionals, philanthropists, lay reformers, professional organizations, and government agencies became involved (Connery, 1968; Foley, 1975). The lobby embarked on a most dramatic path: it formulated and sought to implement a mental health policy unprecedented in scope, an attempt at a unified national policy. As this book will argue, this was an *attempt* which never succeeded. And, despite claims of officials and planners, the attempt was never a unified one.

ORGANIZING THEMES

We are now experiencing the medium- and long-range results of that attempt, as well as the prior faults of the mental health care system. As highlighted earlier in this chapter, there have been a number of major shifts in the types and locations of mental health care. These shifts resulted from fiscal realities, as well as conscious efforts to alter the nature of psychiatric services. In this process, the traditional state hospital inpatient wards no longer occupied first place as the primary location of mental health care. CMHCs, general hospitals, outpatient clinics, private psychiatric hospitals, and nursing and boarding homes grew in importance. The clearly defined two-class system of public and private care also became less distinct, as public funds and private insurance opened up private facilities to a wider range of persons, and as new forms of government health planning intervened to coordinate a new *public-private allied sector.*

This set of circumstances can be understood as various types of *transfer of care.* This transfer of care has several negative aspects. Given the widespread dissatisfaction with the previous array of mental health services, and given the dramatic promises of the new mental health lobby, much more progress should have occurred. Also, despite various shifts within the multi-faceted mental health system, professional privilege, institutional conservatism, and drastic underfunding continue to dominate the environment.

There has been a transfer of chronic patient care from the mental health system to other social service systems and to non-system settings. Deinstitutionalization of state hospital patients represents an attempted transfer of financial responsibility from state mental health budgets to federal Medicaid and Social Security Supplemental Security Income budgets. The relocation of chronic psychotics to nursing homes, boarding homes, flop houses, and the street represents a transfer of social responsibility from professional psychiatric providers to low quality, non-psychiatric facilities. This relocation is a transfer of responsibility from public authority to private control. Even though there is government regulation of nursing homes (but very little regulation of boarding homes), that regulation is less authoritative than is governmental power in direct service. Further, it is a transfer of responsibility from state mental health departments to public health and public welfare departments. This transfer results in less attention to the psychiatric and psychological needs of patients, since those other departments may be very concerned with official inspection checklists and reimbursement practices. Of course, patients need a wide range of social services — housing, health care, food assistance, income supports, recreation, rehabilitation, and employment training. If the welfare and health departments provided those services, these would be important adjuncts to psychological services. Indeed, for many chronic psychotics, those other social services are often the most important ones. True, the old system provided sparse therapeutic treatment, but it did house, feed, and otherwise care for the patients, even if poorly. This is not an apology for the comprehensive custodial asylum, but rather an expectation that much more should have been done in the recent decades of mental health reform. It also contributes to a transformation of the public perception of clients from mental patients to welfare cases, thus demeaning them even more than they already are. As is most evident in nursing and boarding homes, the transfer of care often involves a shift of location, yet retains traditional forms of personal control and institutional rigidity.

In terms of acute care (and some chronic care) there has been a shift within the mental health system. This has involved the growth of private sector care (especially general hospital psychiatric care) to replace and/or augment public services. Even though this has largely centered around a new public-private alliance, it is a transfer of power and authority to a private sector which is less accountable to government and public scrutiny.

Some of these transfers of care have been intended, while others have been wholly or largely unintended. *The Transfer of Care* will provide a comprehensive analysis of these phenomena. This analysis is unique in that it conceptualizes mental health practices as the result of three main structural forces which operate at different levels on the mental health system and/or on the larger society: 1) political-economic factors which operate on both the mental health level and the social level; 2) professionalist forces, which function primarily at the level of the mental health system but are part of a generally accepted societal faith in professionalism; and 3) institutional factors which operate primarily at the level of the psychiatric system and its individual facilities. These three influences often interact with each other. Within these three organizing themes, especially that of political economy, I also locate another important element of this book — the *role of popular forces* in the critique and restructuring of mental health policy.

I will first provide an overview of the three organizing themes. Following that I will explore conceptions of mental health *policy*, since much of the analysis presented here turns on what extent of policy — if any — actually exists in the mental health field.

Political-Economic Forces

In recent years a rich tradition of political-economic analyses of the health care system has emerged. A good deal of this perspective may be applied to the mental health system as well. Political-economic approaches argue that the health care system cannot be viewed in isolation, but that it must be understood as arising from underlying elements of the social structure. The pioneering work of the Health Policy Advisory Committee (Health-PAC) emphasized the profit motive by which health care services enrich large sectors of capital in the pharmaceutical, medical supply and equipment, insurance, and finance industries. Through the economic and political power of these firms, and through the political power of the professional and institutional components of the health system, medical institutions exert enormous political power. For example, hospital expansion may displace poor and working class people; private hospitals are able to replace municipal ones at the expense of serving the very needy; drug firms can profit from dangerous products. Despite the nonprofit status of most hospitals, profit is generated through their consumption of medical commodities. Further, both well-known research hospitals and community hospitals seek to attract better staff and to fill beds by attracting patients. This results in competition for newer facilities and more modern equipment, even if this equipment receives less than optimal use. Such processes lead to extremely high inflation in the health sector, approximately double that of the economy as a whole (Ehrenreich and Ehrenreich, 1970; Kotelchuck, 1976).

Political-economic approaches argue that the role of the federal government is integral in the organization, regulation, and financing of health services. This is particularly evident with reimbursement mechanisms of Medicare and Medicaid, and in the role of research and institutional support from a variety of government bodies such as the National Institutes of Health and the National Institute of Mental Health. Although much power remains in the hands of professionals and institutions, state and federal controls have made important alterations in health care (Navarro, 1976). As will be evident, this governmental role is very central to mental health services. This government involvement may be positive, such as when it expands accessibility to underserved populations and breaks down local and state racist discrimination. But federal health care intervention can have negative effects, such as when it bureaucratizes services or restricts them due to fiscal austerity measures.

According to political-economic analyses, health professions and institutions function to reinforce and replicate existing class, gender, and race stratification. This may occur due to unequal provision of health services, as well as due to pre-existing structural forces which produce differential well-being. Stratification also stems from biased treatment, a phenomenon most clearly studied in regard to women's health issues, such as obstetric and gynecological care (Wertz and Wertz, 1977; Dreifus, 1977; Doyall, 1981). Related to the continuation of race, class, and gender inequality is the professionalist monopoly of knowledge (which will be treated as a separate but related theme) and the individualist conception of health problems. This individualist ideology blames people for their health status, rather than locating the causes of ill health largely in the society's structural forces (Ryan, 1972; Navarro, 1976; Crawford, 1979).

The problems mentioned above are exacerbated by the fragmented nature of the health care system. Due to governmental conservatism and physicians' fears of loss of power and wealth, there exists no national health plan. This shortcoming exacerbates the existing problems and generates a multitude of very short-range and partial solutions, such as 'determination of need' (DON) programs and frequent revisions of Medicaid eligibility. As Ryan (1972) notes, human services in this society are governed by 'particularist' rather than 'universal' criteria, and are meliorative rather than preventive. The political-economic analysis of social services augments the political-economic perspective on health care, since it deals with the whole complex of human services. Piven and Cloward (1971) advanced the viewpoint that social welfare programs are a necessary function for capitalist societies in that they regulate the labor force and provide responses to social unrest. This is relevant to mental health concerns because the 1963 and 1965 Community Mental Health Centers Acts were components of the larger social welfare package of the New Frontier/Great Society programs of Presidents Kennedy and Johnson. Psychiatric facilities certainly had their own problems which required reform, with or without a larger social welfare context. But the 1960s welfare state initiatives allowed psychiatric restructuring to advance much further than if left to its own devices.

While the political-economy perspective is employed here to analyze recent mental health trends, it is useful to note that political-economic forces have always played a strong role in the provision of psychiatric carc. Foucault (1971) and Rosen (1968) have discussed the creation of the European asylum in the seventeenth and eighteenth centuries as a response to the economic dislocation of early industrialism and the political unrest associated with that process. Rothman (1971) has done similar work on the nineteenth-century American asylum. If political-economic *origins* of the mental hospital are not always clear, the *ongoing effects* of such social forces are. Rothman (1971;1980), Morrissey et al. (1980), and Scull (1981a) have shown how changes in the economic life and political structure have led to changes within institutions and in whole institutional systems. Such changes include new financing mechanisms, curtailment of expansion of facilities, differential treatment of immigrants, and the development of public-private splits in mental health care.

Professionalist factors

Medical and psychiatric sociology have put much effort into studying professional development. In fact, the medical profession is often used as a prototype for studying other professions. Central to this area of work is the notion that the medical profession's skills and knowledge are not entirely scientific and unchallengeable, and that medical practice may mask and perpetuate oppressive social structures. This holds true for psychology as well, and this book considers professionalist forces to be common to psychiatry and psychology, even if the former is more powerful.

Historically, the mental health field has had a tradition of employing its power to enforce the existing social order. Nineteenth-century psychiatry applied medical concepts to defend slavery, oppose women's rights, and attack immigration (Chesler, 1973; Thomas and Sillen, 1972). Such social control was by no means restricted to the last century. The entire body of anti-psychiatry critiques developed in the 1960s and 1970s exposed the many past and present problems in mental health theory and practice. Critics such as Laing (1959), Szasz (1961), Scheff (1966), and Leifer (1969) have explored how professional definitions of mental disorder frequently focus solely on the individual, with little regard for social factors. Further, these critics argue, the professional definitions of what constitutes a psychological problem often lead to labeling other social problems as mental health problems. This expansion of the psychiatric domain proved to be very important in community mental health programs, as Chapter 3 will discuss.

Expanded definitions of mental disorder are problematic since they may be unwarranted intrusions into other areas of personal life. Also, they may be based on incorrect diagnosis. Rosenhan (1973) and Temerlin (1968) have demonstrated the manners in which institutional structures and prestige suggestion can cause misdiagnosis. This problem of diagnostic bias, along with the race, sex, and gender issues mentioned earlier, point to the flaws in psychiatry's myth of value-neutrality. Antipsychiatric critiques of professionalism also emphasized the impersonal detachment and authoritarianism of much therapeutic interaction (Laing, 1959; Cooper, 1967); these problems mirrored many flaws in mental institutions, as pointed out by the widespread critique of custodialism.

New directions in mental health practices would need to take into account the above issues if deep alterations were to be made. But the mental health field has not changed so dramatically in its fundamentals. Services and personnel expanded, but there were few alternatives to ingrained traditions of caregiving. Freidson's (1970) work on professional dominance argues that physicians seek to solidify and expand their status, power, and wealth through a monopoly of knowledge and skills. This often takes precedence over what one might prefer to be mainly patient-oriented goals. In conjunction with the institutional forces to be discussed next, professionalist factors often impinge on quality care through selective choices of who will receive care, and what kind of care they will receive. Another aspect of the professional-institutional linkage is the use by professionals of new mental health programs and government aid in the 1960s as vehicles for advancing their professions.

The Institutional Framework

In studying the institutional forces operating on the mental health system, there is relevant material at several levels: the individual facility, groups of facilities, and the system as a whole. While this book is more concerned with groups of facilities and the entire system, what happens in individual institutions is both cause and effect of the other levels.

At the system level, this book looks at the attempted creation of a national mental health policy and at the various overarching elements of existing services. It is therefore important to trace the development of the mental health lobby and its widespread influence. This book also puts forth the notion that most state mental health systems faced and dealt with relatively similar problems at approximately the same time; further, this was potentiated by federal efforts via the National Institute of Mental Health. Also at the system level is the issue of psychiatric expansionism, whereby mental health agencies and institutions widened their nets to cover a variety of larger social problems and to increase the supply of clinicians, researchers, and their training and work sites in academic and caregiving institutions (Chu and Trotter, 1974).

At the level of the individual facility, we are confronted with many forms of uncertainty and unclarity, problems which also affect the whole system. Perrow (1963) has emphasized the 'multiple leadership' which characterizes general hospital structure. This multiple leadership derives from the co-existence of a small number of centers of power which seek to achieve their own goals, goals which are themselves imprecise. Perrow noted that this multiple leadership could cause accommodation to group interests, which could lead to organizational drift or opportunism and to the lack of long-range planning. It could also lead to the compromising of the hospital's original goals. The hospital is a likely site for multiple leadership due to the power bases of trustees, physicians, and administrators. Strauss et al. (1963) add to this a 'multiplicity of purposes': not only do groups have differing goals *between* them, but there is also variability *within* groups due to competing professional orientations, work habits in their institutional practice, and extent of practice outside the institution. Strauss et al. also pay attention to nonprofessional staff groups and to patients as a group. Altogether, then, there is a 'negotiated order' in the psychiatric (or other) hospital as daily life goes on. The apparent common goal in the psychiatric hospital is 'to return patients to the outside world in better shape.' But while 'This goal is the symbolic cement that, metaphorically speaking, holds the organization together,' this symbol in fact 'masks a considerable measure of disagreement and discrepant purpose.'

At various times there is a 'periodic appraisal process' which Strauss and his colleagues view as a mechanism by which the 'daily negotiative process' is regularized in 'long-standing policy.' There are often specific points of such regularization; for instance, the death of a chief of staff might be the occasion to re-evaluate past and present negotiation between medical and administrative priorities (Perrow, 1963).

In Perrow's (1979) later work, drift of goals is less important than a pre-existing divergence of goals which involved some not even apparently part of the institutional fabric. We err in searching for bureaucratic rationality and for specific goals when studying human services:

> *Public service organizations such as schools, hospitals, and armies are under little constraint to achieve 'official' goals, since their outputs are hard to measure and their real value lies in the multitudes of usages that groups outside them and within them can put them to. (Perrow, 1979: 245).*

In this sense, then, organizations are interactive and fragmented, rather than rational, and they include 'large opportunities for accident and short-term opportunism.' The bureaucratic ideal of objective, universalistic, and rational criteria is not typically operative. Instead, there are many particularist elements of organizational style which are used to pursue many goals other than those which are officially stated or assumed.

Morrissey et al. (1980) emphasize the multiple usages of state hospitals. They find that the state hospital serves many different groups, and does not have a uniform goal of treating patients in the best possible fashion. An extension of this application can be made to the entirety of mental health services. The development of a 'mental health lobby' or 'mental health establishment,' as will be addressed later in the book, produced a large number of persons and groups with vested interests in maintaining the *system* of services, even if they did not share a uniform set of *goals*. For instance, a general hospital may wish to preserve Community Mental Health Center funding since that money fills some of the hospital's psychiatric beds; administrators may constantly support new demonstration projects as a mechanism for providing a continual stream of 'soft' money into the facility or agency; union officials and members may oppose deinstitutionalization for fear of job loss and union membership loss. In these three examples, one could expect in some cases that there might be a congruence of these organizational goals with other goals of positive patient care. This is not, however, to be automatically assumed. If anything, the agglomeration of policies and programs may have resulted in a situation in all social services where general social goals are increasingly hidden by special interest goals.

This should not be read as an argument for the existence of 'pluralism.' There remain the dominant social values and structures which have been mentioned earlier; the dynamics of the mental health system and other social service systems tend to reinforce and reproduce existing class, gender, race, and professionalist power. To the extent that some persons and programs of a critical nature enter into the picture, they are a minority of participants who are often constrained to act through proper channels. Since rational and equitable social planning rarely occurs, individual policies have effects which are divergent from original goals. This holds true for the largest levels of national planning, as well as for specific areas such as mental health.

It is interesting to note that a number of studies of mental hospital structure have found that the apparently centralized hierarchy was in fact somewhat decentralized, with much daily control in the hands of nurses and aides (Belknap, 1956; Strauss et al., 1964; Perrucci, 1974). Other research has found that patients themselves exert a good deal of influence, even if on minor events, and are often an important source of information for staff (Braginsky, Braginsky, and Ring, 1969; Perrucci, 1974). While it is important to take into consideration this diversity of knowledge and power, it still remains that the hospital is a custodial, often counter-therapeutic place. The freedom that staff and patients have to act is therefore still constrained and delimited freedom. Still, it is useful to know about the limited autonomy of staff and patients, in order to understand the difficulties in implementing administrative change, which typically begins from the higher professional and/or administrative levels. With a multiplicity of group actors, new methods may be thwarted in the actual treatment and/or the evaluation of the treatment. Innovative personnel practices may be countered by employee work habits. Such problems do fit with this book's overall assumptions, though, since the fragmentation of the psychiatric institutions is in this case self-perpetuating. Overall, the uncertainty of goals and structures in the individual institution thwarts concerted planning and coordination at the group and system levels.

At the level of groups of institutions, this poor planning and coordination has jeopardized many attempts at comprehensive service delivery. The CMHC program counted on most centers to be collaborative arrangements between several pre-existing services. But divergent goals within each organization made it difficult to specify what exactly any one agency would do. Added to this is the problem of boundary conflicts between facilities. Greenley and Kirk (1973) have developed a useful approach which sees some agencies as having 'high boundary control' and others as having 'low boundary control.' High boundary control agencies — usually in the private sector — are able to select the best clients and to regulate inter-agency relations. Low boundary control agencies — usually in the public sector — have less client selection discretion and less control of inter-agency relations. These imbalances have produced many barriers to effective cooperation, as Morrissey at al. (1980) demonstrated in the case of mental health services in Worcester, Massachusetts.

Also relevant here is the Health-PAC analysis of 'medical empires,' whereby a university medical school and its major affiliated teaching hospitals control much of an area's health facilities. Such control may sometimes promote increased and improved services, but it may also sacrifice certain services (typically outpatient clinics which produce relatively low revenue) to the empire's other goals (such as specialized treatment and research activities).

These aspects of the institutional framework — individual, group, and system — interact with each other, as well as with both political-economic factors and professionalist forces. An example of the critique of custodialism can demonstrate these linkages, as well as introduce the discussion of what is mental health policy.

The critique of custodialism has been one of the major aspects of institutional analysis in the mental health field. Recapturing a reform impulse from the eighteenth and nineteenth centuries in Europe and the U.S., mental health professionals in the 1950s devoted much attention to the iatrogenic and dehumanizing nature of state hospital care. Belknap (1956), Goffman (1961), Strauss et al. (1964), and other social scientists and clinicans described the poor conditions of public mental health care and the ways in which such care was harmful to the patient. Hospital life inculcated institutionalized characteristics which robbed people of self-esteem and made them incapable of most autonomous activity. These behavioral scientific analyses were quite similar in ideology to the more popular, muckraking work of journalists (Deutsch, 1948) and lobbyists (Gorman, 1956), but they went further in that they described the actual mechanisms of hospital life. In a short span this anticustodialism became widely accepted in professional and governmental circles, and informed the planning by the National Institute of Mental Health and the Joint Commission on Mental Illness and Health. This acceptance led to a basic consensus on new forms of psychiatric care, thus changing a very old pattern. Attempts were begun to improve individual hospitals, and to restructure the whole system, including the development of alternatives to hospitalization.

To be sure, anticustodial perspectives existed before. Morrissey and Goldman (1980a) have written of Merrick Bemis's nineteenth-century attempt to pursue a cottage system of community care in Massachusetts based on the Geel colony in Belgium. Despite the apparently beneficial aspects of this model, a leading psychiatrist, Pliny Earle, successfully organized his colleagues to fight Bemis's plan for fear that the resulting decentralization would encroach on the asylum superintendents' power. Public officials agreed with Earle's opinion that a decentralized hospital would increase, rather than decrease costs, and that it would provide a dangerous amount of liberty for patients (Grob, 1966: 218-220). At the time, mental hospital superintendents were a very powerful force, and their restrictive professional association fought against proposals for public interest involvement (e.g. commitment law reform). The superintendents' group concentrated on increasing professional status and power, and in maintaining their autocratic, architecturally rigid, well-ordered asylums. In recent decades, too, as this book will argue, anticustodialism has been blocked by political pressures, economic forces, and social choices. But of perhaps greater interest, the ideology of anticustodialism would not have received the support it did had it not been for the grave economic threat posed by growing state hospital censuses.

In looking at anticustodialism as a confluence of political-economic, professional, and institutional forces, we see in anticustodialism the hint of a mental health *policy*. Let us now explore whether or not alterations in mental health services in the post-World War II era do in fact represent a coherent policy.

IS THERE A MENTAL HEALTH POLICY?

Mental health services in the post-World War II period may appear as more policy-directed than earlier periods, because that was the first time that the federal government took on a role as a policy-maker. Previously, states' provision of public mental hospitals was a checkerboard of divergent approaches. Still, state systems had policies of their own, and often shared similarities. Legislative and administrative debates over hospital construction and financing, relations between jails and hospitals, admissions practices, commitment statutes, and orientation towards immigrants have been well described by Rothman (1971; 1980) and Grob (1966; 1973). These same issues have returned in the period under discussion here, providing evidence that recent policy matters are by no means new. Rather, this is evidence that there are repetitive 'cycles of institutional reform' in the mental health arena (Morrissey et al., 1980).

But the federal role in mental health planning and financing has brought these issues to light in a more national fashion. National legislation and appropriations have involved far more people and institutions, with more at stake. Perhaps federal mental health policy would not have become so noticeable if not for the fact that its cornerstone — the Community Mental Health Centers (CMHC) program — was part of the 1960s New Frontier/Great Society complex of social welfare programs, the largest such effort since the New Deal of the 1930s. At the same time, state deinstitutionalization practices became just as noticeable. These actions came to look like a policy because they occurred in many states at roughly the same time, and were coterminous with the CMHC program. Further, both state and federal efforts manifested the underlying problems of public mental health care — lack of adequate planning, dramatically rising costs, uncertainty over treatment methods, and growing professional and public criticism of traditional custodial institutions.

For a definition of policy, we will use David Gil's (1976) approach to *social policy* in general. From that background we will examine some specific elements of mental health policy, as well as other human services policies which can be applied to mental health.

Gil notes that most discussion of social policy separates social welfare services from economic issues. The focus, then, is on specific programs oriented toward specific social problems. But for Gil this is inadequate, since social policy means the totality of how a society deals with its social and economic relations. In this sense, he writes that 'social policies are, therefore, not merely potential solutions of social problems but are also their powerful underlying causes' (Gil, 1976:3-10). Gil begins by defining *policies* as 'guiding principles or courses of action adopted and pursued by societies and their governments, as well as by various groups or units within societies.' These policies govern, or attempt to govern, domains of a society, a process which may or not be legally codified (12). But *social policies* are special types of policies:

> *policies which deliberately pertain to the quality of life and to the circumstances of living in society, and of intrasocietal relationships among individuals, groups, and society as a whole. And any specific social policy, irrespective of its unique content, objectives, and scope, is thus one discrete instance of this type of policy (13).*

According to Gil's framework, there are three major mechanisms through which all social policies develop. First, *resource development* involves the basic resources needed for survival. Second, *division of labor* deals with the breakdown of tasks and roles by which society is maintained and reproduced. Third, *rights distribution* includes the allocation of resources and privileges in the society (15-16). Gil's formulation is valuable because it grounds social policy in the primary economic, political, and work status elements of society.

Policy, then, is largely a matter of examining actual practices and the forces behind them. Within this formulation we can locate legislation, actions of administrative planning bodies, financing mechanisms, activities of professionals and professional organizations, citizen and industry lobbying, philanthropic activities, patients' rights activism, and many other phenomena. From this examination we can understand how and why the forces in the mental health field operate. This understanding can be applied toward current and future attempts to be more comprehensive in planning, equitable in service delivery, and knowledgeable in dealing with the underlying social determinants.

It may be argued that in actuality, there have been *competing policies*, using a restricted meaning of policy as programming. As will be pointed out often in this book, spokespeople for CMHCs and state hospitals were typically at odds with each other, if in fact they were even communicating at all. Within the federal orbit, the CMHC emphasis on outpatient and preventive care was countered by Medicare and Medicaid reimbursement practices which encouraged inpatient care. Within state governments, deinstitutionalization was often thwarted by legislative refusal to allow mental health departments to transfer state hospital savings to community care budget lines.

Yet despite such counterforces, there is a broad notion held by many involved in mental health services: older state mental hospitals were at best custodial and more typically were harmful; these should be replaced, as widely as possible, with a new system whereby inpatient treatment would be a minority of services, and both outpatient and structured community living would become dominant. If we could pursue an ideal view of policy, this might approximate *stated* mental health policy in the last three decades. Spinning off from this basic concern were issues of providing more and better technologies and modes of care. Federal research and educational training funds were crucial here, even if most of that support did not result in direct benefits for federally funded CMHCs. The above example of the critique of custodialism and its earlier defeat is but one case out of many where the overall social goals of better patient care are not attained. Perrow (1979) might argue that this was due to the initial existence of several sets of goals, whereas the 'institutional school,' which Perrow criticizes, might consider it an example of subversion of an original consensual goal.

While Perrow is generally correct in addressing the issue of multiple goals, we must observe that mental health planners and their governmental and philanthropic allies have *claimed* to seek a coherent set of policy goals. NIMH and other federal planning documents reveal this notion of coherent and rational policy-making. Studies of the policy and history of community mental health (e.g. Connery et al., 1968; Foley, 1975; Bloom, 1975; Wagenfeld and Jacobs, 1982) also emphasize this coherence. Key CMHC planners' retrospective analyses of the period likewise argue for a rational, comprehensive policy approach. Stanley Yolles (1975), past NIMH chief, wrote that the community centers were to be a *national* public policy, 'the first national effort to create a nationwide network of mental health services.' President Kennedy (1963) stated that the goal was a 'national mental health program to assist in the inauguration of a wholly new emphasis and approach to care for the mentally ill.' This approach involved prevention, increased research and personnel, service improvements (in state hospitals) and service innovation (especially CMHCs). Foley (1975: 76) argues that the CMHC Act was a 'new innovative policy...The policy was nonincremental. The mental health leaders had recommended a *national* community mental health care system, a totally new concept' (original emphasis). Foley (137-142) believes that the 'mental health oligopoly' successfully centralized power via NIMH and with the aid of presidential and bureaucratic initiative. In this way, the oligopoly pursued a cohesive, rational policy. While Foley did not see this as a completely centralized decision-making process, it was, he thought, a 'partisan oligopoly' with a professional lobby at its core. Unlike Foley's focus on the federal CMHC Acts of 1963 and 1965, Connery (1968: 546-564) examined six state community mental health programs. He, too, found professionals to play the main role in leading a plurality of group interests.

The point of the above material on perceived goals — at the time and in retrospect — is to show that there were *beliefs* in coherent, national policy, and perhaps even *attempts* at such planning. Even if these were idealist initiatives, enough people have conceived of these plans as large-scale, long-term policy so that the conception has taken on a life of its own. Certainly these persons failed to see the multiple functions of mental health services and varying agendas of interest groups in the field. Rothman (1980) has observed that such naivete has characterized mental health reform efforts throughout U.S. history. If reformers were unable to grasp the complexity of mental health restructuring, then they might not understand why their efforts bore too little success. Reform pressures alone would not alter such an entrenched system. Much of this book deals with the contradictory beliefs and programs of the reformers, and with the structural forces which thwarted them.

It may appear too easy to criticize the actors now for lack of foresight two and three decades earlier. There is more to be learned by examining the other social structural elements which, largely unbeknownst to the leaders, played an equal role in psychiatric reform. This is a more useful lesson precisely because no matter what new psychological theories, psychiatric technologies, and sociological knowledge we now have, future change efforts can still be derailed by forces which may never enter into professionals' awareness.

Major reports, such as the Comptroller-General's (1977) report for the GAO, the Senate Subcommittee on Long-Term Care (1976) and the Report to the President of the President's Commission on Mental Health (1978) have made it clear that mental health efforts are characterized by lack of coordination among a multitude of separate agencies, and a wide degree of poor implementation of mental health goals. In this light, is it accurate to discuss mental health *policy*? If all the agencies involved did not pursue a unified set of goals, can we call their disparate practices a policy?

DiNitto and Dye (1983: 3-11) argue against those who demand that a set of specific goals be evident in order to demonstrate the existence of social policy. Such a perspective, they argue, presupposes a well-planned, rational policy based on consensual values. Yet policy making is not so well-planned in reality. Further, policy-making is more political than scientific-rational. This results from the conflicting values of groups in an unequal social structure where there are no consensual values, no common recognition of social problem areas, and thus no agreed-upon solutions. Bureaucratic inertia and lack of coordination between agencies also mitigates comprehensive planning. Additionally, those who make and carry out policy often have their own self-interest and biases which prevent the clear implementation of policies that may have been mandated in a more specific sense. Due to these considerations, much public policy is *incremental* in that existing programs are changed, or even replaced, but no new developments truly take place from the ground up.

Vladeck (1980) emphasizes that health policy is marked by 'interest group incrementalism,' though not all interest groups have equal power. His particular focus — the growth of the nursing and boarding home industry — demonstrates that the dominant profit motive, in the hands of smart entrepreneurs, has been able to transform the U.S. health care system by adding to it a vast new set of facilities.

As Dye (1972:2) sees it, we can rarely visualize a governmental goal; we can only witness what a government actually does. Therefore,

> *Realistically, our notion of public policy must include* all *actions of government — and not just stated intentions of governments or government officials. Finally, we must also consider governmental inaction — what a government chooses not to do — as public policy.*

While Dye's unit of analysis is the federal government, the same notion can be applied to a private agency (such as a private general hospital) or to a whole service arena (such as the mental health delivery system as a whole).

The above formulations accord with Gil's conceptualization of policy as the totality of practice, and that policy analysis implies a discovery of the political, economic, and normative influences on that policy. Underlying the totality of practice, then, one may logically expect to find a codification of the values and social structures which permeate the society at large. This does not, of course, presuppose a monolithic arrangement whereby political officials and economic leaders consciously plan social control mechanisms in psychiatric forms. Nor does it mean that some programs critical of the status quo will not make it through the myriad channels of public program production. Rather, the above formulation means that the basic power arrangements of the society will be represented — and often replicated — by mental health practices. This is much like the reproduction of the status quo in other social programs such as income maintenance. The primary factors which are reproduced are class, race, gender, and professionalist power bases of the society. Clearly there will be variation in the degree and form of such power representation. Occasionally a few people may seek to use the policy and practice arena to alter or temper the underlying social order. Such was the case with the radical approaches to community control of Community Mental Health Centers (a topic which will be discussed in Chapter 3). Such attempts will be relatively infrequent, and rarely successful. Throughout the book I will show occasions where these dominant class, gender, race, and professionalist relations are played out. All these aspects of policy inform the book's discussion of its three main themes: political-economy, professionalism, and institutional inertia.

Incrementalism, as noted by DiNitto and Dye, is a major facet of social service policy. In the mental health field this is certainly true. Even when there is an innovative, major step forward — such as the CMHC program — it is largely an incremental addition to the entrenched state hospital system(s). This particular point will be developed in various parts of the book. The new CMHC program did not alter the existing professional structure of mental health practice; if anything, it increased the range of practice of those providers. Incremental approaches often result from the inability of a single legislative and/or executive effort to fundamentally restructure an existing human service area. This is largely a matter of what such change would do to the traditional social order. It may also be a matter of agencies and organizations which resist real or perceived threats to their autonomy and future security. Thus, bureaucratic inertia results as agencies and facilities seek to protect their part in the service delivery or planning system. Again, our efforts at defining policy leads to a discussion of the book's treatment of the three major determinants of mental health practices.

There are two interconnected types of mental health policy, as Kiesler (1982a) points out. *De jure* policy is the legislated programs, essentially favoring non-hospitalization and outpatient care. *De facto* policy is the actual operation of the system, dominated by insurance reimbursement mechanisms, which undercuts the progressive goals of the de jure policy. We can extend Kiesler's model to include a wider range of programmatic de jure policies and a larger number of structural de facto barriers. Using such a model we can think of mental health policy as having many *unintended consequences* — practices which diverge from intentions. In other words, there are many humanitarian goals proposed in mental health planning, as one can read in the reports of the President's Commission on Mental Health, for instance. Yet the structural forces of political-economy, professionalism, and institutional obstacles deflect policy from its intended goals. Unfortunately, we are only in the earliest stages of recognizing these unintended consequences for what they are. As Kiesler (1982a) writes:

> *As with most national policies, mental health policy is not a carefully planned and coordinated set of laws resting on the best of scientific knowledge. A good deal of what we do in the name of mental health rests on historical accident, political pressures, and unintended consequences of well-meaning acts.*

David Rothman's (1980) research allows for an elaboration of Kiesler's formulation. Rothman demonstrates that the idealist reform notions of the Progressive Era — 'conscience' — were subverted by the actualities of mental health practice — 'convenience'. He notes that early twentieth-century mental health reformers failed to examine the complexity of the problems facing them, and could conceive of the state as only a benevolent and not a repressive agent. Thus these reformers repeated past errors and plunged forward without adequate preparation. Similarly, Morrissey et al. (1980) emphasize the 'cycles of institutional reform' in which modern professionals and planners repeat early nineteenth-century errors due to their inability to see the practical limits of idealistic goals. Further, such reforms often begin with therapeutic innovation but are subverted by political-economy structures.

With this approach to mental health policy in mind, we can turn to the development and outcome of that policy. First, however, a word of caution: this book contains a great deal of criticism of the mental health field, but it is not meant to disparage the well-meaning beliefs and actions of persons working in the system. As in most other areas of society, the institutional structure overrides the individual's best intentions. The critique provided here is meant to enable persons in the system to better understand that system, which envelops them and is therefore so difficult to analyze.

PLAN OF THE BOOK

This introductory chapter has presented a picture of the problems presently facing the mental health system, as well as pointing to the overall progress in the field. Further, it has laid out the conceptual framework within which the mental health system will be analyzed. Chapter 2 will provide a capsule summary of the development of federal mental health policy from the end of World War II to the Community Mental Health Center Acts of 1963 and 1965.

With this background material in place, I look at the organization and functioning of the mental health system in Part II and discuss the structures and functions of its different components. Chapter 3 in turn examines the neotraditional public sector of community mental health centers. Chapter 4 studies the traditional public sector of state mental hospitals. Chapter 5 proceeds to the new custodial private sector, comprised of nursing homes, boarding and care homes, and single-room occupancies. Chapter 6 explores the new alliance of public and private sectors, mainly manifested in private psychiatric hospitals and general hospital psychiatric care (both public and private). Part III explores various social aspects of mental health practices. Chapter 7 looks at public attitudes toward the mentally ill, and at the effects of deinstitutionalization on mental health staff, especially at the lower levels. Chapter 8 examines psychoactive drugs, psychotechnology, and the new emphasis on biologistic approaches. Chapter 9 addresses the responses of antipsychiatry and the patients' rights movement to the mental health system, and evaluates the impact of those movements on psychiatric care. In each of these chapters I apply the three elements of the conceptual framework: political-economy, professionalist factors, and institutional problems. The conclusion discusses the possibility of significant alterations and reform of the mental health care system.

CHAPTER 2

Formulating a National Mental Health Policy

As I passed through some of Byberry's wards, I was reminded of the pictures of the Nazi concentration camps at Belsen and Buchenwald. I entered buildings swarming with naked humans herded like cattle and treated with less concern, pervaded by a fetid odor so heavy, so nauseating, that the stench seemed to have a physical existence of its own.
— *Albert Deutsch (1948), The Mentally Ill in America* (p. 42).

The crises of depression and war had left their mark: the state hospital system remained largely in ninetenth-century condition. With the exception of the Public Works Administration and other Depression-era federal jobs programs, few resources had been appropriated for the asylums. Gigantic, prison-like dayrooms, forgotten back wards, and the indiscriminate use of restraints were typical practice in these massive custodial warehouses. Underbudgeted and understaffed, the huge hospitals merely continued their traditional maintenance functions. Therapy was rarely a conceivable part of hospital life.

Recognizing that state governments were having difficulty operating mental health and retardation facilities during the Depression, the Public Works Administration (PWA) put much energy and funding into mental hospitals. According to the PWA, 'More than 50 per cent of the PWA hospital allotments have been made for construction of hospital facilities for nervous and mental patients.' From 1933 to 1939, PWA projects in forty of the forty-eight states added 49,725 beds for mentally ill persons and 8,304 beds for the retarded. The PWA spent over $14 million on projects ranging from small additions to massive construction involving dozens of buildings, powerhouses, barns, farm buildings, and even railroad stations and freight depots. Some hospitals were built nearly from the ground up in this fashion. Additional funds also came from the Federal Emergency Relief Administration, the National Recovery Administration, and the Works Progress Administration (Deutsch, 1948: 159; Massachusetts Department of Mental Disease *Annual Reports*, 1930-1940; Short and Brown, 1939: 347-403; Public Works Administration, 1939: 146-14.)

After World War II, professionals, government officials, and mental health advocates were able to look critically at the disgraceful nature of their state mental institutions. Georgia's Central State Hospital at Milledgeville, with 9,000 inmates, was one of the world's largest mental institutions. Eighty-three patients were typically squeezed into a twenty-person ward; many people lived and slept in the corridors for lack of bedrooms. Byberry (Philadelphia State) Hospital contained 6,100 patients, 75 per cent over the 'normal' maximum of 3,400. Its male incontinent ward held 300 men who never received clothing. Elsewhere in Byberry, 400 inmates were packed into a dayroom intended for forty. New York's Rockland State Hospital 6,100 residents, Manhattan State's 4,000, and Cleveland State's 2,750 patients were a small population in that era of decaying bedlams (Deutsch, 1948: 4-43, 57, 64, 84, 88, 104). The women's admitting ward at Phoenix State Hospital contained forty beds, each 'enclosed in diamond mesh-wire partitions in which patients are detained for complete examination before assignment to wards.' (Short and Brown, 1939: 403).

REFORM EFFORTS PRIOR TO WORLD WAR II

Although this book focuses on post-World War II practices, it is also concerned with historical cycles of reform. A brief discussion of significant reforms in the Progressive Era and the 1920s can help situate the subsequent events. One stream of reform was with state governments. In the 1890s and the first decade of the 1900s, State Care Acts were passed in a number of states, providing for states to centralize mental health services. This forced localities to release mentally ill persons from jails so that they could receive more appropriate care in state hospitals, and sought to provide more coherent psychiatric practices throughout each state's asylums (Morrissey and Goldman, 1980a). This rationalization of public psychiatry was part of the overall rationalization of social services in the

Progressive period, so well described by Lubove (1965). This was not only a governmental matter, for professionals played a major role in such changes.

The second stream of reform initiatives came from professionals. Neurologists and a new breed of psychiatrists in the last two decades of the nineteenth century challenged the custodial superintendents of the asylums, seeking hospital reform and offering new forms of treatment, most notably office-based practice. Beginning at the turn of the century, Adolf Meyer led efforts to integrate mental hospitals with medical and welfare services in the community. Meyer also pioneered the state hospital's development of outpatient clinics, social service departments, and research units. Meyer's approach joined psychology and physiology, informed by a social and somewhat psychodynamic perspective. Stemming from such an approach were parole and family care for state hospital patients, as well as preventive community services and child guidance clinics. Social workers found a new role in the modern psychiatric environment. Further, a new type of mental hospital was devised — the psychopathic hospital — to function as a short-term receiving hospital. This facility would treat acute cases on the premises, and direct chronic cases to the state hospitals. Originators of the psychopathic hospital hoped that it would diminish the stigma and fear of the asylum and therefore encourage earlier treatment which would lead to more rehabilitation and even cure (Rothman, 1980: 293-316; Morrissey and Goldman, 1980a).

Public involvement in mental health care was the third stream of reform, a stream intimately connected with the professional inputs. Clifford Beers' (1907) autobiography, *A Mind That Found Itself*, attracted much attention to hospital reform. With Adolf Meyer's support, Beers directed his efforts towards a public-professional alliance to spread ideas of education prevention, and more modern treatment. Under Beers' leadership, the National Committee for Mental Hygiene was founded in 1909 to pursue those goals (Rothman, 1980: 317-320; Dain, 1980).

Rothman's (1980) analysis of Progressive era psychiatric reforms, as mentioned in several places in this book, is that they largely failed due to unbridled optimism, failure to examine possible resources and support, and uncritical reliance on the government's benevolence. To the extent that Rothman is correct, the psychiatric reformers of that era provided the foundation for a post-World War II mental health lobby to commit some of the same mistakes.

POSTWAR REFORM EFFORTS

The conditions found in post-World War II mental hospitals were inconsistent with liberal public opinion in the war's wake. A decade and a half of depression and war had prevented much attention being given to asylum conditions, but in the postwar period impetus was provided by journalists' exposés of the hospitals and by lobbying efforts of the mental health professions which had expanded in wartime service. The strongest exposes had been appearing since the 1930s from the pen of Albert Deutsch. As a *PM* (later the *New York Star*) columnist in 1945, Deutsch had published a series on Veterans Administration hospital abuses. The series nearly landed him in jail for contempt of Congress because he refused to divulge the names of VA doctors who had provided him with the documentation. Deutsch's 1948 volume, *The Shame of the States*, was one of the main mental health reform polemics of the time. Its popularity led to the 1949 republication of Deutsch's 1937 work, *The Mentally Ill in America*, which had been prepared for the American Foundation for Mental Hygiene.

Deutsch pointed out the tremendous economic and social costs of mental illness. Noting the then current inpatient population of 538,629, he cautioned that one out of seventeen Americans were destined to spend some time inside a mental institution. The nation's 190 state hospitals cost $200 million annually, and costs were rising just as dramatically as their inpatient censuses. At the same time, staffing was totally inadequate, thus making decent treatment impossible. Milledgeville's 9,000 patients, like Byberry's 6,100, shared 14 doctors. Byberry had only 41 nurses and 180 attendants. Manhattan State provided a comparatively large staff for its 4,000 patients, with 432 attendants and nurses. At Rockland State, one night attendant worked eight wards. Aides often worked a regular shift of a twelve-hour day with every eighth day off. Forced patient labor was typical; patients worked twelve and fourteen hours a day and were paid in candy and tobacco (Deutsch, 1949: 41-43, 60, 69, 85, 97).

With daily per-patient expenditures in the 1940s as low as 76 cents, it was no wonder that restraints were so commonplace, or that patients often went shoeless, clothed in hospital-issue gowns, and sometimes naked. Food was cold, tasteless, and non-nutritious. At Cleveland State ward toilets doubled as pantries and dishwashing rooms. In Milledgeville, syphilitic and tubercular patients aided in food preparation. Poor health conditions and vermin infestation contributed to the spread of infectious diseases (Deutsch, 1948: 57-63, 92, 97-110).

The Shame of the States is a useful document for observing some of the contradictions in the ideologies of mental health reformers. Deutsch provided a devasting expose, yet did not believe that administrators, clinicians, or even politicians were much responsible for the poor status of mental health care. Deutsch lauded the various shock treatments of the day — electroshock, insulin shock, and metrazol shock — and believed that 'Shock therapy constitutes the most important development of the last decade in the institutional treatment of mental disease' (163). Thus a leading reform polemic calls for increased use of procedures which would later come in for much criticism for being therapeutically questionable, and often punitive. In a similar vein Milton Greenblatt, a leader in mental health reform, was convinced of the usefulness of psychosurgery. A 1948 survey by the Council of State Governments found that 102 of 187 state hospitals polled performed psychosurgery (Lerman, 1982: 87). In an important anthology (Greenblatt et al., 1955: 91-105), the section 'Toward a Therapeutic Community' included a favorable discussion not only of ECT but also of lobotomy. This seeming contradiction arose since the advocates of better psychiatric treatment were enamored of technical methods. Thus new techniques were equated with improved care, without taking into account those techniques' potential dangers.

Terrible conditions of mental hospitals, exposed by the muckrakers and reformers, produced much public outrage. Daily papers, weekly magazines, and films such as the 1946 'Snake Pit' made it clear that asylum reform was on the agenda. Particularly following a war supposedly fought for a better life, it was hard to tolerate such terrible institutional conditions. But exposes alone were not sufficient to improve conditions. World War II provided a strong impetus for changing the pattern of mental health care. World War II played a major role in the development of psychological and psychiatric services. As in World War I, IQ testing was employed, but on an ever larger scale, with the assistance of bodies such as the William Alanson White Foundation and the American Psychiatric Association (Deutsch, 1949: 464; Gorman, 1956: 24). Leading psychiatrists served the wartime needs: General William Menninger was Army chief of psychiatry, Captain Francis J. Braceland (later president of the American Psychiatric Association) headed the Navy services, and Jack Ewalt (later director of the important Joint Commission on Mental Illness and Health) served as psychiatric consultant to the Air Force. They and others, such as Maxwell Jones in England, established new psychiatric treatment services in the medical corps, and offered new treatment forms, including narcosynthesis (with sodium amytal and sodium pentathol), hypnosis, short term therapy, and group therapy. The Public Health Service set up hospitals for the merchant marine to treat emotionally disturbed seamen. World War II mental health staff discovered that treating acute symptoms at the front resulted in greater return rates to combat than did the previous method of removing soldiers to the rear for treatment. Further knowledge was gained concerning psychosomatic syndromes, as well as social aspects of mental illness (e.g., secondary gain, isolation, leadership, group identification, job motivation). Innovations in training included short training periods for mental health professionals, and the origin of the psychiatric team of psychologist, psychiatrist, and social worker. And at the same time that professionals feared the high prevalence of mental illness, they sought to combat stigma towards it (Grinker and Spiegel, 1945; Brand, 1965).

Veterans Administration (VA) advances were also instrumental. As chief of the psychiatric division, Daniel Blain recruited many psychiatrists from private practice, started intern and resident programs, opened psychiatric wards in VA general hospitals, and affiliated VA services with medical schools. The VA was the first body to put into practice various wartime innovations such as short-term therapy and group therapy, and Blain became a leader of the new community mental health perspective. VA expansion of psychiatric services created the need for more professionals. Those services also furnished a model of centralized, standardized mental health programs which the National Institute of Mental Health (NIMH) planners came to emulate, since such centralization and coordination were crucial to any national policy. And no one could fail to see the benefits of a psychiatric program which spent three times as much per patient as the state hospitals (Deutsch, 1949: 474-478; Joint Commission, 1961: 166-192; Blain, 1975).

The large influx of psychiatrists and psychologists fleeing the tide of fascism in Europe since the early 1930s provided additional advocates of innovative mental health services. Further, the psychologists stimulated the postwar development of clinical psychology as a major professional area.

Besides the specific promptings of wartime and postwar mental health services, a more general point about wartime influences needs to be made. Wars, as severe manifestations of existing political, economic, and ideological structures, have a great impact on many areas of social structure and state activities. The ordinary limits of governmental activity are transcended by wartime exigencies. Thus wage and price controls, rationing, rule by executive order, and partial nationalization are commonly accepted. In general, there is massive state intervention into areas previously less touched by state activities, and into some areas where no state intervention has ever occurred. This intervention carried over into the immediate postwar period when the legacy of state intervention was still strong, and when the state still retained more power due to the necessities of reconstruction.

National mental health policy formation is better understood in light of state intervention into new aspects of social life. This is because the wartime experiences of military psychiatry played such a strong role, as discussed above. Further, postwar mental health planning involved the federal government's taking much power away from the separate states and focusing that control in a centralized, standardized manner. In addition, the mental health planners were among the first health planners to urge the federal government and burgeoning hospital complexes to challenge the individualistic, free enterprise mentality and practices of the American Medical Associaton, an organization which preferred the individual doctor's autonomy over any form of health planning. Hill-Burton funds for hospital construction, introduced in 1946, were a significant aspect of the federal government's immediate postwar health programs. Apart from medical-surgical beds, Hill-Burton funds between 1946 and 1965 built 19,300 state hospital beds and 10,000 general hospital psychiatry beds (Connery, 1968: 26-27). This background facilitated the attempted formation of a national mental health policy. The Community Mental Health Centers program was especially significant in that it was the first time that the federal government provided continuing support for a nationwide civilian health program.

THE MENTAL HEALTH LOBBY

Postwar mental health policy formation centered around the growth and development of the National Institute of Mental Health. The Joint Commission on Mental Illness and Health also played a major role as a research and promotional body, although its work largely ended in 1961 with its final report, *Action for Mental Health*. A 'mental health lobby' developed, with NIMH as its core, and included professional organizations, political leaders, lay mental health reformers, philanthropists, and voluntary organizations, all of whom had some desire for more and improved mental health services. This lobby provided the overall initiative for creating an innovative national policy which greatly extended the network of mental health services, augmented the power of mental health professionals, and increased NIMH's organizational autonomy.

In 1946 the Mental Health Act created the National Institute of Mental Health as the building block of the new mental health program. NIMH was to initiate and support research in the cause, diagnosis, and treatment of mental illness; to train mental health personnel via institutional grants and individual fellowships; and to assist the states through grants and technical assistance, including the establishment of clinics and pilot programs. There would be no grants for state hospital maintenance but only for new programs, especially for community mental health. Each state was required by the Mental Health Act to designate a single mental health authority to receive and disburse grants (Foley, 1975: 4-5). This was the origin of NIMH's influence over state mental health departments. Forward-looking professionals considered the existing multiplicity of different mental health authorities to be detrimental to reform.

Professions were not in solid control of the mental health lobby in developing new programs. NIMH director Robert Felix had to accept compromises due to pressure from philanthropist/lobbyist Mary Lasker and her ally, National Committee Against Mental Illness director Mike Gorman, on issues such as establishing a Psychopharmacology Service Center, or in using NIMH funds to train non-physicians (psychologists, nurses, social workers); the American Psychiatric Association opposed that training program. Thus, the mental health lobby was in fact divided, with professionals in the NIMH and APA sometimes unable to hold their own against philanthropists and lobbyists who had influence with Congressional appropriations committees. Some of these disagreements concerned professional autonomy, such as in the APA's attempt to prevent competition from clinical psychologists. In the case of the pharmacology center, Lasker and Gorman's innovations challenged the cautious attitudes of NIMH scientists. Nevertheless, as most studies of the lobby indicate, it presented a united front to Congress and the public for fear of having its divisions used against it (Connery, 1968; Felicetti, 1975: 54-56; Foley, 1975: 8-9; Armstrong, 1980).

In its early years the mental health lobby directed much energy towards the state governors. In the late 1940s and early 1950s a series of studies by the Governors' Conference and the Council of State Governments provided wide coverage of deficits in the psychiatric care system. The reports targeted overcrowding, inadequate funds, poor staff resources, sparse research, and public misinformation. They established an Interstate Clearinghouse on Mental Health to compile and distribute data, provide consultation, formulate model legislation, and pool facilities between states. These early efforts brought results. Thirty-eight of forty-two states responding to a questionnaire had 1955 increases in mental health appropriations, ranging from 10 per cent to 45 per cent, mostly for new state hospital construction. Community mental health and clinic facilities were also being built, often for the first time. New York's Community Mental Health Services Act was considered a milestone in that it gave permanent state aid to local community mental health programs at a 50 per cent matching rate, with maximum total funds of $1 capita of local population. Training and research also grew rapidly, doubling in funds in only two years between 1953 and 1955. Total expenditures for the nation's state hospitals increased more than threefold over the decade 1947-1957, expenditures per patient rose 150 per cent, and the staff-patient ratio doubled. California, Minnesota, and New Jersey followed New York's lead in matching funds for local community programs. More states expanded research and training programs, and more mental health departments were reorganized. Along with this came increasing professionalization, such as legal requirements that state hospital directors be psychiatrists. State certification of mental hospital attendants in California set the stage for greater professionalist control, even at the lowest levels of the state hospitals' personnel (Interstate Clearinghouse, 1956: 1-11; 1958: 1-8; 1960: 2-10; Gorman, 1956: 162-166, 186-187).

The series of Governors' reports on *State Action in Mental Health* is very striking. The extremely positive tone and the near-absence of substantial criticism is representative of the mental health lobby's reform ideas during that period. In their eyes, a custodial past was rapidly disappearing into a straight path of future improvements, and government and professional leaders were running the system in the best possible way. As Scull (1981a) points out, this linear progress approach to medical and psychiatric history has failed to grasp the issues of professional dominance, economic pressures, political involvement, and the general complexity of social policy formation in recent decades. Much the same was true for past generations of mental health reform (Rothman, 1980).

The National Institute of Mental Health was the first tangible embodiment of the mental health lobby; NIMH then developed into the most concrete manifestation of the lobby, directing most of its work. NIMH was also the one site where psychiatric efforts could be measured in terms of nationwide impact. The institute's phenomenal growth was largely a result of highly organized planning. As Foley's (1975: 137-138) study of community mental health legislation concludes,

> *The Community Mental Health Centers Act did not evolve out of a series of marginal moves and uncoordinated decisions that necessitated only vague agreement on broad goals. Rather, the mental health oligopoly provided a public policy responsive to technical knowledge and congressional sentiment that it had molded.*

This was, then, a consciously created policy. Of course, much policy has been less consciously created. Many persons and agencies, performing small roles in a complex system, may be unaware of how their work fits into a larger picture, and may reject the evidence which might make that picture manifest to them. In this sense, the creation of public mental health policy is a combination of conscious and non-conscious activities, of intended and unintended consequences. Despite the unity of various components of the mental health lobby, psychiatry itself was far from unified. State hospital psychiatrists dominated the profession and the American Psychiatric Association until the 1950s. At that time, NIMH efforts raised community psychiatry to greater influence, partially through clinical training funds to medical schools (Gruenberg, 1982). Overall, however, organically-oriented psychiatrists remained in most dominant positions of the profession. By the mid-1970s a resurgence of medical model approaches clearly dominated the field. Psychoanalysts had remained more attached to individual treatment rather than community approaches (Light, 1980).

The professional dominance of the related professions developed in tandem with this institutional dominance of NIMH. Psychiatry, of course, achieved the greatest degree of professional power. This was due to its residual power from nineteenth-century control of state hospitals. In more recent times, this power stemmed from psychiatry being a branch of medicine, even if a marginal branch. Psychiatry may be a low status medical specialty, but it ranks on top of the hierarchy of the mental health professions. Since much psychology and social work were dependent upon the forward-looking psychiatrists who dominated NIMH and the lobby in general, members of those professions could be counted on to place much effort into relatively unified support for NIMH's directions. Thus, it is not surprising to see this interlock of professional and institutional dominance as a key element of postwar mental health planning.

THE JOINT COMMISSION ON MENTAL ILLNESS AND HEALTH

In the latter half of the 1950s and into the first five years of the 1960s, the Joint Commission on Mental Illness and Health (JC) played a major role in psychiatric planning. This quasi-governmental, interdisciplinary body was, next to NIMH, the major professional organization involved in mental health planning. Formed in 1955 by the American Psychiatric Association and the AMA's Council on Mental Health, the Joint Commission was charged by the 1955 Mental Health Study Act with assessing the United States' mental health needs and pointing to methods of meeting those needs. *Action for Mental Health*, the JC's 1961 final report, taken together with its earlier monograph series, provided much of the necessary coordination of research to justify increased government intervention. Even though the JC's emphasis was more on improvement of state hospitals (as compared to NIMH's later focus on CMHCs) the two bodies shared many assumptions. The legwork of the JC can therefore be seen as very important to the CMHC program as well as other future mental health developments.

The assumptions underlying the Joint Commission's establishment were addressed in American Psychiatric Association president Kenneth Appel's 1953 appeal for a survey that would give mental health the same kind of results as the 1910 Flexner report gave to medicine. The American Medical Association agreed. Its head, David Allman, told the Senate, 'What the Flexner Report did for medical education is what we hope to accomplish with the Joint Commission on Mental Illness and Health' (Foley, 1975: 16). The Flexner Report, sponsored by the Carnegie Foundation, fits into early twentieth-century higher education reforms, which, through the scientific rationalization of knowledge and skills, put educational control into the hands of a select few institutions which were certified by, and supportive of the medical profession and its governmental and corporate allies. The Flexner Report capped several decades of professional rationalization and governmental control, a period in which education and licensing laws were passed which drove out most non-physician medical personnel and formed the basis for present day elitism in the medical field.

Beginning in 1900, the AMA grew dramatically, from 8,400 members at the turn of the century to 70,000 a decade later. Arguing that doctors were poor, and that their poverty was caused by overcrowding within and without the profession, the AMA sought to abolish medical training institutions of which it did not approve, and to curtail the number of 'regular' schools (Ehrenreich and English, 1973; Markowitz and Rosner, 1973). Midwives, osteopaths, naturopaths, chiropractors, and others were deprived of their power to practice the healing and prevention of illness.

Traditional apprenticeship methods of physician training were outlawed, and with that went the potential for greater equity in medical care, since women, blacks, and practitioners of working class background were forced out of medical practice and therefore were unavailable to serve their constituencies. A number of the medical schools closed in that period were institutions which trained many black and female physicians; proprietary night schools for working-class medical students were also shut down. These schools had been founded in the first place because women, blacks, and persons of working-class origins rarely gained admittance to 'regular' schools.

Doctors also feared the wide use by immigrants and the native poor of hospital clinics, charity clinics, and benevolent society prepayment plans. The professionals thus worked to achieve university medical school control of hospitals, especially public ones, in order to keep those patients in the fold of regular medicine — largely for use as teaching material. Physicians increasingly turned to the Rockefeller and Carnegie Foundations, whose massive funds successfully transformed medical schools and hospitals into the models of scientific, rational efficiency which both capitalists and physicians wanted (Markowitz and Rosner, 1973). These alterations in medical education and practice were largely for the benefit of doctors, not patients. The practitioners — coming from increasingly higher class backgrounds — were concerned with issues like the 'doctor surplus' rather than with the poor health of the majority. Psychiatrists, as physicians, understood the rapid advancement gained by their early twentieth-century colleagues from the Flexnerian restructuring. Thus a mid-1950s proposal for a 'Flexner-type' reorganization of mental health care found much support among psychiatrists.

The Joint Commission produced an important set of monographs on a broad array of mental health topics. The series dealt with popular conceptions of mental health and illness, the extent of mental health resources in social agencies, schools and churches, the mental health workforce, inpatient care, research, economics, and epidemiology. This collection of studies, the largest such project of its kind, made a case for a greater recognition of the pervasiveness of mental illness, and for expansion of services throughout the society. Such an approach was typical of the 1950s and 1960s mental health planners: their vision was to expand their role into all areas of life, and the definition of which areas of life were appropriate for psychiatric intervention was a matter for the mental health planners to decide. This psychiatric evangelism and expansionism was more than simply a human concern for the mentally ill. It was also a search by a growing set of allied professions and their institutions for more clients, facilities, legitimacy, and funds (Szasz, 1961; Chu and Trotter, 1974).

Nineteenth-century psychiatrists had followed a similar path of expansionism. They asserted themselves as guardians of sexual morality and behavior, marital relations, social class stratification, and nativist racial/ethnic purity (Grob, 1966; Rothman, 1971). Much of this social concern served to cement the medical superintendents' control over state hospitals. Ironically, mid-twentieth-century psychiatric expansionism sought to break the control and power base of the conservative, asylum-centered section of the profession.

The Joint Commission pursued these changes within the context of a general acceptance of the medical model, exhibited in such notions as the desire for a universal diagnostic and classification system. And in order to win financial backing, it posited the cost-benefit approach at a very early point. This viewpoint sought to contain future costs of mental illness, such as lost labor of the mentally ill, by direct expenditures at present. Such justification was necessary, since increased state spending in the early 1950s had already become a problem for state governments.

Action for Mental Health urged vast increases in research, especially basic research. It sought an increase in person-power by a redefinition of who could treat mental illness: social workers were to be more included in the mental health workforce. More psychologists and psychiatrists needed to be recruited, trained, and given scholarships. The JC planners sought increased emergency services, community mental health clinics, state hospital improvements (with no hospital to exceed 1,000 beds), and early return to the community with aftercare, partial care, foster families, and rehabilitation programs. To further this, the JC urged greater public education to diminish the stigma of mental illness. And to fund the dramatic changes it posed, the Joint Commission asked that mental health spending be doubled in five years, and tripled in another five, largely by federal support. To obtain that federal funding, states would have to change their laws in accordance with JC perspectives: they would have to encourage outpatient treatment and, for inpatients, voluntary admission. They would be required to serve persons regardless of state of origin. States would have to budget certain amounts of federal funds for personnel training and for research, and to limit hospital populations to the JC's 1,000-patient maximum (Joint Commission, 1961).

While not all of these proposals were accepted, subsequent developments clearly showed the extent to which federal agencies could control large parts of state programs. The positive aspect of this phenomenon was that it began to replace the often parochial and backward programs of many states, and offered a national distribution of knowledge and methods. The negative aspect was that it led to mandatory types of programs which might not always be suitable for all areas; this would particularly be the case for the CMHC program's mandate of five required services, and after 1975 of twelve required services. These new initiatives did not always find easy channels, since many institutional psychiatrists in powerful positions blocked the modern approaches.

NIMH had already laid some groundwork for its influence over the states. State planning grants began as early as 1948, with states qualifying for grants of at least $20,000 for which they had to provide matching funds. In fiscal year 1948 $1.6 million was allocated; by 1955 the total reached $2.3 million, and by 1962 $6.6 million, with $65,000 minimum grants. All states took advantage of these grants, which were one of NIMH's first methods of certifying proper mental health authorities in each state, and thus laying the base for the coming federal CMHC program (Connery, 1968: 25-26; Foley, 1975: 12-13).

Action for Mental Health was more than a summary of recommendations. It was the culmination of a period in which, as Foley (1975: 20) notes:

> *The mental health elite and their lobbies had made a persuasive case for the care of the mentally ill to become a national responsibility. As a combined force these groups knew how to attract the attention of people who could influence the crucial decisions — the elected decision-makers. These politicians, adhering to the values that had developed in the 1950s concerning the care of the mentally ill, believed that they should enact a program that would constitute a radical shift in the delivery of mental health care in the United States.*

According to most psychiatric and psychological opinion, no major shift in mental health services would have been conceivable without the advent of psychotropic drugs. The dominant viewpoint considers that 1956 was the turning point in the inpatient state hospital population largely because of such drugs. The national inpatient population fell by 7,500 from its historic high of nearly 559,000, and patient population fell in three-fifths of the states (Lander, 1975). Scull (1976) notes that the psychiatric establishment and its supporters have frequently cited drugs, along with the contemporary anticustodial theories, as being reponsible for the large-scale decarceration of institutionalized mental patients. According to Scull, however, administrative policies had already begun to empty out

English and American hospitals before the advent of widespread drug treatment. In his view, financial incentives were key: public hospitals were costing too much, and new capital expenditures would soon be necessary. Such incentives led mental health departments to favor tighter admissions and looser discharge policies. Psychotropic drugs were surely a key technological companion, but not the primary causal factor (these issues will be addressed in detail in later chapters).

Reserpine, a derivative of Rauwolfia serpentine (snakeroot), was the earliest of the psychotropic drugs. Rauwolfia had been used for centuries in India for the treatment of epilepsy, mental illness, insomnia, diarrhea, and headaches. In the U.S. it was given clinical trials in the early 1950s. Chlorpromazine (Thorazine) was the real 'wonder drug,' discovered in France in 1951 in the search for an antihistamine without side effects.

Mental health officials were amazed at the initial successes of psychiatric drugs. So were the budget-minded governors and legislators, fearful of continued increases in inpatient population which meant ever-expanding costs. In the early years of psychotropic drugs, professionals were oblivious to the side effects of those drugs, but still remained somewhat restrained in administering them, at least compared with the nearly three decades since. Certain patients never before reachable were considered more amenable to psychotherapy. Unfortunately, very few of them would ever receive individual or group therapy since staffing would never reach adequate numbers. A large number of patients were, however, able to be discharged since some of their hallucinations and bizarre behavior were controlled by drugs, even if little would be done for them on the outside.

NIMH AND THE COMMUNITY MENTAL HEALTH CENTERS PROGRAM

A political base was also necessary for professionals, planners and officials to embark on such an accelerated course of mental health transformation. By 1960, NIMH and the Joint Commission had succeeded in winning much public acceptance, professional cooperation, and government support. But this was for incremental programs, and the forward-looking planners had a larger vision. NIMH leaders felt that the JC was traditionalistic, too focused on rehabilitation, lacking emphasis on prevention, and wedded to the archaic state hospital system. Jack Ewalt, for example, was Commissioner of Mental Health in Massachusetts immediately prior to heading the Joint Commission. NIMH believed that a new program was necessary, with federal funds to pay for building and staffing community clinics. This faced opposition from the National Institutes of Health (NIH), NIMH's parent body, and from the Health Insurance Institute and American Medical Association, both of which had recently defeated the King-Anderson bill, an early attempt at Medicare legislation (Foley, 1975: 14-31; Musto, 1975). Part of the reason for opposition to staffing grants, quite likely, was that no other NIH institutes had a service delivery component, and NIMH would therefore have a very privileged role. NIH may have also feared that NIMH's budget would outgrow that of its entire parent institute, a phenomenon which did occur.

Following President Kennedy's election, an NIMH task force was set up in 1961 to proceed on the community mental health idea. NIMH deputy director Stanley Yolles held a far-reaching notion of setting up 2,000 centers, one per 100,000 population, with permanent federal subsidies rather than only seed money. As part of his keen sense of the political patronage needed to ensure NIMH autonomy, Yolles urged that there be at least one CMHC in each congressional district in order to give each representative a pork barrel interest in the program (Foley, 1975: 30, 35-36). This task force led to a presidential planning body, spurred by Kennedy's interest in mental illness and retardation. Kennedy's 1963 State of the Union address promised a mental health and retardation package, and a month later he introduced it in a message to Congress. The president asked for a CMHC program with federal funds, training and research programs, and a small amount of state hospital support (Kennedy, 1963).

Hearings on the CMHC Act were without significant opposition, except for the AMA which opposed federal staffing grants for psychiatrists' salaries; these conservatives feared that staffing grants were but another step in the development of 'socialized medicine.' The lack of other opposition is interesting. At the time very few people could envision very rapid growth of the new policy, and therefore little threat was perceived, even in other conservative circles. Also, the magnitude of other social programs blurred the potential impact of mental health service expansion, since mental health services were less visible and less familiar than other social services such as welfare. Even if it looked to some legislators and officials as if mental health programs were going to represent a large investment, the phenomenal expansion of Kennedy's New Frontier health and welfare services made it more acceptable. When the act was signed into law on October 31, 1961 as PL 88-164, the AMA had succeeded in defeating the staffing grants, and it would take two years until the 1965 Amendment provided those funds. But in the meantime Congress had enacted the mental health lobby's first major component of an attempted national mental health policy.

When NIMH published the regulations for the CMHC program six months later, the center's five 'essential elements' were first defined: inpatient services, outpatient services, emergency services, partial hospitalization (day and night), and consultation and education. Catchment areas were defined as between 75,000 and 200,000 people. Coordination with state and local health planning agencies, welfare departments, and urban renewal agencies was urged. But despite official requirements for federal-state coordination, the CMHC program actually sought to bypass the states due to their entrenched institutional systems. Residence requirements were not to be used in order to deny anyone the services of a CMHC. Psychiatrists won a professional and medical victory by obtaining a proviso that a psychiatrist was to be the head of each CMHC (Connery, 1968: 56-57).

Chu and Trotter (1974, 26-27) argue that the most striking parts of these regulations were what was left out. The regulations were extremely vague in terms of community participation, services to the indigent, and coordination with other public and private agencies. No plans, procedures, or mechanisms were formulated for CMHC relations to state hospitals. 'Indeed,' remarked Chu and Trotter, 'the regulations contain not a single reference to the goal of supplanting state hospitals.' There was no way that the CMHCs would supplant the state hospitals if attention was not given to their relationship. This again demonstrates the NIMH de-emphasis of the states' roles, and the expanded federal-level control. Thus, from the beginning, the major federal initiative was flawed, and would lead to a mental health system dangerously split into unconnected services and facilities. There was no realistic appraisal of how state and local governments would take over funding:

> *If any NIMH official did recognize that long-term federal support would be needed to bail many centers out of insolvency, they concealed the fact, since it would have been politically unfeasible to suggest that the federal government foot the bill for the centers indefinitely.*

a situation that came to pass in short time (Chu and Trotter, 1974: 21-27). It had always been assumed that the states' large hospital expenditures would somehow be redirected. This assumption was derailed by the 1970s crisis of the welfare state, and in the 1970s state governments sought to save whatever budget items they could; savings from state hospitals went into the general treasury, not into community facilities.

The CMHC program was still incomplete without the staffing grants which the AMA had deferred. Lyndon Johnson's landslide 1964 election and the AMA's major emphasis on defeating the Medicare bill made it feasible to win that important CMHC component (Foley, 1975: 106-108). Government-sponsored health care, underwritten by private insurance companies and Blue Cross, and provided by the growing medical-industrial complex, was the new trend. The mental health planners were quick to understand that trend and to devise ways of working with it. Also, the mental health lobby had grown very strong. In a relatively short period of time, an extraordinarily strong mental health block of professionals, associations, legislators, lobbyists, and other allies was able to press the federal government into embarking upon the country's first national mental health policy. Referring back to discussion in Chapter 1 of multiple goals, we can understand the problems of this mental health lobby. It was a coalition of forces uniting for a brief period, despite their differences. This would make for opportunism in the short run and for disruption and discontinuity in the long run. NIMH's national coordination of the CMHC program was a unique form of public policy. It was the first time that a federal program provided ongoing support for a nationwide health service program, and a dramatic manifestation of federal programs bypassing state mental health authorities. We now turn to the implementation and results of this major national policy.

PART II

The Changing Structure and Organization of the Mental Health System

CHAPTER 3

The Neotraditional Public Sector: Community Mental Health Centers

CHANGES IN THE PSYCHIATRIC LANDSCAPE

In the past twenty-five years, the psychiatric landscape has changed in many ways: location of treatment, type of treatment, average length of stay, and number of admissions are some of the most noticeable changes. Nineteen fifty-five was the first year that psychotropic drugs came into wide use in U.S. mental hospitals,and the following year was the first in which the century-long constant rise in inpatient state hospital population began its permanent decline. In that year, 77 per cent of all psychiatric episodes were inpatient, and the remainder were outpatient, as shown in Figure 3.1. By 1971, largely due to the growth of CMHCs and other sources of outpatient treatment, only 42 per cent of all episodes were inpatient, with 55 per cent outpatient and 3 per cent day treatment. In 1975, the pattern continued, with the inpatient episodes equaling 27 per cent, the outpatient episodes 70 per cent, and day treatment stable at 3 per cent. For 1977, the last year in which complete data are available, the breakdown was the same (Witkin, 1980).

State hospitals are no longer the major location of total psychiatric episodes, or even of inpatient episodes, as they were in 1955 when they accounted for 49 per cent of all episodes, as shown in Figure 3.2. By 1971, they were down to 19 per cent, while the new CMHCs already accounted for 20 per cent. The largest location of episodes then, as today, was in the combined outpatient locations of freestanding clinics, general hospitals, and psychiatric hospitals. By 1975, CMHCs continued their climb to provide for 29 per cent of total episodes while state hospitals fell to 9 per cent. And in 1977, CMHCs accounted for almost one third of all

Figure 3.1 Per Cent Distribution of Patient Care Episodes in Mental Health Facilities by Modality: United States, 1955, 1971, 1975, 1977

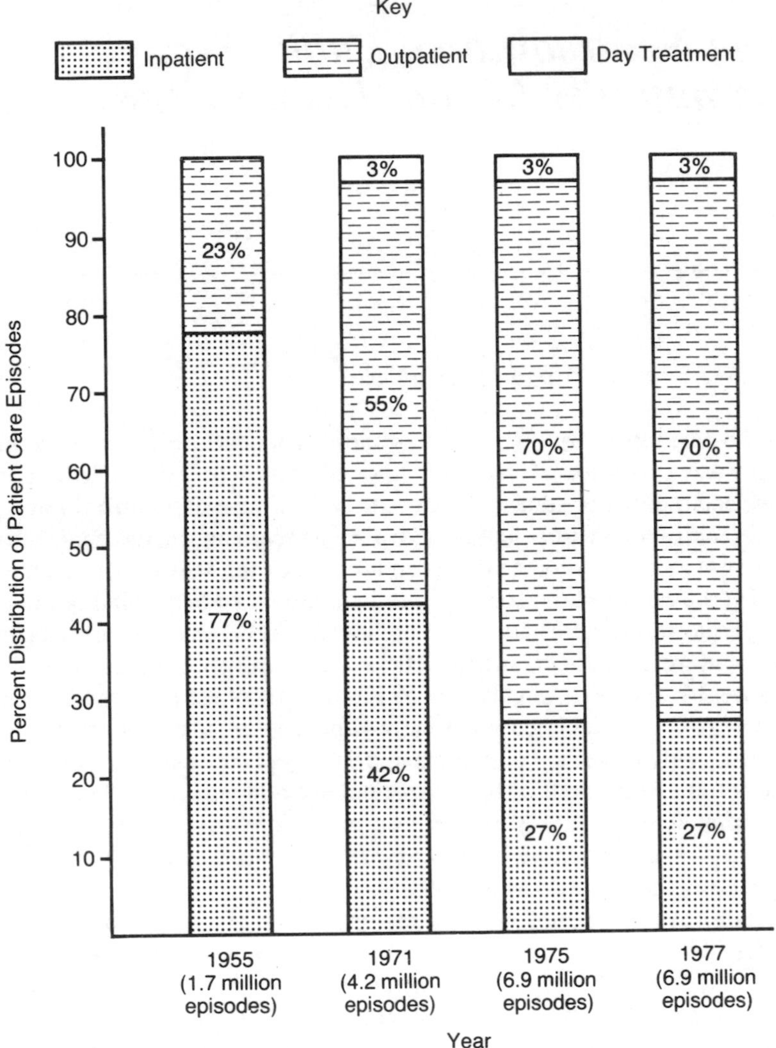

Source: Witkin, 1980

Figure 3.2 Per Cent Distribution of Inpatient and Outpatient Care Episodes[1] in Mental Health Facilities by Type of Facility: United States, 1955, 1971, 1975, 1977

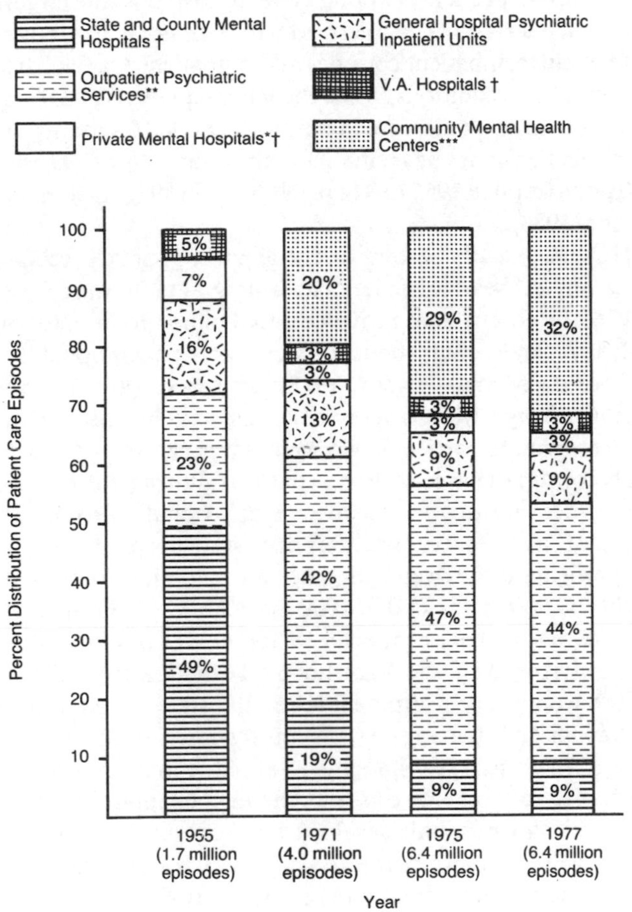

* Includes residential treatment centers for emotionally disturbed children.

† Inpatient services only.

** Includes freestanding outpatient services as well as those affiliated with psychiatric and general hospitals.

*** Includes inpatient and outpatient services of federally funded CMHCs.

1/ Excludes day treatment episodes and V.A. psychiatric outpatient services.

Source: Witkin, 1980

episodes (Witkin, 1980). If we count only inpatient episodes, we see that public and private general hospitals combined, including both psychiatric and nonpsychiatric units, account for 60 per cent of episodes, and state hospitals only 19 per cent. Among general hospitals, the largest volume is in non-psychiatric units (Kiesler and Sibulkin, 1982). It is, however, inaccurate to compare inpatient episodes and outpatient episodes. The former equals census plus additions, while the latter equals visits. Of importance here is that despite an increase in new services and locations, the rate of total inpatient episodes has remained fairly stable from 795 episodes per 100,000 population in 1955 to 842 per 100,000 in 1977 (Goldman, Adams, and Taube, 1983).

CMHCs have clearly become a central part of public psychiatry. In the first eleven fiscal years of federal staffing grants funding for CMHCs, 1966-1976, the government provided $1.48 billion to initiate 650 centers (NIMH, 1977c), although about 100 were not yet operational (President's Committee on Mental Health, 1978). It is necessary to observe that changes *involving* CMHCs are not the same as changes *initiated* by the CMHC program. In particular, CMHCs have been affiliated with general hospitals for inpatient services so that certain transformations in psychiatric services are attributable to general hospitals' directions. As these new types of facilities were proliferating, state hospitals were declining. More significant is the decline in patient population from its 1955 peak of nearly 559,000 to 138,000 in 1980 (see Table 3.1). From 1971 to 1977 alone there was a 50 per cent drop (Witkin, 1981a). Figure 3.3 provides a graphic portrayal of the state hospital changes from 1950 to 1980. CMHCs have not been responsible for the state hospital decline. The centers have picked up many new, previously unserved clients who account for most of their increase; state hospital reductions are a separate facet of psychiatric services. As this and the next chapter will examine, the CMHCs and state hospitals developed on very separate paths, and only recently have the centers begun to work with hospital dischargees.

It will be noted that admissions, as shown in Figure 3.3, rose sharply even as patient population fell. This is the well-known 'revolving door syndrome' where patients enter the hospital a number of times for short stays. However, after 1974, even admissions fell. Tables 3.2, 3.3, and 3.4 show additions for 1971, 1975, and 1977, for inpatient, outpatient, and day treatment services. Also included are percentage changes over time. As state hospital additions fell in all these categories, CMHCs rose in all

Table 3.1 State Mental Hospitals — Resident Patients, Admissions, and Patient Care Episodes, United States, 1950-1980

Year	*Resident Patients*	*Total Admissions*	*Patient Care Episodes* (PCE)*	*Percentage Change PCE*
1950	512,501	152,079	664,580	–
1955	558,922	185,597	744,519	+12.0
1960	535,540	252,742	788,282	+ 5.9
1965	475,202	328,564	803,766	+ 2.0
1970	337,619	402,472	740,091	- 8.0
1975	193,436	376,156	569,592	-23.0
1980	137,810	332,920	470,730	-17.4

Source: Adapted from Morrissey (1982)
*Patient care episodes=resident patients plus total admissions

modalities. Public general hospital psychiatric wards fell in all services, while their private counterparts showed mixed results, increasing in inpatient additions and decreasing in the other types (Witkin, 1981b).

Average length of stay fell drastically for state hospitals, from 421 days in 1969 to 189 in 1978. At the same time, CMHC stays fell slightly, but from a short 17.4 to 13.6 days (Kiesler and Sibulkin, 1982). Seen in a different fashion, a person diagnosed as psychotic in 1950 would spend an average of twenty years in a state asylum, compared to nine months in 1975 (Redlich and Kellert, 1978).

Having presented these basic changes in the psychiatric landscape, we will turn to the services and policy developments which produced these changes. The two major segments of the public mental health sector will be examined, first the CMHC program in this chapter, and then the state hospital system in Chapter 4. Although CMHCs are newer than state hospitals, it makes sense to discuss them first in order to provide continuity with the discussion in Chapter 2 and the beginning of this chapter.

THE COMMUNITY MENTAL HEALTH CENTERS PROGRAM AND THE RISE OF NIMH

The new CMHCs, cornerstone of modern mental health planning, were geared to be an alternative to traditional reliance on inpatient care. It is often claimed that the centers succeeded in that goal, since in 1975 80

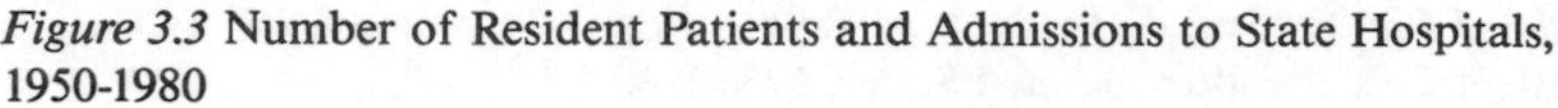

Figure 3.3 Number of Resident Patients and Admissions to State Hospitals, 1950-1980

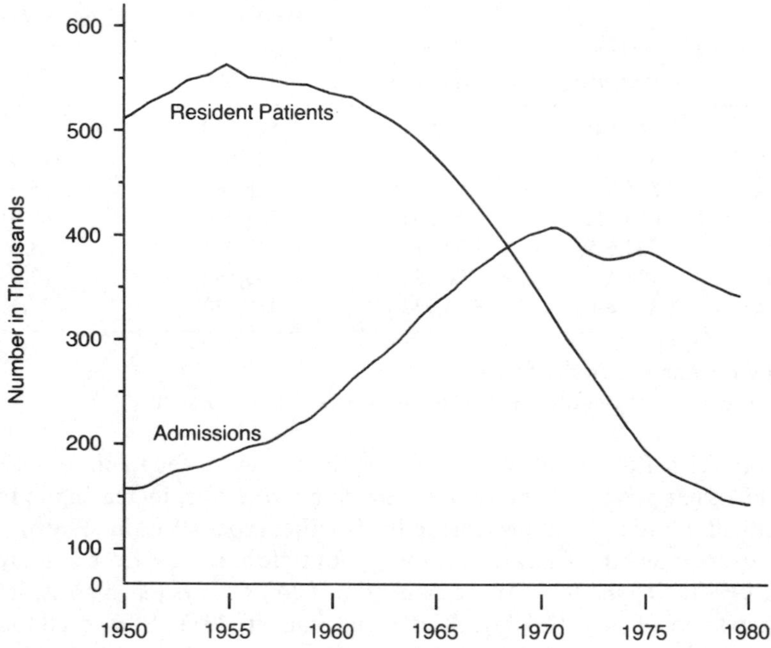

Source: National Institute of Mental Health, 1982d; Morrissey, 1982.

per cent of all CMHC episodes were outpatient, 13 per cent inpatient and 7 per cent partial (day or night) treatment (NIMH, 1977d). However, as noted earlier, CMHCs were choosing new populations to serve, rather than treating the same group as were treated in state hospitals. The approximately 550 operational centers were just over one third of the 1500 authorized in the original legislation, and as late as 1967 NIMH director Stanley Yolles sought an eventual complement of 2000 (Foley, 1975: 125-126). Through the latter half of the 1960s, CMHCs flourished in the Great Society environment, until the Nixon Administration began to challenge the program. Various amendments up until 1970 added new services for alcohol and drug abuse and children, extended staffing grants from the prior maximum of fifty-one months to a new maximum of eight years, and allowed poverty area CMHCs greater percentages of federal funds (Hesse, 1976).

Table 3.2 Inpatient Additions to Selected Mental Health Facilities 1971, 1975, 1977, and Changes Over Time

	1971	1975	1977	% change 1971-5	% change 1975-7	% change 1971-7
State hospital	474,923	433,529	414,703	− 8.7	− 4.3	− 12.7
VA hospital	134,065	180,701	183,461	+ 34.8	+ 1.5	+ 36.8
Public general hospital psychiatric ward	211,158	141,024	135,460	− 34.5	− 3.9	− 37.0
Private general hospital psychiatric ward	304,768	402,707	416,977	+ 32.1	+ 3.4	+ 36.8
Private psychiatric hospital	87,000	125,529	138,151	+ 44.3	+10.1	+ 58.8
Community Mental Health Center	75,900	236,226	257,347	+211.2	+ 8.9	+239.1

Source: Adapted from Witkin (1981b)

NIMH director Yolles' efforts to increase the CMHCs' status as the Institute's central program included urging the center directors to form the National Council of Community Mental Health Centers (NCCMHC) in 1968 as a lobbying body to prevent cutbacks. In summing up the CMHC expansion through 1972 Foley explains:

> *The primary factors in this expansion are the development of a CMHC interest group and the pragmatic style of the mental health leaders. Directors of federally funded centers formed themselves into the National Council of Community Mental Health Centers. The council quickly became an effective lobby: its primary purpose was to guarantee the continuation and expansion of the centers program. It worked in tandem with other interest groups in the mental health oligopoly, especially the NIMH, the State and Territorial Mental Health Program Directors, and the National Association for Mental Health (Foley, 1975: 126-127).*

Yolles resigned under duress in 1970, claiming that administration policies were harming mental health services by withholding funds (Bloom, 1975: 50). As Yolles (1975) later put it, 'the Administration wanted to kill the program.' At least some of the background to Nixon's antagonism was

Table 3.3 Outpatient Additions to Selected Mental Health Facilities 1971, 1975,1977, and Changes Over Time

	1971	1975	1977	% change 1971-5	% change 1975-7	% change 1971-7
State hospital	129,133	146,078	107,692	+ 13.1	- 26.3	- 16.6
VA hospital	51,645	93,935	120,940	+ 81.9	+29.8	+134.2
Public general hospital psychiatric ward	139,077	122,976	106,866	- 11.6	-12.8	- 23.2
Private general hospital psychiatric ward	143,600	131,689	123,299	- 8.3	- 6.4	- 14.2
Private psychiatric hospital	18,250	32,879	33,573	+ 80.2	+ 2.1	+ 84.0
Community Mental Health Center	335,648	784,638	876,121	+133.8	+11.7	+161.0

Source: Adapted from Witkin (1981b)

his general dislike of the social psychiatry approach. In 1969, Yolles opposed Nixon's proposal for long prison sentences for drug offenses, preferring instead a social psychiatry approach involving community mental health programs (Rumer, 1978). In the 1971 fiscal year, no funds were used for new construction, and the $90 million in staffing grants went only to previously funded centers (Chu and Trotter, 1974: 102). In 1973, Nixon illegally impounded CMHC funds already appropriated by Congress. The administration claimed that the CMHCs were ineffective, and were only intended as a time-limited trial program. Nixon's impoundment merely capped a trend in which appropriations increasingly fell far short of authorizations. During the nine years in which CMHC construction funds were in effect, 1965-1973, $600 million had been authorized, but only $245.5 million had actually been appropriated. During 1965-1969, the $195 million in appropriated funds equalled 75 per cent of $260 million in authorizations, but from 1970 to 1973, only $50.5 million was budgeted out of $340 million in authorized funds, a mere 15 per cent of the possible total (Bloom 1975: 51).

Table 3.4 Day Treatment Additions to Selected Mental Health Facilities 1971, 1975, 1977, and Changes Over Time

	1971	1975	1977	% change 1971-5	% change 1975-7	% change 1971-7
State hospital	16,554	14,205	10,697	- 14.2	- 24.7	- 35.4
VA hospital	4,023	7,788	6,978	+ 93.6	- 10.4	+ 73.5
Public general hospital psychiatric ward	4,291	3,299	3,480	- 23.1	+ 5.5	- 18.9
Private general hospital psychiatric ward	7,272	10,917	9,244	+ 50.7	-115.3	+ 27.1
Private psychiatric hospital	1,897	3,165	3,842	+ 67.1	+ 21.4	+102.9
Community Mental Health Center	21,092	94,092	102,493	+346.1	+ 8.9	+385.9

Source: Adapted from Witkin (1981b)

Gerald Ford's continuation of the Nixon Administration included a pursuit of Nixon's attacks on the CMHC program. Ford vetoed a routine two-year extension in 1974. While the reintroduced bill was being debated in 1975, Ford sought to impound funds which were running the CMHCs on an emergency monthly Congressional appropriation; that impoundment had been illegal under Nixon, but a 1975 law permitted it. Ford vetoed the bill, and was then overridden by Congress (Bloom, 1975: 52-55; NIMH, 1977d). The result, PL94-63, overhauled the CMHC program, with mixed results. While it authorized an expansion of funded catchment areas, it added more mandatory services, so that the previous five became twelve. Some conversion grants were authorized to aid that change, while regular operating grants were changed from a single eight-year grant to eight one-year grants for new facilities (Hesse, 1976).

Federal cutbacks in CMHC funding were matched by cutbacks in other areas of national mental health policy. CMHCs had been the main vehicle through which NIMH achieved a dominant position in psychiatric policy. Its rapid development as a powerful agency included significant research and training programs. From 1948 to 1974, NIMH spent over $1 billion on research, mostly on outside grants and contracts. By 1974, research budgets had already been steadily reduced for five years. Similar reductions affected training funds, which reached $120 million by 1969 when the cutbacks began. By 1976 those funds were down to $85.1 million, a 52 per cent cut since 1969, figuring inflation. NIMH had awarded 6,600 fellowships through 1972. Those awards, together with the research grants, made NIMH a central factor in academic psychology and psychiatry, and a considerable backer in sociology, anthropology, and social work, a position it no longer holds due to the drastic cutbacks (NIMH 1975).

Despite the large cutbacks, NIMH's institutional growth and autonomy were unique in social service programs. As ex-director Yolles (1975) recalled: 'From its beginnings, the National Institute of Mental Health staff chose to establish the agency as a focal point from which a global point of view regarding the mental health field could be developed.' NIMH succeeded to a large degree. Its budget grew from $18 million in 1956 to $315 million in 1967, nearly an 1800 per cent increase (Chu and Trotter, 1974: 7). But NIMH's power was curtailed in 1978, when it was merged with two agencies previously under NIMH control — the National Institute of Drug Abuse (NIDA) and National Institute on Alcohol Abuse and Alcoholism (NIAAA) — into the Alcohol, Drug Abuse, and Mental Health Administration (ADAMHA). Upon taking office, ADAMHA head Gerald Klerman fired NIMH chief Bertram Brown, thus ending the continuity of original and aggressive NIMH leadership *(APA Monitor*, 1978a; Herbert, 1978a). While NIMH still plays an important role in mental health services, it has been less able to initiate new programs. One aspect of that decline in initiative is due to recognized failures in CMHC operations, as noted by the GAO, Congressional committees, the President's Committee on Mental Health and the 1980 Mental Health Systems Act. Even though the Mental Health Systems Act curtailed the primacy of the CMHC program, it still kept NIMH in a position of responsibility. The new federal block grant procedures for health and social services, as legislated in the 1981 Ommibus Reconciliation Act, further eroded NIMH's power in program initiation. Under the new structure, federal funds go directly to the states in large blocks, to be allocated according to the states' priorities. This reversed two decades of practice and policy in which federal programming bypassed the states and enabled NIMH to play a large role in directing public mental health services (Wagenfeld and Jacobs, 1982).

Federal block grants are both an economic and ideological practice.

The Reagan Administration has argued against large-scale public human services, in order to cut federal spending and to end federal responsibility for policy-making. Human services with broad social goals have been particularly targeted for retrenchment, since current federal conservative leaders oppose such social action. The social action component of the CMHC program has been criticized from the right as an unwarranted involvement in seeking the amelioration of racial and economic injustices, and from the left as either a social control intrusion or a cooptation of radical social change efforts. The social action model was a very significant part of the overall CMHC program, either in the promise or in the practice. It therefore deserves attention for that reason. Additionally, this social action approach provides data for an interesting example of professional dominance and institutional expansion.

Psychiatric expansion and community mental health ideology

Various observers have pointed to the psychiatric expansionism which dominated federal mental health planning in the formative years of community mental health. The mental health professions have often had a crusading aspect, a sense of mission which has led mental health professionals sometimes to pursue increased services without adequate attention to social, political, and economic factors. At other times planners have sought to influence those factors or to bring them partly under control. Community mental health presented itself as a thoroughly new approach which had answers not only to mental health problems, but also to a wide range of other social problems — poverty, racism, juvenile delinquency, community-police relations, and educational problems. The broad conceptual framework which allowed community mental health professionals to extend themselves in this fashion was one which considered these other social problems to be psychiatrically involved. This is a form of medicalization, the phenomenon of applying medical definitions and practices to areas which are not clearly medical (Conrad and Schneider, 1980). This could be justified by pointing to epidemiological studies which demonstrated a dramatic prevalence of mental illness. For instance, the famous Midtown Manhattan Study (Srole et al., 1962) found that 80 per cent of the population had some psychiatric impairment. While this was not all serious impairment, the spreading of the net was important in demonstrating the ubiquity of mental illness throughout the society. As one well-known textbook put it, 'community mental health refers to all activities undertaken in the community in the name of mental health' (Bloom, 1975: 1-2).

Stanley Yolles (quoted in Bloom, 1975: 257), NIMH head from 1964 to 1970, proclaimed in the early years of community mental health:

> *There will be no effective national progress in community mental health unless psychiatrists and other core mental health professionals accept their responsibilities as professionals to practice as community leaders and activists as well as clinicians.*

In the words of the next NIMH director, Bertram Brown (1977: 12):

> *NIMH, and the mental health field generally, has historically held a unique position that straddles the health/biomedical fields on the one hand, and the human services/social problems fields on the other. We are unique in our ability to go where the problems are, where the needs are.*

Mental health planners and practitioners in the post-World War II era have asserted themselves as a major social movement. They have compared the 'mental health movement' to movements for suffrage and civil rights, which were bent on changing some fundamental values and practices of the society. But despite their new concepts and methods, the mental health planners and practitioners were doing what professions generally try to do: advance the profession. That the mental health planners and practitioners should see themselves as activists of a sort is by no means a recent phenomenon. Mental health reform was previously attached to other social movements, and sometimes defined itself as a movement in its own right. Benjamin Rush and Philippe Pinel placed their asylum reforms firmly in the context of their nations' late eighteenth-century bourgeois-democratic revolutions. Dorothea Dix led a nineteenth-century reform campaign to improve state hospital conditions. Clifford Beers, in the early years of this century, did likewise, but added the notion of 'mental hygiene' as a social movement. Whereas previous reformers sought primarily to improve asylum conditions, Beers and his allies also aimed at prevention and rehabilitation.

In the tradition of histories, textbooks, commentaries, and planning documents of the postwar psychiatric scene, Bloom (1975: 231) discusses the mental health movement as 'part of a larger social revolution' that includes the civil rights movement. This is combined with a 'revolution in prevention which includes an interest in the prevention of poverty and malnutrition.' It is also seen as a 'geopolitical revolution' of local community responsibility, as a 'revolution in participation,' and as 'part of a planning revolution that now includes highway planning, general hospital construction planning, urban redevelopment, and other projects.'

Actually the 'planning revolution' sounds like a major counterrevolution, if one counts the large numbers of poor and working class people displaced by highways, medical empires, and urban renewal. Such destructive attitudes also take place in mental health expansion, since planners sometimes assume that their programs are sufficiently important to justify destruction of neighborhoods. A case in point is the 1964 planning for a $7 million addition to the Massachusetts Mental Health Center. These plans included demolition of homes in Boston's working class Mission Hill neighborhood which would displace 200 families (Connery, 1968: 392-393). Mission Hill residents, furious at yet another in the long series of medical facility incursions into their neighborhood, organized 3,000 persons to demonstrate at the State House, but neither the governor nor the mental health planners took heed, and the mental health center was built on the site of those 200 families' homes.

The crusading element of the 'mental health movement' provides a self-contained history whose view of linear progress can justify the current campaign. It also serves, intentionally or not, to mask whatever deep-seated political, economic, or other motivations are involved. But movement status is more than just a vehicle for mental health professionals to establish and expand their programs. Movement status is an ideology which perpetuates the entire apparatus of mental health facilities, professionals, and organizations once they attain regular status in the society, and allows for uninterrupted expansion.

Kingsley Davis (1938), writing when the mental hygiene 'movement' was little more than the National Committee for Mental Hygiene, already understood much of this. Davis discerned that the movement had assumed the society's dominant values, mores, and class relations. Psychiatric textbooks took for granted a mobile class structure, and regarded competition as fundamental to human nature. Various types of psychological maladjustment were seen as resulting from inability to compete. This stemmed from an individualism which assumed that people were themselves responsible for their own destiny, that individual happiness was the ultimate good, and that human behavior could be seen in isolation from society. This last point, what Davis termed a 'psychologistic conception of human nature', was 'a means whereby an unconsciously held ethic may be advantageously propagated under the guise of 'science'.' Mental health professionals ignore those elements of reality which do not fit into their social concerns. This did not surprise Davis, who noted that 'If human personality is understandable without reference to social reality, then naturally social reality need not be analyzed.' The criteria of mental health were always social criteria which pervaded the overall society, such as class and gender structures. Foreshadowing the popular antipsychiatry doctrines and labeling theory of the 1960s, Davis wrote that 'Sanity lies in the observance of the normative systems of the group.' Davis' implication was that psychiatry would therefore serve as a social control mechanism rather than as a purely scientific healing profession. Szasz (1961) later amplified this perspective.

In many respects, the professionals and the rest of the mental health lobby really do feel themselves to be part of a social movement with a progressive political impact similar to the civil rights movement, albeit one enamored of drugs and other technical solutions to human problems. For instance, as late as 1976, a prominent community mental health founder, state hospital superintendent, and Massachusetts Commissioner of Mental Health, Milton Greenblatt (1976), could still include ECT, insulin shock, and lobotomy as part of the 'therapeutic-egalitarian model' of mental health practice which began in the 1930s.

Further, while mental health professionals understood that psychiatric problems often stem from social problems, they incorrectly assumed that individual treatment and community liaison work, rather than social change, would eradicate those social problems. Such solutions would only deal with cases of disorder, rather than preventing them via deep reform. Similarly, they assumed that mental health professionals were the chief responsible change agents. These personnel believed in many of the social values of the society, and thus might reproduce — even if unwittingly — what needed to be changed.

Another contradiction in this outlook is that while the planners acknowledged the CMHC program as a partly political movement, they ignored the potential of a political opposition on the left and/or right. So they saw their opponents as ignorant at best, and mentally ill at worst (Musto, 1975). Attempts at labeling political opponents 'mentally ill' rather than dealing with the actual opposition is a very self-serving way of looking at the world. 'Psychohistory', as a recent example of this, focuses on psychopathology in political leaders such as Nixon and Hitler, rather than on the real political and economic forces represented by those leaders.

One dangerous extension of this outlook can be seen in the psychologistic explanations of the black liberation, antiwar, and student movements of the 1960s. In the middle of the political upsurge resulting from the civil rights movement and anti-Vietnam war movement, student activism on campuses increased. At the University of Chicago, students occupied buildings to protest the firing of Marlene Dixon, a popular teacher long active in the antiwar movement. The students' program centered on the demand that the school end its research and development for war-related matters. Most opponents of this action simply argued against it on political grounds: the students were trying to overthrow legitimate authority, the Vietnam war was a justifiable defense against communist aggression, the university was value-free and thus above partisan politics. Bruno Bettelheim (1969), the noted psychologist, had a different opinion. In his understanding of the demonstration and of campus activism in general, the students had no real political points to make. As Bettelheim told a Congressional subcommittee:

> *The symbolic meaning should not be overlooked of students' invading the dean's or president's office, violently, or by means of sit-ins, big in age and size, who inwardly feel like little boys, and hence need to play big by sitting in papa's big chair.*

But the students hated their parents and themselves, Bettelheim continued. Thus they would not really 'sit' in the surrogate father's chair. As a result, the students were attacking the university as a surrogate for attacking their fathers. Therefore, Bettelheim explained, it was unnecessary to treat the protest as a political event. It was, instead, a manifestation of psychopathological behavior. Bettelheim also equated the behavior of antiwar activists with Nazi youth who helped bring Hitler to power. Psychologist Gustav Gilbert (1969), formerly a U.S. witness at the Nuremberg war crimes trials against Nazis, pursued a similar logic on the Nazi analogy. Turning to the Detroit ghetto uprising of 1967, Vernon Mark and Frank Ervin suggested that individuals' innate violence ('episodic dyscontrol syndrome') caused the riots, and that preventive psychosurgery could prevent further outbreaks.

Such attitudes, quite common in the middle and late 1960s, led people like Kenneth Kenniston (1968) to write in humorous fashion, 'How Community Mental Health Stamped Out the Riots — 1968-1978', in which he forecasted the creation of a psychiatric police force which took over urban counterinsurgency functions under the guise of medical/scientific treatment. Kenniston later turned against the radicals as well. In an article with Michael Lerner (1970), he accused the student left of being in an 'unholy alliance' with the right, an alliance whose motive was to destroy the university by the severe pathology of terrorism. As will be seen in the next section these ideological issues involving professionalism, institutional expansion, and political-economic matters played important roles in various outcomes.

COMMUNITY MENTAL HEALTH CENTERS IN PRACTICE

NIMH planners had a grand range of social goals in mind when they designed the Community Mental Health Centers program. They sought to increase the quality, range, and continuity of services; coordinate federal, state, and local roles; link mental health and medical services; make accessibility to mental health services a basic right, without regard to location or ability to pay, by replacing the 'two-class' system of care with a single, high-quality program; and to emphasize community participation and social concern (Feldman, 1974; Windle et al., 1974). Weighing those intentions against actual functioning of the CMHC program, we will explore how successful the policy has been.

Services and accessibility

NIMH's high expectations were in themselves a problem for the CMHC program. Chu and Trotter (1974: 51) argue that the five essential services (inpatient, outpatient, partial treatment, emergency services, and consultation/education) were possibly a good idea for some catchment areas, but by no means a necessary comprehensive program for all areas. Similarly, the 1975 amendments added seven more mandatory services: screening (to prevent inappropriate hospitalization), follow-up services (for released patients), transitional services (such as halfway houses), alcoholism services, drug abuse programs, special programs for children, and elderly services. Centers unable to make the transition faced loss of all federal dollars. While the comprehensiveness of the twelve services is ideal, it might have been impractical for certain centers, given the generally underfunded and undeveloped mental health care system, as well as different local needs.

Another blind spot in the original planning concerned future funding. Federal support began at a high level, and tapered off to zero over eight years. The assumption was that CMHCs would become so integral to states and localities that they would take up the centers' support, and that centers would also generate direct payments. This 'seed money' concept was typical of many human services programs of the period, but none of the other programs were as grandiose in attempting a national network of facilities as large as the CMHCs. CMHCs typically made no plans for that future period (Jacobs, 1974; Comptroller General, 1974). By the late 1970s, some CMHCs were bankrupt and in receivership. Further, matching funds meant that poor areas weren't likely to generate enough money to open and operate facilities (Chu and Trotter, 1974: 87). Contrary to the planners' expectations, state and local funding fell from 45.4 per cent of 1969 CMHC funds to 37.9 per cent of 1975 funds (NIMH, 1977c: 26). From 1971 to 1975, the federal share of CMHC support fell 9 per cent, as direct service receipts rose 9 per cent. But in absolute terms, direct receipts have not made up for federal cutbacks (NIMH, 1977d).

Federal support for the CMHC program has not extended to designing other federal programs so that they could contribute to appropriate community care. Medicaid and Medicare reimbursement biases play a fundamental role here. Medicare permits an annual expenditure per patient of only $250 on outpatient mental health care, and this is accompanied by a 50 per cent coinsurance rate (coinsurance on other medical care is only 20 per cent). For inpatient care in a hospital, there is no such restriction. Therefore elderly mentally ill persons are often unable to use outpatient care, and are either admitted to unnecessary inpatient services or are left untreated and thus at greater risk for more serious developments. As a result of this reimbursement restriction, Medicare accounted for a mere 2.3 per cent of all CMHC receipts in 1975. Medicaid also has restrictions on outpatient care, though not as excessively restrictive as Medicare. Still, Medicaid only accounted for 10.1 per cent of 1975 CMHC receipts (NIMH 1977d; President's Commission on Mental Health, 1978; Comptroller General, 1977).

Another important reimbursement restriction prohibits CMHCs from being paid for case management and central intake services. In a well-designed collaborative CMHC arrangement in Worcester, Massachusetts, planners intended that the non-reimbursable, yet vital, functions of case management would be billed as direct services through the eight collaborative providers. But the other agencies did not readily do this, leaving the CMHC in financial distress (Morrissey and Goldman, 1980b). As a result of the biases against all but inpatient services, some authors (e.g. Landsberg and Hammer, 1977) have considered that 'graduate' centers — those which have exhausted their eight years of federal support — will turn to increased inpatient care.

This may not be entirely without benefit. Heiman (1980) suggests that CMHC inpatient units may become 'private hospitals for the poor.' In an Arizona city, Heiman compared a CMHC unit (located in a general hospital) with other inpatient units in the city: a public general hospital, a VA general hospital, a university hospital, and two psychiatric hospitals. The CMHC patients shared age, sex, and diagnostic characteristics with the other private inpatients: a predominance of middle-age persons, more women, and a higher number of neurotics. This is in contrast to the public facilities with more males, a younger population, and a predominance of schizophrenics. The only differences the CMHC patients had from the private patients were income and education: 53 per cent had less than a high school education and 68 per cent earned less than $5000 per year. Heimann concluded that the CMHC inpatient unit thus serves a clientele that would otherwise be underserved. Clinics referring to the CMHC inpatient unit (a Neighborhood Health Center and the CMHC's outpatient service) act as casefinders, locating patients who would not be otherwise recognized since they are low-income people whose non-bizarre behavior would not ordinarily bring them into contact with treatment.

As discussed earlier, CMHCs have provided a large number of services, especially emphasizing outpatient and partial care. From 1970 to 1978, centers' greatest increase was a 525 per cent rise in partial care. Outpatient care rose 242 per cent, while inpatients treatment grew by 111 per cent (Wagenfeld and Jacobs, 1982). Yet this mainly occurred by selecting new populations, rather than serving the chronic psychotics then being discharged from state hospitals. This has been one of the key complaints in analyses of the CMHC program, documented by the GAO, the President's Commission and many NIMH studies as well. Basically, the CMHC program and the new policy of state hospital deinstitutionalization proceeded somewhat separately, to the detriment of both. This has been changed in theory in recent years, as a result of the President's Commission on Mental Health, though the Commission-sponsored Mental Health Systems Act has been effectively repealed by the block grant system. CMHCs are beginning to serve many of the chronic street psychotics and are attempting to coordinate their planning and service delivery with health and welfare agencies. A recent ADAMHA service delivery assessment team visited sixteen CMHCs in seven states. While the investigators concluded that CMHCs in general still serve a non-seriously ill, never-hospitalized population, there was some improvement in serving the chronically ill. In five of the sixteen centers, chronics composed from 10 per cent to 25 per cent of the caseload, in ten others 26 per cent to 50 per cent, and in one CMHC 70 per cent (Bean et al., 1979). The same study discussed reasons why CMHCs had not improved sufficiently. Centers had very poor relationships with state hospitals, with health services, and with social services, although there had been some improvement in the latter due to federal mandates. Lack of proper coordination with health care facilities was determined to result from physician distrust of CMHC methods, health facilities' fear of competition, CMHCs fear of absorption, and reimbursement biases which favor health facilities over CMHCs (Bean et al., 1979).

While studies such as the above point to serious flaws in the CMHC program, there has been too little evaluation of it. As the GAO study (Comptroller General, 1974: 32) put it, 'NIMH has had little success in developing an effective program for measuring the accomplishments of the CMHC program.' According to its own reports, NIMH's years of evaluation have provided 'only a little evidence beyond that which initiated the Centers program concerning the validity of the program's basic concepts' (Windle et al., 1974). NIMH site visits have been largely uncoordinated, too infrequent, minimal in scope, and largely fiscally oriented. They have looked at one point in time, and have failed to provide follow-up to solve problems which they encountered (Comptroller General, 1974: 32-40; Swenson et al ., 1975). The GAO report (Comptroller General, 1974: 40) noted that NIMH contracted for twenty-nine evaluation studies from July 1969 to December 1973, at a total cost of $2.9 million. Most were done by consulting firms, universities, and psychiatric facilities. Due to those contractors' self-interest in future NIMH funding, they held back from criticizing fundamental problems of the CMHC program. One evaluation which did point to deep flaws was conducted by the Health Policy Advisory Center (1972). It was so critical of individual centers and systemic problems that NIMH disavowed the final report. There is a big difference between looking at increases in services, which mainstream evaluation studies do, and looking at underlying problems, which we observe in other evaluations from outside NIMH control. Another problem in evaluation is that center staff often felt that NIMH was 'policing' them. At the other end, many federal officals at the Institute preferred to view themselves as program developers and consultants rather than evaluators (Wagenfeld and Jacobs, 1982).

NIMH sought to end what it termed the 'two-class system' of mental health care, by which public facilities served those without resources, and better private institutions treated people with means. As Chapter 6 will demonstrate, there has been a significant interchange of public and private care. This phenomenon, however, has not resulted from conscious NIMH policy. Rather, it stems from the structure of private and governmental reimbursement practices which allow for private sector care by persons covered by insurance or publicly-funded health programs. Related to this is the ability of private sector institutions to garner governmental funding, a function of the present welfare state.

It is true that CMHCs have served many persons who might not have previously found services very accessible. In 1971, 62 per cent of all clients had incomes under $5000 (Bachrach, 1974), though this dropped to 53 per cent the following year (Foley, 1975, 127). And the nonwhite additions to CMHCs increased from 15.5 per cent in 1972 to 17 per cent in 1976 (NIMH, 1978). But the notion of breaking down class and race barriers originally went deeper in that it sought to provide culturally responsive treatment to persons who might otherwise be wary of a mainstream psychiatric facility. The training and employment of community paraprofessionals was one part of this strategy. Yet even one avid supporter of CMHCs (Bloom, 1975: 222-223) observes that often third-world paraprofessionals treat mainly low income clients (often third world), while white professionals cater to middle class white patients. Similar data are found in studies from a wide range of perspectives (Redlich and Kellert, 1978; Chu and Trotter, 1974). For paraprofessionals to serve culturally similar clients would be consistent with NIMH's stated goal of cultural responsiveness. But the paraprofessionals were limited in work autonomy and were used for other purposes. Lang's (1975, 64, 100-103) year-long field study of a Boston CMHC showed that paraprofessionals were often used as a means of deceptively obtaining client information which professionals could not draw out. She also observed that paraprofessionals were used to lend legitimacy to the CMHC's claim to be non-elitist and community-oriented. Yet the paraprofessionals were the only clinical staff not allowed to select their own patients; they often treated chronic patients and mothers' groups, populations which professionals did not expect to benefit from the psychotherapy which professionals preferred to practice. Also, paraprofessionals are paid far lower salaries than professional staff who often perform similar work.

At the same time as some poor and working-class persons are receiving treatment, NIMH training funds have functioned to train psychiatrists and psychologists who would soon leave and enter private practice where they would serve a significantly higher class clientele. As Chu and Trotter (1974: 61) note:

> *NIMH has spent over $300 million in the last decade (1964-1974) to support psychiatric residency programs, half of whose graduates turn exclusively or primarily to private practice. In this sense, tax money has been used to subsidize psychiatric care for the wealthy.*

While this training has not taken place primarily at CMHCs, it comes from the same general federal expansion of mental health care.

Community-based treatment and involvement

To provide more egalitarian services to the widest range of people, CMHCs tried to create a new form of service planning and delivery. This was to be achieved through the catchment area concept. According to one advocate of this approach (Zusman, 1972), it has many advantages. Catchment areas encourage a progressive reorganization of mental health care so that services are located close to the patient's home, are more egalitarian, allow for continuity of care since the same facility would work with the patient through various phases and types of treatment, provide for preventive work due to knowledge of local characteristics, provide a more humanized environment due to small unit size, and allow for easier accountability and community involvement. However, the catchment area has been an artificial concept, since communities are not defined by merely having 75,000 to 200,000 people. CMHC catchment areas do not mesh with other health planning units, nor with existing political boundaries, thus preventing adequate coordination. The GAO report (Comptroller General, 1974) urged the abolition of catchment areas for these and other reasons.

Scheper-Hughes (1981) adds an interesting dimension to the problem of the definition of community. Her ethnographic research of a cohort of Boston State Hospital patients discharged in South Boston found that the ex-patients were negatively affected by the exclusionary and rigid notion of community prevalent in the neighborhood, known for its strong racist attitudes and actions. The long-time racism of that community, rekindled by the 1970s school busing controversy, was extended to a prejudice against mental patients as outsiders. Additionally there was considerable anti-Jewish feeling towards staff members. As a result of South Boston's insularity, and also due to the general failure of communities to take in ex-patients, the day treatment patients had little exposure to the community, and most of their relationships and support networks were with each other.

Robert Connery (1968: 489), supportive of the basic thrust of the CMHC program, nevertheless understood the limitations of the catchment area concept. In his opinion, 'Evident in the discussion of the relationships of the new community mental health centers to their 'communities' is the ideal of the New England town of the nineteenth century.' In other words, the catchment area concept assumed a fairly homogeneous and tight-knit community which would exert both a preventive and healing environment. But a culturally homogeneous community can be antagonistic to its own disabled members, as Scheper-Hughes' example shows. Overall, the complexity of modern urban living arrangements does not fit well with the planners' ideal notion of community.

CMHCs' consultation and education (C & E) component was to be another aspect of community orientation and preventive mental health. Centers would work with community agencies, schools, police, courts, religious centers, and medical facilities to aid them in serving mental health needs of their constituencies. Early detection of problems would be beneficial since treatment could begin before a crisis was reached. Mental health care would be viewed as more integral to people's daily lives and to local institutions' regular operations. C & E has been a difficult part of the CMHC program. It has often been loosely structured, and frequently resulted in nonproductive contact between mental health professionals and leaders of other facilities and institutions. In the 1960s minority populations sometimes distrusted CMHCs due to their cooperation with the police and courts. To the extent that CMHCs have not generally coordinated local mental health services or linked them with other social services, C & E has failed to fulfill its far-reaching goals.

Another grand promise of CMHC planners was that community participation would be central. The combination of community participation and the program's concern with neighborhood social structure was to aid in political reform as well as psychiatric care. In fact, the few popular attempts at expanding preventive mental health to include such areas such as tenants' union organizing, campaigns against lead paint poisoning, and welfare counseling were met with opposition from hospital and agency sponsors, and dismantling of activist storefront CMHC satellites. In the early years of community mental health programs, many progressive people were attracted by the rhetoric and possibility of real community involvement and political change. That notion was contradictory, since the supposedly scientific nature of psychiatric treatment was geared to individual and group treatment, whereas the task of social change was a larger political and economic phenomenon. For conservative professionals, this contradiction was not an issue, since they did not seek social change through mental health services. For the liberals who founded social psychiatry, social change was desirable, but their notions of reform were well within the mainstream of the American social order. Further, the liberal mental health ethos placed professionals in the guiding role of social change. For radical professionals and students, the contradiction between individual treatment and social reform was more apparent, since they believed that social reform involved fundamental restructuring of corporate domination, military aggressiveness, and racial polarization (Kunnes, 1972). Many radicals probably saw the CMHCs as merely one of many possible vehicles for community organizing.

Lincoln Hospital, in New York City's impoverished South Bronx, was perhaps the key struggle in which progressive and radical forces sought to achieve the promise of political reform and community participation. Lincoln Hospital Mental Health Services (LHMHS) started in 1964 with Office of Economic Opportunity (OEO) funds, in coordination with the New York City Department of Hospitals and Yeshiva University's Albert Einstein College of Medicine (Einstein is the nucleus of the medical empire which dominates most of the Bronx's medical care, Ehrenreich and Ehrenreich, 1970: 62-76; Kotelchuck, 1976: 22-24). Storefront preventive services, staffed by 140 black and Puerto Rican community paraprofessionals, were popular with South Bronx residents. But when the OEO grant was about to run out, LHMHS obtained CMHC funding which meant a total program change. The storefronts were to be phased out, and community political action ended. One specific directive against tenant organizing was prompted by the fact that a targeted landlord was a large contributor to Yeshiva University. Elections for a representative community board were cancelled by Yeshiva's general counsel around the same time. When several third world paraprofessionals were fired for disciplinary reasons, a revolt broke out in the CMHC which NIMH had designated as one of the nation's eight model centers. In March 1969, nearly 200 mental health workers, professionals, and community supporters occupied the mental health center, demanding the return of previous programs and of popular control over the center (Chu and Trotter: 1974, 174-181; Ehrenreich and Ehrenreich, 1970: 253-267). Hospital and university administrators invited the police in, who wounded and arrested dozens of people.

The Lincoln situation was not typical of attempts at deep community involvement, but it was a rallying point for those who believed in such a model. It was a watershed for those who took seriously the CMHC promise of political reform and popular control; such people would no longer take the promise seriously. But even in moderate forms of community involvement, CMHCs didn't live up to their stated goals. The GAO (Comptroller General, 1974) found significant community involvement in only two out of twelve centers studied. Health-PAC (1972) found that in only two out of six CMHCs studies was there any consumer participation, and then only in the early planning stages.

As Nassi (1978) sees it, 'The true meaning of community control has been diluted in the community mental health literature through interchangeable usage with the concepts of community involvement and participation.' Nassi borrows from Holton et al.(1973), who pose three models of community practice: elitist, advisory, and consumer control. The elitist model consists of community involvement, where token board members from the community are used to raise funds and provide legitimacy. The advisory model consists of community participation on the basis of 'maximum feasible participation,' although the definition of those words is left up to the professionals. In the consumer control model, the community chooses the programs and controls finances and jobs. Nassi extends this latter category to a more radical perspective by adding Rick Kunnes' (1972) proposition that real community control means also that such control extends to general political and economic issues of the area, such as substandard housing and police brutality. Holton et al. (1973), in studying six CMHCs, found only the first two models, the elitist and the advisory. Two studies in 1973-1974 surveyed 130 mental health boards in two states, finding them to be generally all of the elitist model, as well as very unaware of their area population's needs (Mazade and Sheets, 1975). A survey of advisory boards of four CMHCs and one mental health clinic found that board members had a distinct provider orientation, and rated existing or potential clients at the bottom of the list for membership on advisory groups (Pinto and Fiester, 1979).

The obstacles to community control, then, can be understood in light of the book's organizing themes of political-economy, professionalism, and institutional structure. Maintenance of the political-economic status quo is fostered by the medical model paradigm which utilizes a 'blaming-the-victim' approach which blames the mentally ill person, rather than the socio-political conditions precipitating his/her state (Ryan, 1972; Nassi, 1978). In some cases, professionals have considered the desire for community participation as itself a sign of psychopathology. Professionalist forces are at work in the professionals' domination of community boards and of community practices. This stems from their belief that mental health professionals can and should guide these aspects of community mental health. The entrenched institutional structure, consisting of agencies with control over professional and financial resources, operates mainly to preserve its own power. This is carried out by the techniques of rejection, co-optation, or giving lip service to reform while acting to stem that reform movement through bureaucratic and technical roadblocks (Nassi, 1978).

Relations between state hospitals and CMHCs

So far we have seen how CMHCs added new services to the mental health system, which took some load off the state hospital sector. We have also seen how the centers promised much larger social reforms than they could deliver. Now we will turn to relations between CMHCS and state hospitals. This relationship involves both of the above issues — new services and social change — since CMHCs were supposed to be not merely additions to the psychiatric establishment, but a new type of facility that would change the manner in which society dealt with mental illness.

Ever since the NIMH planners rejected the Joint Commission's emphasis on improving state hospitals, the CMHC program and the state hospital systems have developed along separate paths. This has been detrimental to the entire mental health system, particularly in the failure of CMHCs to treat the large numbers of chronic patients discharged from state hospitals. Even though the CMHC program intended to reduce the state hospital use, a 1972 questionnaire to CMHCs found that centers did not give priority to that goal. One hundred seventy-five centers responded, ranking the ten goals of the community mental health centers program. The goal of reducing state hospital utilization was ranked next to last (Comptroller General, 1977:72).

Regional NIMH officials have reported that private psychiatrists use their affiliations with CMHCs to provide inpatient CMHC service for their private patients, while remanding indigent persons to the nearby state hospital (Chu and Trotter, 1974: 89-90). The Health-PAC study (1972) found many similar cases. Inadequate CMHC services account for higher than necessary state hospital admissions. A 1975 study of one Massachusetts hospital showed that nearly 50 per cent of admissions were made during the evening and weekend hours when the local CMHC was closed (Comptroller General, 1977: 71). As mentioned earlier, CMHCs have often preferred to serve new populations, and therefore have ignored the problems of chronic patients. They don't usually do their job of following up patients discharged from their catchment area's state hospital, and have given very few aftercare services to those discharged patients they did serve (Comptroller General, 1974: 46-49). This was most noticeable for elderly persons. Although persons over sixty-five accounted for almost 60 per cent of the state hospital patient decline from 1966 to 1970, only 5 per cent of CMHC patients in that period were in that age group (Chu and Trotter, 1974: 41). Although the 1975 amendments mandated service to the elderly and to discharged inpatients, CMHCs have been deficient in serving their needs. An ADAMHA survey (Rotegard, 1979) found that CMHCs were not providing any clinical services to large numbers of mentally ill residents of nursing homes in centers' catchment areas. Rather, CMHCs offered a limited amount of C & E to nursing home administrators. While it was only with the 1975 amendments that CMHCs were *expressly* required *by law* to serve the discharged hospital patients, this existed as a more *general* requirement under the initial program design.

To emphasize these flaws is not to minimize the positive programs of some centers. Rather, it is to show that there was no comprehensive national policy that could produce innovative services for the chronically mentally ill in a general way. Bassuk and Gerson (1978) express this point well:

> *There are, to be sure, a few centers that have devised innovative programs to enhance the quality of life for chronically ill patients; there are some experimental programs that offer total care for discharged patients in a community setting. Such centers and programs are few, however, and they are the result of efforts by particular individuals or institutions, special funding or other special circumstances rather than of any consistent plan.*

Senate hearings on the 1980 Mental Health Systems Act (U.S. Senate, 1980) looked at the many critiques of CMHC practice, and formulated a rationale for a new form of community mental health service, one which would fund a variety of community treatment and rehabilitation services rather than remain wedded to the CMHC concept. The logic behind this approach is correct, though the goal will not be fulfilled. First of all, the Mental Health Systems Act has not been implemented, due to the block grant funding and its resultant cutbacks. Second, hearings on the 1975 CMHC Amendments had taken cognizance of critical reports, and then proposed to ameliorate the situation. However, this was not feasible on a large scale, since the correctives remained within the existing system, which had not been able to sufficiently correct its past flaws. Morrissey et al. (1980) discuss how 'cycles of institutional reform' perpetuate the old system by using ad hoc rather than deep reform strategies. CMHCs are only the most recent example of this problem. Psychiatric reform movements of the nineteenth century also promised dramatic new methods of treatment. Early in the nineteenth century the state asylum itself was the new alternative. Early in the twentieth century the psychopathic hospital promised great reform. And in the 1960s CMHCs repeated the problem, since 'each movement was launched with little or no appreciation of the practical limits to which the core ideas could be pushed.[7] As Morrissey et al. continue:

> *These reform movements shifted attention from one administrative solution to another, from institution to community and from centralized to decentralized services. Each expanded and diversified the mental health system but none fundamentally changed the two-class system of care.*

The legacy of Community Mental Health Centers is a mixed one. They have indelibly marked the contemporary structure of mental health services with a new type of facility which offers both traditional and newer modes of treatment. The centers have expanded the availability of services to areas previously unserved or underserved. They have played a slight role in depopulating state hospitals, as they encouraged a shift to more local institutions, though hospital admission and discharge policies were more significant factors. Yet the CMHCs failed to achieve a thorough restructuring of mental health care due to their own limitations and have failed to achieve their deeper social change goals. It is now time to study the other major part of the public psychiatric sector — state hospitals.

CHAPTER 4

The Traditional Public Sector: State Mental Hospitals

While federal policy concerned itself primarily with the CMHC program, the most dramatic results of recent mental health practices, both intended and unintended, have been state hospital deinstitutionalization and the growth of large numbers of discharged chronic psychotic patients in the community. We will look at how state and county mental hospitals (New Jersey, Michigan, and Wisconsin have county hospital systems which operate like state hospitals in the other forty-seven states) have decreased and transformed their inpatient populations, changed their admission policies, and are being phased out.

STATE HOSPITAL DEINSTITUTIONALIZATION

As discussed earlier, the old mainstay of the psychiatric system has drastically changed. Figure 3.3 (Page 52) showed the path of state hospital inpatient population reduction and changes in numbers of admissions. One of the most striking elements is the reduction of state hospitals as a dumping ground for unwanted elderly people. From 1955 to 1968 admissions of persons over sixty-five fell nearly 20 per cent from 33,140 to 26,593. During this same interval, admissions of those under sixty-five rose more than 55 per cent from 89,144 to 138,474 (Scull, 1976). This change in first admission rates by age can be illustrated by Figure 4.1 which demonstrates that in both 1946 and 1955, the rate rose dramatically at age sixty-five, but in 1972 the jump at that point was very slight. While it is important to have ended the role of the state hospital as a convenient dumping ground, there is serious fallout in the growth of the elderly

Figure 4.1 First Admission Rates Per 100,000 Population by Age, State and County Mental Hospitals, United States, 1946, 1955 and 1972

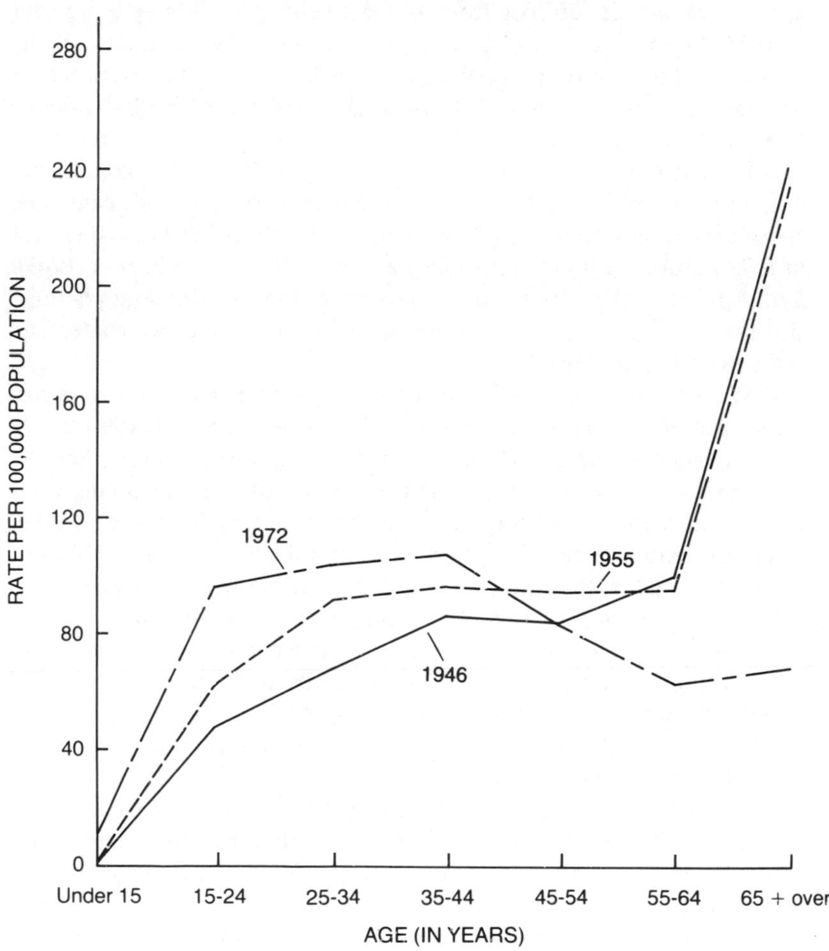

Source: NIMH, 1976d

mentally ill population in nursing homes, boarding homes, and single room occupancies (to be discussed in the next chapter). There are now between 1.7 and 2.4 million chronically ill persons in the U.S. (Goldman et al., 1981), many of them found in nursing and boarding homes and SROs.

Readmission rates to state and county mental hospitals have risen while total admissions have dropped. Nationwide, readmissions as a percentage of total admission rose from 47.1 per cent in 1969 to 60.3 per cent in 1975 (Weinstein, 1983), showing an increase in what many call the revolving door syndrome. Looking at some individual state figures over a longer interval, we observe that Massachusetts' rate of readmissions as a per cent of total admissions moved from 23 per cent in 1955 to 36 per cent in 1965 and to 55 per cent in 1976. New York in 1955 had a 27 per cent rate, in 1965 a 35 per cent rate, and in 1980, a 67 per cent rate. Maryland experienced a large rise from 43 per cent in 1963 to 70 per cent in 1974 (Taube, 1974; Comptroller General, 1977: 23; Weinstein, 1983). Critics of mental health practices have pointed to these rising readmission rates as signs of a flawed system which is unable to provide adequate services to those in need.

Psychiatric authorities often offer an alternative view: it is less harmful for patients to have many readmissions, since they do better outside the hospital and only return when they are in serious difficulty. There is an element of truth in this, though too many of these revolving door patients are living in non-hospital situations equally as bad as the hospital. There is some evidence that rising readmission rates are an artifact of other phenomena. For instance, as first admissions decline, readmissions will become a larger fraction of total admission. Also, the fact that each year brings larger numbers of people who have previously been hospitalized produces a higher population at risk. Rosenblatt and Mayer (1974) examined readmission studies for twenty-five years in the U.S., Canada, England, and Wales; they found that the only predictor of readmission was number of previous admissions.

In addition to the drop in first admissions and the increase in the population at risk, A. Weinstein (1983) notes that the high New York readmission rate is a result of two artifacts. First, better data management improved the state's ability to identify persons as previous patients. Second, since 1967 most patients leaving state hospitals were discharged outright, rather than merely being placed on 'convalescent leave'; thus the return of such patients has since 1967 swelled the ranks of readmitted patients. Weinstein suggests that the other measures may be more appropriate to examine multiple admissions. One such measure is the percentage of patients who return to state hospitals within three months; this figure has remained stable at between 20 per cent and 21 per cent from 1972 to 1979. A second indication is the percentage of persons admitted three or more times within one year; this figure rose from 6.5 per cent in 1972 to a high of 9 per cent in 1976 and 1977, but then fell again to 6.9 per cent in 1979. But even if high readmission rates to state hospitals are an artifact, a revolving door system still exists in that chronic patients move in and out of multiple locations, ranging from state hospitals to nursing homes to general hospitals to CMHC inpatient units. State hospitals only account for one-fourth of all inpatient episodes (Kiesler, 1982c).

To maximize patients' ability to remain outside the hospital, officials would have to have available a large number of alternative care modes. These have not existed. State hospital discharges have too often been large-scale, unplanned releases which have earned the epithet of 'dumping'. There has been insufficient study of discharge policies and subsequent follow-up for geriatric mentally ill persons. Markson and Cumming (1976) studied 2,174 discharged mental patients in New York. Their modal age, accounting for 29 per cent of the sample, was sixty to sixty-nine, and an additional 14 per cent were seventy or over. In general, they found that hospital discharge rates, rather than patient characteristics, was the decisive factor in release. State hospitals were divided into high, moderate, and low discharge categories, based on the percentage of their patients discharged in the first ninety days of a statewide discharge plan. Hospitals with high rates discharged more patients over fifty years than did hospitals in the other two categories. Patients didn't differ significantly by diagnosis, nor was there any difference in mortality of discharged, non-discharged, and already discharged patients. Significantly, high discharge hospitals placed 71 per cent of their patients in nursing homes, compared to only 7 per cent and 10 per cent in the moderate and low categories.

QUALITY AND COST IN STATE HOSPITALS AND IN ALTERNATIVE CARE

While nursing home placements are often detrimental, dynamic alternative modalities are often positive. The critics of institutionalism believed that active treatment in smaller, more personal units was one of the core elements of mental health reform. Not enough of these new forms are available. In those services that are available in limited numbers — half-way houses, hostel care, day treatment, and supervised group apartment living — outcomes are always equal to or better than state hospital care, as Kiesler (1982b) found in his review of ten randomized studies. Quality measures included rehospitalization, psychiatric status, probability of subsequent employment, independent living arrangements, and staying in school. More will be said on this question in Chapter 10.

One of the great promises of community care was cost savings. Evidence is mixed on the outcome. Studies of individual facilities show that alternative care costs are equal to or less than state hospital costs. A day treatment program at McLean Hospital near Boston in the early 1970s averaged $14,000 per patient for an 18-month period, compared to a $22,000 average for inpatient care. A 1978 report on day care by Washington, D.C. Blue Cross found that it cost 38 per cent less (Kiesler, 1982). But savings on many alternative programs may not be due to transfer to federal funding, since the types of intensive, alternative care involved are often not covered by federal programs (Stein and Test, 1980; Kiesler, 1982b). Other scholars have found higher costs for alternative services. In northwestern Illinois, treatment costs in regional mental health centers are $1000 more than state hospital costs (Bloom, 1975: 218). Kirk and Therrien (1975), based on studies of Hawaii and California, claim that monetary savings are a 'myth' of community mental health. In California, some studies have shown CMHC costs for deinstitutionalized patients to be 250 per cent higher than state hospital costs (Chase, 1973; Kirk and Therrien, 1975). These data are problematical, since the types of services can not be compared very well. To the extent that CMHCs are serving discharged chronic patients, they are only beginning to do so, and their costs will reflect the early stages of high expenses for a small population until the programs become stabilized. The same holds true of high start-up costs for other alternatives.

Transfer of costs from state to federal ledgers is clearer in the case of nursing homes and boarding homes, since the funding sources there are Medicare, Medicaid, and Supplemental Security Income (this will be discussed further in the next chapter). Nevertheless, state and local governments must still pick up additional costs in their shares of joint federal programs (such as Medicaid) or federal programs which many states supplement (such as Supplemental Security Income). Because of this, Lerman (1982: 95-96) calculates that there are not even short-term savings. However, this must be evaluated in terms of what states would have had to spend if state hospital censuses had continued at anything near their pre-1955 growth. Even with the huge reduction in patient population from 1969 to 1979, total state hospital costs fell by only $37 million in constant dollars (NIMH, 1982a); expenses such as maintenance and fuel do not decrease in the same linear fashion as does the patient census.

In 1976, an average state hospital spent $12,000 annually per patient. Massachusetts' 1977 average was $17,520 per patient. NIMH's St. Elizabeth Hospital, serving Washington, D.C., spent $24,000 per patient

(Massachusetts Department of Mental Health, 1977a; U.S. Senate, 1976: 723). As discussed earlier, federal work programs in the Depression took a certain burden off state mental health departments. After World War II, some states acquired Army facilities, as was the case with California's Modesto and DeWitt State Hospitals. Such acquisitions brought problems, since the temporary wartime construction of those buildings made for enormous repair and maintenance bills in the future (Weiner et. al., 1973: 234).

States would be facing enormous financial problems now, if they had to continue construction and maintenance for what would certainly be a growing inpatient census. Prior to the inpatient population decline in 1956, it was feared that new construction would be very difficult, since construction costs would be much higher than in previous years, due to the general inflation of construction costs, as well as increased unionization of workers. Public workers organized rapidly in the 1960s and 1970s and the once impermeable mental hospitals now have union locals. The pre-World War II sixty-hour week for Massachusetts attendants (Grob, 1966: 326) was ended, and Scull (1976) estimates that the advent of the eight-hour day has nearly doubled unit costs.

Further, court decisions on patient labor and minimum standards for state hospitals, particularly the 1973 Supreme Court decision in *Souder v. Brennan*, led to cost increases for state hospitals. Policy directions were changing even before that decision — as early as 1967, New York added $1 million to its mental health budget for replacing laundry workers. Pennsylvania estimated an annual expense of $12.8 million to replace 10,000 patient workers; Ohio figured on $13 million to make up the difference; and Minnesota expected to budget $1.6 million to replace 2,143 patients with 397 regular workers (Lander, 1975; U.S. Senate, 1976: 723). The Supreme Court effectively nullified the Souder decision in a 1976 case, *National League of Cities v. Usery*, when it ruled against the extension to state and local workers of the wage and hour standards under the Fair Labor Standards Act. That ruling eliminated the basis for requiring that minimum wage scales be applied to patient workers (American Psychological Association *Monitor*, 1976), though the ideological and policy effect has already eroded the traditional reliance on exploited patient-workers. (A longer discussion of the impact of patients' rights on mental health practices is found in Chapter 9.)

Increased government regulation has also increased hospital costs. For example, Pennsylvania's Retreat State Hospital lost Medicare certification due to staff and plant deficiencies. To correct only plant deficiencies

— violations of the Life and Safety Codes — the hospital's annual budget would have increased 16 per cent had it not been closed (Frank and Welch, 1982). Additionally, mental health planners since the 1950s have been concerned with indirect as well as direct mental health costs. In NIMH data:

> *Indirect costs are the income or income-equivalent losses which result from deaths due to mental illness, total disability due to mental illness, and loss of productive time to those individuals who are institutionalized or who utilize outpatient therapy for mental illness. (Levine and Willner, 1976).*

Overall costs of mental illness have been measured in studies by the Joint Commission, NIMH, and the Social Security Administration. Levine and Levine (1975) compared those findings, including their own study of 1971 costs. That data, plus data from Levine and Willner's (1976) study of 1974 costs, are shown below in Table 4.1. Figure 4.2 provides a more detailed breakdown for 1974. It was believed that the longer a person was kept in a custodial asylum, the more likely he or she would be to be disabled permanently, and thus become a permanent contribution to higher indirect costs. Alternative care was therfore aimed at reducing this aspect of the mental health bill. Apart from the somewhat speculative nature of the calculation of indirect costs, it should be noted that at present there are many chronic mental patients of a new type who are not graduates of long-term state hospital care, yet are still completely disabled. This 'new chronic' patient, to be discussed more fully in Chapter 10, is typically a young male with many short admissions to various types of facilities, rather than the classic type of older chronic discharged after many years in state hospitals.

Table 4.1 Comparison of Direct, Indirect and Total Costs of Mental Illness in Six Studies, 1956-1974 (in thousands)

year studied	Fein (1958) 1956	Rice (1966) 1963	Conley Conwell & Willner (1970) 1968	Yett & Levine (1972) 1969	Levine & Levine (1975) 1971	Levine & Willner (1976) 1974
Direct costs	$1,188,789	2,401,700	4,030,974	8,984,086	11,058,299	16,973,059
Indirect costs	1,926,452	4,634,000	16,906,000	not computed	14,179,382	19,812,768
Total costs	3,115,241	7,035,700	20,936,974	—	25,237,681	36,785,827

Source: Levine and Levine (1975), Levine and Willner (1976)

Figure 4.2 The Cost of Mental Illness, 1974

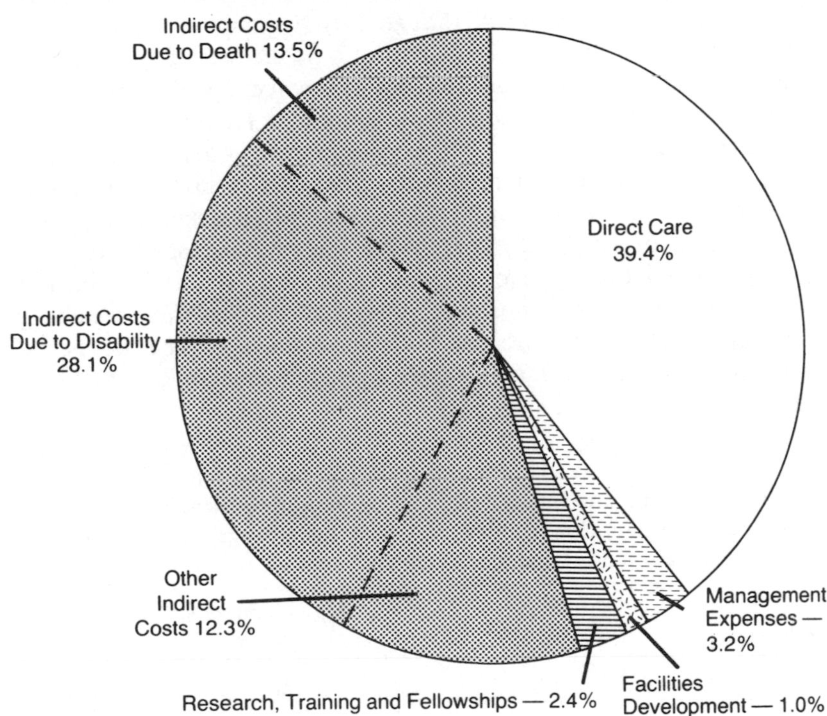

Total Cost (in 000's)	$36,785,827
Direct Care	14,506,028
Research	607,003
Training and Fellowships	284,842
Facilities Development	385,230
Management Expenses	1,167,298
Unallocated Expenditures of NIMH	22,658
Indirect Costs	19,812,768
Due to Death	4,942,320
Due to Disability	10,345,951
Due to Patient Care Activities	4,524,497

Source: Levine and Willner, 1976

CURRENT STATUS OF STATE HOSPITALS AND PROBLEMS OF COORDINATION

For those patients still in state hospitals, some of the worst snake-pit conditions have been alleviated, though they are still very poor living environments. As mentioned in Chapter 2, public mental health policy largely ignored state hospitals in favor of the new CMHCs. It was felt that efforts to improve the hospitals might lead to retention of the traditional asylum model. Table 4.2 shows the increase in daily expenditures per patient. The more than threefold increase in constant dollars is one indication of improvement. In 1977, total state hospital expenditures were $3.33 billion, of which only $100 million was capital expenditures. The average daily patient expenditure was $55 (Witkin, 1981a). Yet much of the cost in running state hospitals is in inflation in salaries, materials, utilities, and supplies; a decrease in patient population does not necessarily diminish many maintenance costs for the large, out-of-date facilities.

Table 4.2 Daily maintenance expenditures per resident patient expressed in current and constant (1967) dollars, inpatient treatment of state and county mental hospitals: United States, 1967-1977

Reporting	*Index**	*Daily maintenance expenditures per resident patient*	
		Current dollars	Constant dollars
1967	100.0	$ 8.84	$ 8.84
1968	106.1	10.47	9.87
1969	113.4	12.59	11.10
1970	120.6	14.89	12.35
1971	128.4	17.59	13.70
1972	132.5	20.68	15.61
1973	137.7	25.20	18.30
1974	150.5	30.86	20.50
1975	168.6	37.54	22.27
1976	184.7	43.55	23.58
1977	202.4	56.47	27.90

*Medical care component of the consumer price index, 1967 = 100.
Source: Witkin (1981a)

Frequent exposés of public asylum conditions are still commonplace, providing evidence that higher costs, smaller populations, and greater knowledge cannot basically change the custodial state hospital. Many state Departments of Mental Health were prompted by this evidence to attempt to close all state hospitals but such proposals have been quickly retracted. Table 4.3 illustrates the numbers of hospitals and yearly phase-outs from 1970 to 1977. It will be noted that despite closings, there are some new facilities as well. There have been decreases in the number of state hospitals over the last four reported years, though not the larger number of phase-outs originally hoped for.

Despite some concerted efforts, state hospitals have been unable to work successfully with other mental health facilities in providing a wide range of coordinated, quality services. Morrissey et al. (1980) examined Massachusetts' Worcester State Hospital (WSH) in its recent attempts at transformation to a more dynamic model of service delivery. WSH's cooperation with a local general hospital psychiatric unit was plagued

Table 4.3 Number of State and County Mental Hospitals, 1970-1977

Year	Number of operating hospitals at end of period	Number closed during year	New facility	Newly identified	Net change in per cent
1976-1977	297	15	11	1	- 3
1975-1976	300	15	1	1	- 13
1974-1975	313	16	4	2	- 10
1973-1974	323	13	—	2	- 11
1972-1973	334	7	11	3	+ 7
1971-1972	327	2	5	3	+ 6
1970-1971	321	4	7	3	+ 6

Source: Witkin (1981a)

by the psychiatric unit's practice of 'creaming.' This involves the selection of less disturbed patients who have third-party reimbursements. Similarly, the University of Massachusetts Medical Center creamed off the more 'desirable' patients in a collaborative CMHC in which WSH was involved. The lesser degree of 'boundary control' of the state hospital leaves it prey to such actions by facilities with high boundary control. Morrissey and his colleagues view such processes as a transfer of 'front wards' to private hospitals and some public general hospitals, leaving state hospitals as entirely 'back-ward' institutions. Lamb (1981a) notes that this phenomenon of releasing the least disturbed, while creating an increasingly severely disturbed inpatient population, leads to both renewed custodialism and rising costs. A more disabled patient population requires more special care through more intensive staffing.

EXAMPLES OF 'VANGUARD' STATES

The national data discussed so far are very useful yet do not give us the complete picture. State differences are important, but even more so, the experiences of the 'vanguard' states are significant. California, New York, and Massachusetts were three pioneering states in mental health policy, in terms of deinstitutionalization, community mental health programs, and impact on federal planning by exchange of personnel. Zusman and Bertsch (1975: 3) note that these three states plus Pennsylvania were the states which had planned for the dismantling of their entire state hospital system. Morrissey (1982) also emphasizes the importance of examining these three states.

California

California was the earliest of these three states to engage in rapid deinstitutionalization. California in 1955 had approximately 37,000 inpatients. The 1957 Short-Doyle Act made counties responsible for mental health care, with the state paying 75 per cent (later 90 per cent) of costs. Each county with more than 100,000 population was required to provide mental health services (California State Employees Association, 1972). This was the core of California's early attempts at community placement of mental patients. Beginning in 1962-63, the California Department of Mental Hygiene began planning even more dramatic deinstitutionalization by a depopulation project and geriatric screening (Aviram and Segal, 1977). Geriatric screening to reduce unnecessary admissions began in San Francisco County in 1963. In four years, it reduced the county's commitment of the elderly from 486 per year to 18 per year. Early successes led to its statewide implementation in 1965. As a result, California reduced its sixty-five-plus inpatient population 73.5 per cent from 1955 to 1969, compared to the national average of only 29.6 per cent (Lerman, 1982: 80-91). Smith and Hanham's (1981) time path analysis of deinstitutionalization locates California in the group of states having a moderate decline, tapering off in the 1970s.

California took particular advantage of federal programs which were not designed to produce deinstitutionalization but which came to function as such. For example, the state utilized new HEW regulations which allowed for higher payments for recipients of Aid to the Permanently and Totally Disabled (APTD, later supplanted by Supplemental Security Income). In 1962, California contained only 6 per cent of the nation's APTD clients, but by 1970 it had 20 per cent of all recipients. Also, California allowed for more mental health services under Medi-Cal than did the average state's Medicaid program. Further, state officials found that if they transferred social work programs for the mentally ill from the Department of Mental Health to the Welfare Department, the federal government would pay 75 per cent of the costs. Thus a psychiatric social work system was established in 1967, and by 1969 state funds paid for only 61 per cent of the Bureau of Social Work budget instead of 100 per cent (Lerman, 1982: 89-92).

In 1967, when the state had already reduced its patient census to 22,000, the Lanterman-Petris-Short Act (LPS) was passed. It provided various patient civil rights such as the right to a hearing on a writ of habeas corpus, the right to personal property, to receive visitors, phone use, personal clothing, and the right to refuse psychosurgery and electroshock. The LPS Act allowed only a three-day detention unless two physicians sign a fourteen-day commitment, after which the person must be released unless she or he has assaulted another patient. While not all the many stipulated rights of the Lanterman-Petris Short Act have been complied with, the act has succeeded in depopulating the state hospital system. When LPS took effect in 1969 there were 15,700 patients in nine state asylums. This already represented a 56.4 per cent reduction since 1955, far larger than the national figure of 33 per cent. By 1972 there remained only 7,200 patients in six hospitals, a decline of some 30,000 since 1955. Table 4.4 shows patient population and admissions. Restrictive admissions of the elderly lowered their admissions by 70 per cent from 1963 to 1969 (California State Employees Association, 1972; Aviram and Segal, 1977). By 1980, California's state asylums contained only 5,209 inpatients (Morrissey, 1982). From 1966 to 1972 over 11,000 sixty-five-plus patients were sent to nursing homes, and more than 16,000 under-sixty-five patients to boarding homes. Unlicensed board and care homes alone held 32,000 ex-mental patients (California State Employees Association, 1972).

Table 4.4 State Mental Hospitals — Resident Patients, Admissions, and Patient Care Episodes, 1950-1980, California

Year	*Resident Patients*	*Total Admissions*	*Patient Care Episodes (PCE)*	*Percentage Change PCE*
1950	32,430	14,768	47,198	—
1955	36,927	17,073	54,000	+ 14.4
1960	36,853	23,790	60,643	- 12.3
1965	30,193	26,799	57,424	- 5.3
1970	12,671	42,040	54,711	- 4.7
1975	6,468	27,735	34,203	- 37.5
1980	5,209	18,893	24,102	- 29.5

Source: Adapted from Morrissey (1982)

Like most other states, California's admission rate was up — from 28,000 in fiscal year 1962 to 44,000 a decade later (Aviram and Segal, 1977). But in the 1970s the admission rate fell, to 27,735 in 1975 and then to 18,893 in 1980 (Morrissey, 1982). California had planned to end all state hospitals by 1982, but gave that plan up in 1973, largely due to public, professional, and political opposition (Becker and Schulberg, 1976). Four hospitals had already been closed in the early 1970s — Modesto, Agnews, DeWitt, and Mendocino (Greenblatt and Glazier, 1975). Governor Reagan fought continual battles with state hospital workers, mental health advocacy groups, and local communities — probably the toughest struggle of any state engaged in rapid deinstitutionalization. These concerned workers' demands for better wages, conditions, and job security; advocates' concern over patients' rights issues and service delivery; and localities' fear of economic disruption and the creation of expatient concentrations. Nevertheless, Governor Brown tried to continue the earlier plans. In March 1976 plans were announced to close two more hospitals — Metropolitan and Atascadero (Donner, 1976). More recently, the state has had to again retreat on rapid phase-outs.

New York

New York also had an early plan for introducing community mental health and deinstitutionalization. The state's 93,000 inpatients in 1955 were the nation's highest psychiatric census. A 1954 Community Mental Health Services Act — the nation's first — sought to decrease public reliance on state hospitals in favor of local care, to be reimbursed by the state. Like California, New York also had a 1962 'Master Plan' for discharge, unitization, improvement of living conditions, and revised admission laws. In 1964, a new hospitalization act placed tighter controls on involuntary commitment and granted more rights to patients. In 1965 a new master plan was promoted to make local welfare and mental health agencies responsible for a greater proportion of mental health services via CMHCs (Lander, 1975; Forstenzer and Miller, 1975).

Also, like California, a 1968 plan to reduce elderly admissions was dramatically successful: in one year, over-sixty-five admissions fell from 8,365 to 6,044. By 1972 there were only 2,830 elderly admissions, a 66 per cent drop in four years, compared to a drop in the under-sixty-five rate of only 21 per cent. Table 4.5 provides basic patient data. A 1973 Unified Services Act pursued the goal of deinstitutionalization, and by 1975, New York had reduced the inpatient population to 33,293 and by 1980 to 24,961 (Morrissey, 1982). Median length of stay (the period until one-half of the patients admitted in a given period are discharged), fell from 211 days in 1955 to 75 days in 1966, and then to 38 days in 1973 (Lander, 1975; Forstenzer and Miller, 1975; Morrissey, 1982). In Smith and Hanham's (1981) time path analysis, New York and Washington, D.C. stand alone as having the steepest decline, even through the early 1970s.

Admissions rose from 1955 to 1968, and then fell, reaching 26,861 in 1975 and 22,897 in 1980 (Morrissey, 1982). Through the mid 1970s, New York's extremely rapid deinstitutionalization was accomplished by a climb in the readmission percentage. From 1955 to 1958 it was 27 per cent; between 1959 and 1966 it ranged from 30 per cent to 35 per cent, in 1967 it jumped to 40 per cent, and by 1974 stood at a high rate of 65 per cent (Lander, 1975).

Table 4.5 State Mental Hospitals — Resident Patients, Admissions, and Patient Care Episodes, 1950-1980, New York

Year	*Resident Patients*	*Total Admissions*	*Patient Care Episodes (PCE)*	*Percentage Change PCE*
1950	82,971	20,929	103,900	—
1955	93,379	21,925	115,304	+ 11.0
1960	88,824	27,676	116,500	+ 1.0
1965	84,859	36,466	121,325	+ 4.1
1970	64,257	35,742	99,999	- 14.6
1975	33,292	26,861	60,153	- 39.8
1980	24,961	22,897	47,858	- 20.4

Source: Adapted from Morrissey (1982)

Massachusetts

Massachusetts lagged behind the other two vanguard states, but acted vigorously in response to federal policy, beginning with the CMHC act. The Massachusetts Mental Health Planning Project (MMHPP) was later enacted into law in 1966 as the Comprehensive Mental Health and Retardation Act. Unitization of state hospitals followed in 1969; that method places all patients from the same geographic area into the same ward or unit. The presumed benefits are a sense of community and an interchange of staff with local services in the unit's area. Commitment law revision in 1970 made it harder to obtain involuntary commitments — in 1970 three quarters of all admissions were involuntary, and one quarter voluntary; the ratio reversed in one year (MMHPP, 1974: 11-14).

Hospital closings followed, the first of which — Grafton State — was announced in 1971 to occur the following year. In 1972 the Commissioner of Mental Health announced that inpatient population would be halved in the next two years (MMHPP, 1974, 11-14). That proposal was overly optimistic, but substantial declines were effected. From 1955 to 1973, Massachusetts' inpatient population declined from 22,201 to 7,339, a 67 per cent drop which outdistanced even New York. This large decline is something of an artifact, since Massachusetts started the process later. By 1970 the annual decline rate was 11 per cent. It peaked in 1976 at a 21 per cent drop over the previous year. In 1977 Massachusetts had only 3,729 inpatients (Massachusetts DMH, *Annual Reports*) and in 1980 the census was 3,133 (Morrissey, 1982). Table 4.6 illustrates this data. According to Smith and Hanham's (1981) time path analysis, Massachusetts and the other New England states are typical of the U.S. patient population decline as a whole: gradual decline to the early 1960s, steep decline in the middle 1960s, and again gradual decline through the mid-1970s. Following the closing of Grafton, Foxborough and Gardner were closed in 1975 and 1976; Boston State has been transformed into a few local units operating on the same grounds.

Table 4.6 State Mental Hospitals — Resident Patients, Admissions, and Patient Care Episodes, 1950-1980, Massachusetts

Year	*Resident Patients*	*Total Admissions*	*Patient Care Episodes (PCE)*	*Percentage Change PCE*
1950	23,657	7,208	30,865	—
1955	23,302	7,853	31,155	+ 0.9
1960	22,174	10,485	32,659	+ 5.8
1965	21,406	11,737	33,143	+ 1.5
1970	18,508	12,988	31,496	- 5.0
1975	6,767	8,438	15,205	- 48.3
1980	2,213	6,038	8,251	- 45.7

Source: Adapted from Morrissey (1982)

Admission rates in Massachusetts state hospitals climbed until 1972, and then fell. 1974 admissions of 10,785 were 23 per cent higher than the 1955 figure of 8,753 (Massachusetts DMH, *Annual Reports*), less than half the increase of New York over the same interval. But the 1980 figure at 6,038 was less than half that of a decade earlier (Morrissey, 1982). Massachusetts' readmission rate, though less than New York's, climbed to 40 per cent in 1974 and 55 per cent in 1978.

DIRECTION AND COORDINATION PROBLEMS IN PUBLIC MENTAL HEALTH SERVICES

In the late 1970s, federal and state officials realized the failures of much of the deinstitutionalization program. The Community Support Program (CSP) of NIMH was one response. CSP projects were designed to provide continuity of medical, psychiatric and social services. New York allocated $50 million for fiscal year 1982 to pursue contracted services with local, state, and voluntary facilities. Also, the state sought to reorganize the existing state hospitals (renamed Psychiatric Centers) into acute care, skilled nursing care, and domiciliary care facilities. Massachusetts has recommended more communitization (where wards serve particular localities) as well, but has developed fewer pilot programs than New York (Morrissey, 1982). But such reformulation of mental health policy does not usually lead to examining and correcting the deeper structural flaws in the system. Further, the current cutbacks in mental health and other social services will make it most difficult to promote large numbers of new and innovative service networks, as begun with the CSP program and pursued in the Mental Health Systems Act.

Lack of direction and poor coordination are important aspects of the mental health system's structural problems. As the Comptroller General (1977) found, 135 federal programs, operated by eleven major departments and agencies, are involved in deinstitutionalization; eighty-nine of those are within the Department of Health and Human Services. These many jurisdictions and authorities manifested a definite lack of coordination. Further, there has been no central federal initiative or directive to link them together. The President's Commission on Mental Health and the Mental Health Systems Act were attempts to deal with this problem. While much of the nonimplementation of those proposals can be accounted for by fiscal cutbacks, much can also be seen as deriving from continued interagency rivalry, which is heightened by the Reagan Administration's pursuit of localism as an alternative to federal direction of human service programs. This return to pre-1960s politics is particularly problematic, since there are large discrepancies between states on eligiblity requirements and funding levels for the social welfare programs (e.g., housing, income maintenance, social services) which are necessary components of a total deinstitutionalization effort. When the 1977 GAO report was released, HEW commented on it by largely disavowing deinstitutionalization as a consciously planned policy. The Department argued that it preferred a 'balanced system of care,' rather than a normative approach to treatment in the least restrictive environment (Lerman, 1982: 166-171). This is a curious denial of responsibility. NIMH had not only been an advocate of deinstitutionalization, but through the CMHC program and other funding mechanisms had been the only approximation to a national mental health policy. Even though NIMH's only service delivery program was the CMHCs, the agency exerted enormous influence on mental health care. Most likely, the HEW disavowal was part of the department's disavowal of NIMH in general, following the diminution of the Institute's power and authority as manifested in the creation of ADAMHA. A reading of the President's Commission on Mental Health's (PCMH) *Report to the President* shows the administration's dissatisfaction with NIMH for its inability to adequately plan and deliver a unified psychiatric services program. While the PCMH criticism of NIMH is valid, it is a long stretch of policy intention to disavow deinstitutionalization.

It is true that we cannot entirely do without some form of highly structured asylum for a small portion of the mentally ill population. In addition to psychiatric needs, state hospitals still fill other important functions, such as employment, training sites, local economic support, and the public's felt need for security (Goldman, Taube, Regier, and Witkin, 1983). Despite some earlier optimism, most adherents of deinstitutionalization did not seek the total abolition of all hospitals. In fact, the more intelligent approaches to innovative and noninstitutional care have understood that deinstitutionalization does not necessarily mean *non*-institutionalization, or even a large degree of personal freedom. Scheper-Hughes (1981) notes that while most of her study cohort of discharged patients lived in non-institutional settings, their lives were highly regimented by the day hospital, rehabilitation program, or sheltered workshop. The day hospital program and the parent institution, Boston State Hospital, are thoroughly connected, and the day program has become a permanent status for patients, rather than a transition to independent living. Lerman (1982) argues that although boarding home patients may feel 'freer' than they did in the hospital, boarding homes are new forms of social control in that many patients are involuntary in practice, and that operators are given wide latitude in supervising patients in matters such as curfews, withholding money, cashing checks, visitor privileges, and control of access to clothing. He also considers the well-documented abuse of psychiatric drugs in nursing and boarding homes to be an instance of social control which makes the home similar to the old asylum. Various scholars have remarked that we are witnessing *transinstitutionalization*, the mere shifting of people from one facility to another. This is one of the aspects of the *transfer of care*, whereby the location and some of the phenomena of institutional living change, but the underlying personal control and institutional rigidity remain.

In this process, we may be witnessing a return to earlier patterns whereby little discrimination was applied to differentiate asylum inhabitants. Segal and Aviram (1978) argue that the existence of 'multiple groups' in California sheltered-care settings — mentally ill, mentally retarded, drug and alcohol abusers, physically disabled, and elderly — suggests 'a step back to noncategorical care, perhaps to the old almshouse category where individuals are served indiscriminately.'

State hospital deinstitutionalization, in sum, has been a poorly coordinated practice in which states acted in diverse fashion to discharge existing patients and to restrict admisssions. In Gruenberg's (1982) analysis:

> *In each state mental hospital, directors vied for a better report on a dropping census. The states began to compete with one another for publicity, with one claiming to have dropped its census more than another. A falling mental hospital census became a fetish and an end in itself, without regard for the consequences to the patients.*

Entrenched institutional practices prevented more thorough planning. CMHCs and state hospitals failed to coordinate the two major mental health care delivery systems. This was due both to institutional competition and uncoordination, and to professional disputes over the direction of psychiatric care. These forces, combined with reimbursement practices and the entrepreneurial activities of nursing and boarding home owners, have produced a major transfer of care to nursing and boarding homes. This will be the subject of the following chapter.

CHAPTER 5

The New Custodial Private Sector: Nursing Homes, Boarding Homes, and Other Locations

Recent mental health policies have led to a rapid growth of the private sector. Nursing and boarding homes are the most common institutions. Single-room occupancies (SROs) also play a major role in New York City. This chapter documents these phenomena and shows how the custodial private sector is a key beneficiary of public mental health policy.

GROWTH OF NURSING AND BOARDING HOMES IN MENTAL HEALTH CARE

Nursing homes, boarding homes, and single-room occupancies (SROs) are the largest locus of mental health 'care' and expenditure. This is one of the principal legacies of the national mental health policy, and a clear sign of that policy's failure. Reports by the Senate Subcommittee on Long-Term Care (1976), the General Accounting Office (Comptroller General, 1977), and the President's Commission on Mental Health (1978) have been the foremost federal studies of this situation. Journalistic exposés have been followed by special prosecutors, resulting in some indictments and convictions of home operators guilty of fraud, theft, and deliberate poor care. Recent legislation has called attention to these problems and resulted in requirements for special attention toward discharged state hospital patients, although the necessary funding has not been appropriated. In spite of this attention, little is actually being done to alleviate the mental health system's dependence on nursing and boarding homes. That dependence is too far developed to be so easily altered, and there are not enough alternative facilities to change hospital placement patterns or to receive transfers from nursing homes.

Sheer numbers are shocking: close to one million mentally disabled persons live in nursing and boarding homes, compared to the 1980 state hospital inpatient census of under 138,000. Here is the major transinstitutionalization in the psychiatric delivery system. It also represents the most dramatic transfer of care from the mental health system to the public welfare and public health systems. Whereas in 1963, 53 per cent of elderly mentally ill persons were in homes and 47 per cent in state hospitals, by 1969 the ratio had changed dramatically with 75 per cent of elderly mentally ill in homes and only 25 per cent in state hospitals (NIMH, 1976d). Nursing home residents with mental disabilities increased 48 per cent from 1969 to 1974, from 607,400 to 899,500, according to a 1974 study by the National Center for Health Statistics. NIMH recently estimated that 58 per cent of all nursing home residents had some form of mental disorder. That estimate was broken down as follows: 250,000 with a primary mental disorder, 100,000 with a potentially diagnosable mental condition, and 400,000 with senility without psychosis (Comptroller General, 1977: 10; NIMH, 1980). Estimates of the mentally ill population of nursing homes vary between government agencies, and even within NIMH over time. Generally, the mentally ill percentage is probably underenumerated, since federal rules deny Medicaid certification to any home with more than 50 per cent of the patients having a primary diagnosis of mental illness.

The impact in financial terms is also very evident. The data in Table 5.1 show total direct mental health expenditures and for selected institutions in 1971, 1974 and 1977. The magnitude of nursing home expenditure is clear as early as 1971, with nursing homes making up 28 per cent of total direct care costs at that time, and a slightly higher 29.2 per cent in 1974. This form of transinstitutionalization has been going on since the 1960s, although it is only in the past five or ten years that the phenomenon has been clearly noticed.

The $4.243 billion spent in 1974 on nursing home care outpaced the $2.756 billion spent on state hospital care. The bar graph in Figure 5.1 provides an excellent visual representation of this data. By 1978 Medicare and Medicaid together paid for $8.4 billion of the $15.8 billion nursing home costs. Estimates for 1985 predict that these two major programs will pay for $21.8 billion of the $42 billion total. Medicaid has paid for a growing portion of the nursing home costs, and such costs have also become a larger percentage of all Medicaid costs. In 1972, nursing home bills took 23 per cent of all Medicaid spending, in 1976 33 per cent, and in 1978 34 per cent (Lerman, 1982:184-188; Levine and Willner, 1976). Table 5.2 shows Medicaid expenditures for mental health services.

Table 5.1 Expenditures on Direct Mental Health Care, Total and Selected Types of Institutions, 1971, 1974, and 1977

	1971	% of total	1974	% of total	1977	% of total
Total direct care	$9,525,707,000	—	$14,506,028,000	—	$17,000,000,000	
State and County mental hospitals	2,164,237,000	22.7	2,756,442,000	19.0	3,329,351,000	
CMHCs	285,955,000	3.0	602,054,000	4.2	—	
Nursing homes	2,666,357,000	28.0	4,242,905,000	29.2	—	
General hospitals (Psych. wards)	927,746,000	9.7	1,700,560,000	11.7	—	

Sources: Levine and Levine (1975); Levine and Willner (1976); President's Commission on Mental Health 1978, vol. II, 530; Witkin (1981a).

Nursing and boarding home placements have grown so rapidly due to misconceptions of deinstitutionalization and to the entrepreneurial potential of the nursing and boarding home industry. Most visible is the precipitous discharge of tens of thousands of patients from state hospitals, and the accompanying stringent admissions policies which ended the state hospital's previous function as a location for unwanted, apparently senile, elderly persons. As pointed out several times earlier in this book, these discharge and admissions practices were largely attempts to reduce state mental health budgets and transfer costs to federal Medicaid, Medicare, and Supplemental Security Income funding, and to local welfare spending. Mental health planners did not create sufficient alternative care facilities to provide a choice other than the nursing home. Nor did CMHCs offer a wide range of services for chronic mental patients which might keep them in less restrictive and custodial environments. The availability of federal payment, largely through Medicaid, has attracted the enterprising nursing and boarding home operators. At the same time, federal and private third party payers usually will not reimburse outpatient and alternative service modes which might obviate the need for nursing home care.

The elderly were the first focus of deinstitutionalization. The positive impetus behind this phenomenon was to end the practice of using state hospitals as a dumping ground, a last respite before death, or a nursing home in practice. In the late nineteenth and early twentieth centuries

Figure 5.1 Percent Distribution of Expenditures for Direct Care of the Mentally Ill by Type or Locale of Care, United States, 1974

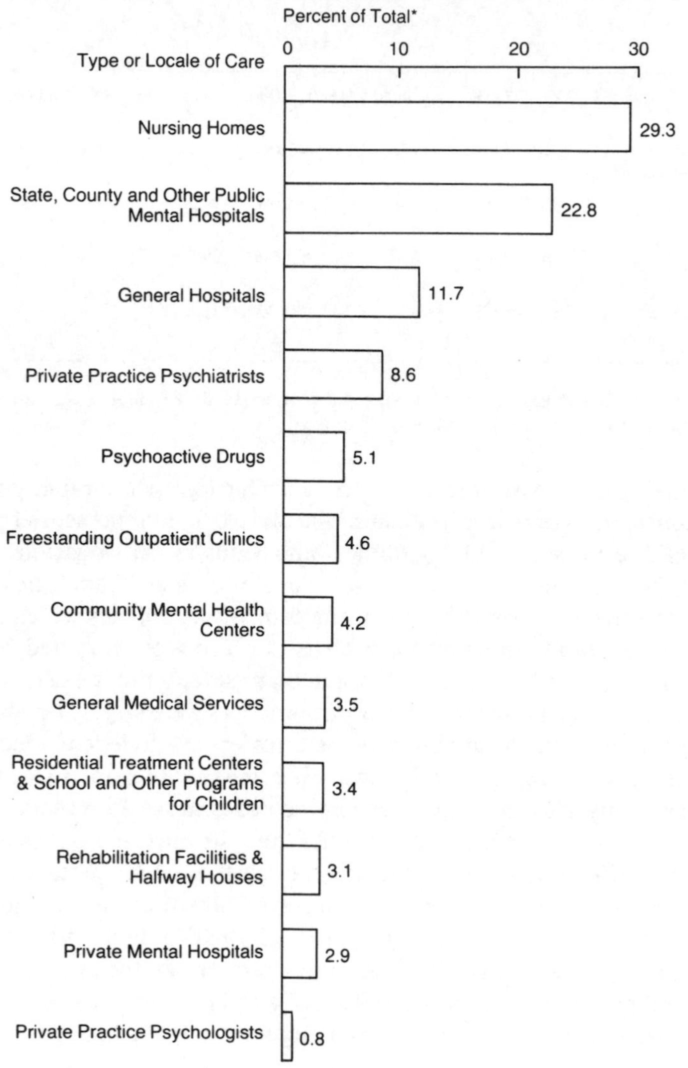

Source: Levine and Wilner (1976)

Table 5.2 Medicaid Expenditures for Mental Health Services, FY 1977 (in millions of dollars)

Public and private psychiatric hospitals	$ 558
General hospital (inpatient and outpatient) and emergency services	185
Community Mental Health Centers	100
Private free-standing clinics	25
Private practitioners	82
Nursing homes	2,189
Residential treatment centers and children's programs	110
Drugs	110
TOTAL	$3,389

Source: President's Commission on Mental Health, 1978, Vol. II, p. 520

Note: $720 millon for nursing homes serving primarily mentally retarded people is not included in this table.

the elderly made up the largest group of inappropriately hospitalized persons, thus contributing to 'warehousing.' When New York began its restrictive admissions of the elderly in 1968, it obtained a 42 per cent reduction in aged admissions within a year. From 1969 to 1974 total U.S. state and county mental hospital inpatient population decreased 44 per cent, from 427,799 to 237,692; over-65 inpatients however, decreased far more rapidly — 56 per cent, from 135,322 to 59,685. In some states the discharge of elderly patients has been much higher than the national average. Over the same period, 1969-1974, Alabama and Illinois reduced elderly inpatients by 76 per cent, California by 86 per cent, Massachusetts by 87 per cent, and Wisconsin's county hospitals emptied 98 per cent of their 4,616 over-65 residents, leaving only 96 (US Senate, 1976: xl,719).

Nationwide, approximately 100,000 (8 per cent) of all certified nursing home residents are ex-mental patients (Friedenberg, 1980). Yet far more elderly persons with mental illness go directly to nursing and boarding homes rather than to state hospitals, as in the past. Massachusetts DMH data for 1977 (February 17 1977 Memo) indicate that at least 5.6 per cent of all discharged patients go directly to nursing homes; the rate of elderly patients taking that route is obviously much higher, but those DMH data are very approximate and fragmentary. Further, such data don't take into account the elderly patients already discharged, but later admitted to homes rather than readmitted to hospitals. In 1975 there were 6,000 ex-patients in Masschusetts nursing homes; these patients were concentrated in homes which had been decertified for Medicaid eligibility due to poor health and safety conditions and to excessive confinement (Dietz, 1975). Schulberg and Baker (1975) report a figure similar to the DMH for Boston State Hospital patients discharged in the early 1970s. Further, they note that 53 per cent of those people were readmitted within thirteen months. Of approximately 4000 Boston State Hospital patients released between 1960 and 1977, 800 (20 per cent) were estimated to be living in nursing homes. This figure is more striking if we take into account that an estimated 1500 (38 per cent) of the released patients were dead, and 200 (5 per cent) returned to the hospital, then 35 per cent of those surviving on the outside were found in nursing homes (Scheper-Hughes, 1981). On Hawaii's main island of Oahu, discharged patients in 1972 represented a huge 68 per cent of all skilled nursing facilities, the highest level of nursing homes (Kirk and Therrien, 1975). In the late 1970s, patients admitted directly from state hospitals to nursing homes accounted for 11.9 per cent of skilled nursing facility (SNF) residents and 28.3 per cent of intermediate care facility (ICF) residents. But looking at ex-patients in general (who may have been elsewhere after mental hospital release), these accounted for 23 per cent of SNF and 65 per cent of ICF patients (Shadish et al., 1981).

These state hospital transfers are not always very long-lasting. Cumming and Markson (1975), in a follow up study of 2,174 discharged New York patients, found a 39.2 per cent return rate within ninety days. When Massachusetts' Grafton State Hospital was closed in 1973, 40 per cent of its patients were discharged (rather than being transferred to another state hospital); of that number, 61 per cent went to level III nursing home and rest homes (no nursing care); and another 16 per cent to landlord-supervised apartments and group residences (MMHPP, 1974, 33-34). During that year, a total of 1,800 patients were sent to nursing homes, with 750 being returned to hospitals within the year (Dietz, 1975).

Ex-state hospital patients are concentrated in some nursing homes. A recent ADAMHA (Rotegard, 1979) study attributed this clustering to three factors. First, absentee ownership or operator indifference about patient mix plays a role. This is particularly important during a period of rapid discharge, when it is easy to fill beds. Second, certain homes are decertified or downgraded due to failure to comply with the Life Safety Code. Waivers of the code are often given for ambulatory patients, and since most ex-mental patients are ambulatory, more of them are admitted to these unsafe homes. Third, a home's proximity to a state hospital makes for easy placement by the hospital.

The growth of nursing and boarding homes is in part an unplanned phenomenon as far as mental health policymakers are concerned. Nursing homes were never intended to be places for psychiatrically impaired persons. Rather, they were a minor extension of the Social Security program. Before the 1935 Social Security Act, there were very few nursing homes. The Act's exclusion of benefits for recipients in public facilities led to the rapid growth of proprietary nursing homes. By 1939 there were 1,200 homes with 25,000 residents. In the early 1950s legislation provided for Federal Housing Authority and Small Business Administration funds to construct and renovate private nursing homes. Thus, by 1954 there were 7,000 skilled nursing facilities (SNFs), containing 180,000 beds. By 1961, 9,582 SNFs existed, with 330,981 beds (Stotsky, 1969: 12; Kramer, 1977). These figures only account for SNFs, which hold about 65 per cent of the total homes population. Also important is federal financing support for nursing homes. In 1956, lobbying efforts by the American Nursing Homes Association won legislative authorization for Small Business Administration mortgages (Lerman, 1982: 214).

In the early 1960s, new programs and new regulations concerning existing programs paved the way for nursing home expansion. In 1960, Medical Assistance for the Aged provided payments for public and private general hospitals and for nursing homes. Two years later, new HEW regulations allowed under-sixty-five persons to receive Aid to the Permanently and Totally Disabled (APTD) if they were convalescing from a hospital stay. Eligible locations included home care, family care, or nursing and boarding homes. Further, funding for social service programs as well as medical care was then allowed for APTD clients (Lerman, 1982: 89-90). As a result, from 1960 to 1970 nursing home facilities increased 140 per cent, beds by 232 per cent and patients by 210 per cent (Senate, 1976: xiii). Much of that growth is directly attributable to Medicare and Medicaid legislation which required skilled nursing facilities and intermediate care facilities for care of poor and elderly persons (Glasscote et al., 1976: 23). Social Security's SSI program proved a boon to boarding homes, particularly when entrepreneurial administrators took advantage of it. In 1972 SSI was created, but it would not take effect until 1974. During the intervening period, states 'blanketed in' a wider range of eligibility types for APTD since SSI would assume all APTD categories. Thus, while from 1962 to 1970, an eight year period, APTD recipients grew 106 per cent nationwide from 421,000 to 866,000 from 1970 to 1973, a three year interval, the program grew 247 per cent to 3 million recipients in anticipation of SSI assumption of the caseload (Lerman, 1982: 94). Such rapid transinstitutionalization has historic precedent; in the 1890s, following state legislation to take over mental health care, senility was defined as a mental problem for which persons were to be sent to the state asylum at state expense.

Adequate data for boarding homes (also called adult homes, rest homes, board and care homes and personal care homes) are sparse since licensing laws are so lax, if at all existent. A 1965 Public Health Service survey counted 18,958 homes of all sorts nationwide (Stotsky, 1969: 10). A more recent survey (NIMH, 1977b) counted a 1973 total of 15,737 facilities with 1,075,900 residents, excluding the lowest level of boarding homes. Glasscote et al. (1976: 23-25) report 16,150 nursing homes and 7,000 boarding homes, for a total of 23,150 facilities.

Nursing homes expanded rapidly in the 1970s, but recent government regulation is slowing them down at present. In New York, the number of adult (boarding) homes nearly tripled from 1971 to 1977, increasing from 8,719 to 24,231, with most of those beds being in homes of 150 or more beds (Hynes, 1977: 11; Marcia Kramer, 1977). Nationally, the number of beds rose 600 per cent (Glasscote et al. 1976: 24). This shows additionally the increase in size of the homes, during the 1970s. 'Determination of need' (DON) procedures are making it difficult to win approval for additional beds. This may stem increase in nursing home size in the 1980s. However, recent federal discussions concerning widescale deregulation of nursing homes might counter such state-level planning.

Data on the number of ex-patients residing in boarding homes are sketchier than similar data for nursing homes. This is because many homes are unlicensed, and even those which are eligible for SSI payments have less detailed reporting requirements than do skilled nursing and intermediate care facilities. On Oahu, the island containing 80 per cent of Hawaii's population, licensed care homes and boarding homes increased, respectively, 31 per cent and 41 per cent in only three years, 1970-1973. While there were no unlicensed homes in 1970, by 1973 there sixty-six (Kirk and Therrien, 1975). In New York State, approximately one-third, or 6,650 boarding home residents are veterans of the psychiatric system; in New York City the proportion jumps to 44 per cent (Hynes, 1977, 23; Baxter and Hopper, 1980). In 1975 in Massachusetts, ex-patients occupied 13.5 per cent of intermediate care facilities and 22 per cent of rest home (boarding home) beds (Dietz, 1975).

In New York City, many patients have been dumped into single-room occupancies (SROs), many of which had been operating as 'welfare hotels'. The city's Upper West Side contains an estimated 7,000 chronic patients living in SROs. Estimates of the citywide population of mentally ill persons in SROs range from 10,000 to 20,000 (Koenig, 1978; Baxter and Hopper, 1980). This kind of community saturation feeds a growing public antagonism to these persons and to the overall thrust of deinstitutionalization.

REIMBURSEMENT BIASES AND RESTRICTIONS

It has been shown how Medicare, Medicaid, and SSI regulations favored the expansion of private, profit-making facilities. Federal reimbursement biases continue to support the private sector by paying for treatment in the most custodial locations, rather than in more innovative care settings. The Joint Information Service survey (Glasscote, et al., 1976:77) found that 85 per cent of ICF patients and 86 per cent of SNF patients were being paid for by Medicaid. Under the Medicaid program, the U.S. government reimburses 50-81 per cent of state costs for services which, within certain limits, the states determine as eligible. Recipients must be under 21 or over 65 to receive inpatient care in any mental hospital. Persons between those ages may receive care in psychiatric wards of general hospitals. Hardly any mental health clinic services, partial hospitalization, or private household care are covered. Many small facilities of 15 beds or less are de facto ineligible since federal regulations requires too much medical orientation, staffing, and equipment for such places to possibly meet their requirements (Comptroller General, 1977: 81-88; Glasscote et al., 1976: 77). These restrictions lead to Medicaid's supporting nursing homes rather than more beneficial placements such as halfway houses or group apartments. New York State in 1973 paid out $560 million in Medicaid funds to 600 nursing homes. Average cost per patient was $10,000 (Santiestevan, 1976). It is general knowledge that since the 1965 passage of Medicare and Medicaid, health costs have risen far out of proportion to past levels of health care, as well as far in advance of general inflation.

Like Medicaid, Medicare's restrictions also hamper proper care for deinstitutionalized mental patients. Maximum yearly payments for outpatient services are $250, a ceiling which has not been raised since 1965 although psychiatric fees have risen 70 per cent. $250 might cover four or five outpatient visits. This encourages mental health professionals to hospitalize elderly patients. Once in a hospital, however, the elderly face a 190 day lifetime limit in psychiatric hospitals, although there is no maximum in general hospital psychiatric wards. First admissions to psychiatric hospitals are limited to 150 days, whereupon the person must leave for at least 60 days in order to qualify for any or all of the remaining 40 days of the lifetime maximum (Comptroller General, 1977: 118-119; U.S. Senate, 1976: 710). Thus a person may be both precipitously hospitalized and then precipitously discharged. The reference point is not the person's health, but the bureaucratic regulations.

Federal SSI benefits are reduced by varying amounts if the person is institutionalized in a facility which could be covered by Medicaid. They are also reduced if the person actually receives any Medicaid or state financed support. If the person lives with a relative, which might be a beneficial setting, benefits are cut by one-third. Further, SSI money can't be used for any publicly funded facilities. This excludes many halfway houses and group living arrangements. This restriction on publicly funded facilities is in part responsible for the poor showing by CMHCs in caring for elderly people, who make up only 4 per cent of total additions. Thus, SSI keeps patients out of potentially beneficial facilities since they are largely public, and to some extent even keeps them out of nursing homes since such homes are Medicaid-eligible. As a result, SSI payments are largely used for boarding homes — the lowest level of living situation. (Comptroller General, 1977: 124-131; U.S. Senate, 1976: 712; Hynes, 1977: 21).

The October 29, 1976 Unemployment Compensation Amendments (PL 94-566) contain provisions freeing up some SSI restrictions. Publicly operated facilities of sixteen or fewer beds may be eligible; state and local subsidies to SSI recipients will no longer reduce SSI payments for persons in institutions which could be covered by Medicaid (Comptroller General, 1977: 132). Other evidence suggests that the government is not prepared to provide an expanded SSI program. The federal maximum payment of $157 is supplemented by some states. California has one of the highest supplements in the nation, $149, for a total maximum of $306.

The mean total maximum in 1976 was $247. Four years later, the average had only increased by $3, while the cost-of-living index rose 41 per cent (Lerman, 1982: 181). Such poor maintenance levels encourage decreasing quality of care.

As part of its budget slashing in the human services, the Reagan Administration has begun drastic cutoffs in disability payments. These disability cutoffs are part of the federal effort to halt the transfer of care from state and local coffers to federal ones. Disability payments have grown dramatically. In 1960 total disability payments were $533 million to 455,000 beneficiaries. In 1970 $3 billion was paid out to 1.5 million recipients and their 1.2 million dependents. In 1980 $15.3 million went to 4.7 million beneficiaries and dependents. The most recent figures for 1981 show $17.3 billion in total Social Security disability, of which $4.4 billion is SSI. A 1980 amendment called for periodic reviews which have been undertaken in excess. Further, a 1981 study by the General Accounting Office estimated that $2 billion in annual payments went to persons without disabilities (Pear, 1982a; Bleyer, 1982). Whether or not the GAO report is accurate, Social Security's cutoff process has generated many stories around the country of persons being declared able to work when they were clearly paralyzed or chronically mentally ill.

In a one-month period in 1981, the Social Security Administration reviewed 436,308 cases and terminated 40 per cent of them. Half of the terminated cases appealed the rulings, and of those, 67.2 per cent were reinstated. Of New York State terminations, 42 per cent were persons with mental troubles (Kihss, 1982). The state's Office of Mental Health reported that increasing numbers of mentally ill applicants were being denied SSI payments by restricted eligibility standards, often based on mere errors in completing application forms. Thirty per cent of New York state's disability cutoffs quickly wound up on state and local relief, and the state Department of Social Services estimated that figure would climb to 40 per cent. New York City Council President Carol Bellamy forecasted that if this policy continues, a total of 5,500 residents of the state would lose benefits, and that if one-half of them enter the general relief rolls, the state would spend $3.5 million and the city $1.5 million additionally each year (*This Month in Mental Health*, 1982; *Newsday*, 1982; Kihss, 1982). Mental health advocates have opposed this policy, and in one jurisdiction have been successful. Federal District Judge Earl Larson in Minneapolis ordered the Social Security Administration to restore benefits to mentally ill persons who had been denied payments since March 1981, and to pay retroactive benefits. He also ordered the SSA to cease using strict guidelines for eligibility which violated constitutional due process (*New York Times*, Dec. 25, 1982). In response to tremendous objections and much litigation, the Department of Health and Human Services announced that 200,000 recipients would be exempt from eligibility review. Among this number are 135,000 persons diagnosed as psychotic (*Mental Disability Law Reporter*, 1983b).

QUALITY OF CARE

Many nursing and boarding homes are dangerous, unhealthy, and oppressive environments. They lack rehabilitative and therapeutic services, provide little or no follow-up by hospitals, offer few recreation facilities, are understaffed, rely on heavy drugging, and are filled with health and fire hazards. As the Moss Senate subcommittee report described boarding homes, 'in some cases they may be converted mobile homes or converted chicken coops', and provide a quality of life 'ranking with prisons and concentration camps as prime examples of man's inhumanity to man'. U.S. Senate, 1976: 753). Senate testimony also noted other abuses: negligence leading to injury and death, misappropriation and theft of money and benefit checks, inadequate control of drugs, assaults on human dignity, profiteering, and to cap it all, reprisals against residents who complain. HEW standards for care were found to be 'so vague as to defy enforcement', and state standards barely exist. Pennsylvania, for example, stopped licensing and inspecting boarding homes in 1967, which was even before the large-scale dumping began (U.S. Senate, 1976: xii-xiv, 752).

The first of a series of devastating reports on New York adult (boarding) homes by state Deputy Attorney General Charles Hynes showed the near total lack of coordination or planning for discharged patients. Mentally ill persons, by law, may not be placed in adult homes if they are a danger to themselves or others. They are supposed to be certified by a physician to be in suitable enough physical and mental condition not to require the nursing care supplied with a higher level of home. Yet this examination is typically ignored, resulting in a number of otherwise preventable homicides, suicides, and other deaths from physical conditions. Discharging institutions rarely coordinate with local social service agencies or the homes. DMH hospital administrators have not even complained about the homes' practice of sometimes sending buses to their institutions to solicit dischargees. The state's Board of Social Welfare and

Department of Mental Hygiene have made several agreements for the DMH to provide services to those homes having 40 per cent or more of their populaton consisting of ex-patients. An early effort has been made to implement these arrangements, through the Community Support Program. (Hynes, 1977: 19, 42-43; Marcia Kramer, 1977). An ADAMHA report mentioned earlier (Rotegard, 1979) found similar failings in CMHC services to catchment area nursing homes with higher populations of discharged patients.

Physicians and registered nurses are a rarity in most nursing homes. Few checkups, tests, diagnoses, or follow-ups on medication are provided. Many reports show, for example, that patients on cardiovascular drugs may go for years without even a simple blood pressure exam. Doctors frequently write prescriptions without seeing the recipient. In the boarding homes where no medical care is required, 80 per cent to 90 per cent of staff are aides and orderlies who are usually paid at the minimum wage and drastically overworked (U.S. Senate, 1975: 251, 280; 1976: xvi-xviii; Glasscote et al., 1976: 82-83).

Federal hearings have found that at least 50 per cent of all homes are substandard, defined as 'with one or more life-threatening conditions'. In 1973 alone, 6,400 fires killed 551 residents. Washington, D.C.'s 180-200 homes are run by owners to whom D.C. authorities provide only six hours of training, and from whom they require no operating standards. These facilities are typically vermin-infested, with many patients in permanent lock-up. Residents often sleep in living and dining rooms. In Michigan, according to the AFL-CIO, 'standards for pet stores are more stringently enforced than for nursing homes'. (U.S. Senate, 1976: xiv, xx, 747; *Associated Press*, 1977).

Psychoactive drugs have been as central to nursing homes as to state hospitals. The average nursing home resident in 1976 took four to seven different drugs daily, spending an average of $300 each per year as compared to the nationwide average of $87 for non-institutionalized elderly. Nearly 40 per cent of those drugs are tranquilizers, sedatives, painkillers, and central nervous system drugs. Overall, more than 90 per cent of psychiatric patients in homes are given some psychotropic drug. Homes often give higher than prescribed dosages of tranquilizers in order to pacify patients; the extra dosages are culled from dead or discharged residents. On the average, 20 per cent to 40 per cent of medication is administered in error, often by untrained staff acting illegally. Patients with no history of heart disease may be given digitalis, and non-diabetics may receive insulin. Theft, misuse, and addiction are common, since medicine cabinets and rooms are often unlocked. Adverse reactions are prevalent, and account for 20 per cent of the nation's total admissions to state hospital geriatric wards. Strong antipsychotic drugs, especially phenothiazines, often produce tardive dyskinesia, dystonia, pseudo-Parkinsonism, and many other extremely debilitating conditions. Uninformed drug experimentation has also been widely documented (Hynes, 1977: 25; U.S. Senate, 1975: 252-274; Redlich and Kellert, 1978).

Schmidt et al. (1977) studied 1,155 psychiatric patients in Utah nursing homes, and determined that all were given increased dosages of psychoactive medication over time, resulting in decreased activity levels. Ray et al. (1980) reviewed 384,325 prescriptions for 5,902 Medicaid patients residing continuously for one year in 173 Tennessee nursing homes. 43 per cent of those patients received psychotropic drugs. Doctors with large nursing home practices (ten or more nursing home patients) prescribed 81 per cent of the total of those antipsychotic drugs. Further, as nursing home practice size increased, doctors prescribed more drugs per patient, and patients received more drugs if they resided in larger facilities. Ray and his associates concluded, as do a large number of researchers in this area, that there is significant misuse of antipsychotic drugs, and that new policies are required which rely less on those medications.

Pharmacist kickbacks to home operators are widespread, averaging 25 per cent of total drug charges, and often reaching 50 per cent. There is also much abuse in drug billing for Medicaid reimbursement, including billing for expensive brand-name items while providing generic drugs at sometimes one-fifth the cost. Pharmacists often charge three to four times the retail store price to nursing homes for government reimbursement. In many cases bills are presented for items never provided (U.S. Senate, 1975: 251, 278-295).

PROFITABILITY AND REGULATION

Nursing and boarding homes are very profitable enterprises. As pointed out at the beginning of this chapter, they gross nearly $16 billion yearly. More than one-fourth of that goes to caring for mentally ill persons, and represents the largest single source of direct mental health expenditures. As the only sector of mental health care which is predominantly private and for-profit, the homes industry demonstrates the structural relations in mental health care which turn chaotic policy into large profit.

Governmental research, such as the Comptroller General's reports and the Senate Subcommittee on Long-Term Care's hearings, and private research such as Vladek (1980) and Mendelson (1975) have documented the fashion in which profit is made. Operators spend less than 60 cents daily per patient for food in some nursing homes, fail to provide clean linen and clothing, keep their homes understaffed, and often steal residents' checks which they endorse and cash. Some home operators even offer per capita kickbacks to mental health officials for deinstitutionalized patients (U.S. Senate, 1976: 741).

As is common in the medical marketplace, monopolization is increasing in the homes industry. In 1973, 106 corporations controlled 18 per cent of total beds and took one-third of the industry's $3.2 billion revenue. Those corporations' income had risen 116 per cent from 1969 to 1972. Beverly Enterprises, starting with three homes in 1964, grew by 1972 to over sixty, netting $79.5 million. Extendicare's forty-one-home business was purchased in 1975 for approximately $15 million by National Health Enterprises, which already owned ninety profit-making hospitals. Holiday Inn's Medicenters Division and American Automated Vending Corp. are among the large conglomerates engaging in the homes industry (U.S. Senate, 1976: xxiv; Chase, 1973; Santiestevan, 1976: 18). By the late 1970s, nursing homes chains owned or controlled between 25 per cent and 30 per cent of all homes and 35 per cent of total beds (Comptroller General, 1979).

Governmental regulation, investigation, and supervision have been weak overall (Vladek, 1980) though some important exceptions exist. HEW's Inspector-General launched an investigation into organized crime involvement in nursing homes (*United Press International*, 1977a), but refused to divulge any information on the issue. In New York state, Deputy Attorney-General Charles J. Hynes was appointed as a special nursing homes prosecutor. In November 1976 he produced twenty-six indictments of home owners, officials, and suppliers for kickbacks, bribery, perjury, and criminal solicitation. Hynes estimated that up to half of the New York City area's 125 nursing homes might be involved, and the amount of fraudulent claims for costs from 1971 to 1976 may total $70 million. These costs, recorded as construction and operation, were covers for the purchase of expensive paintings, foreign travel, mink coats, stocks and bonds, and personal home renovation (Meislin, 1977; Rich, 1976). Through Hynes' efforts, and some court cooperation, some convictions and restitution payments have been won, yet Hynes' prosecution was severely hampered since many homes refused him entrance despite his office. In general, however, lax law enforcement has been common. Regulatory agencies usually lack power to act, and nursing home operators possess a large array of tactics to forestall official action. And despite much governmental and public criticism of nursing and boarding homes, their status as private enterprises gives them a certain acceptability and leeway in a society which is ultimately geared to free enterprise more than to human service. Under the Reagan Administration's antiregulation perspective, Department of Health and Human Services (HHS) funds for nursing home inspection were cut by approximately 65 per cent in 1982. Despite massive evidence to the contrary, HHS will assume that home operators are complying with medical, health, fire and safety codes. As a result, states have had to drastically curtail their inspections and follow-up visits to monitor correction of deficiencies (Pear, 1982c).

Nursing homes, boarding homes, and SROs have become the principal residences of mentally ill persons. Over the last decade and a half they have supplanted state hospitals in this respect. While reformers in the 1950s sought to abolish the traditional 'out of sight, out of mind' function of the state hospital, they have merely transferred it to mini-institutions which replicate many of the custodial and dehumanizing elements of asylum life.

This phenomenon is more complex than merely transinstitutionalization, since it involves more than just a change of facilities. It is a financial transfer from state mental health budgets to federal medical and social welfare budgets. It is a transfer of responsibility from state mental health authorities to state welfare and public health officials, both of which are involved in regulating the homes. Such regulation is insufficient, since it emphasizes facility requirements (such as staffing ratios and life safety codes) more than the provision of comprehensive psychiatric, rehabilitative, and social welfare services. It is also a transfer of responsibility in that there is less direct control of and public authority over patients when they are in private facilities. And, it is a transfer of public perception of these chronically ill people, since they become more of a public nuisance and appear as welfare recipients (Medicaid, SSI, Public Assistance) rather than as more deserving psychiatric patients. This is particularly true for the many chronically mentally ill persons who do not make it into any type of institution. New York State has 79,000 chronic patients in the community, 47,000 of them in New York City. Of the New York City population, state mental health officials estimate that 5,200 are homeless people and dependent on overnight public shelters. According to some public estimates, there are a total of 36,000 homeless people in New York

City (all categories, not just mentally ill). The Men's Shelter, funded in equal part by city and state, serves approximately 10,000 clients annually. New York City serves a total of 12,000 men and 4,000 women per year in homeless care. A 1976 survey of 1,235 clients in the Men's Shelter found that 30 per cent had prior mental hospitalization, but interview research raised that estimate to nearly 50 per cent of the men having overt mental illness (Baxter and Hopper, 1980: 1982). New York City cannot house all these homeless persons, even though it spent four times as much in 1982 as in 1978 to house four times as many. One factor is that the summer demand for homeless shelter now remains as high as the winter demand, a change most likely due to the creation of a larger permanent marginal population of chronic mental patients which does not find alternative living arrangements as did the former homeless population of mainly alcoholics (Daley, 1982).

As Isaacs (1982) points out:

> *nursing home programs should include adequate preadmission evaluation of each client's mental and physical status, individual treatment programs for those judged to have some level of psychological impairment, increased recreational and rehabilitative activities, more direct psychiatric liaison and augmented educational activities, in-service training programs, and joint mental health/long-term care consultations on a regular basis.*

NIMH's (1980) *National Plan* urged such a range of services. Health planners and regulators could enforce such comprehensiveness, especially through 'determination of need' reviews. Nursing homes would then be required to provide evidence of mental health services both internally and by liaison with mental health facilities (Isaacs, 1982). Yet apart from scattered examples of mental health services in nursing and boarding homes, there is little effort to integrate these facilities into a planned psychiatric service system. The clients are the least desirable, the financial incentives are lacking, and the problem is too entrenched. This is in contrast to less disturbed mentally ill persons, many of whom have found some expansion of services in the new and more coordinated *public-private allied sector.* The following chapter examines this sector.

CHAPTER 6

The New Alliance of Public and Private Sectors: Private Mental Hospitals and General Hospital Psychiatric Units

Chapters 3 and 4 have detailed the neotraditional and traditional public sectors of CMHCs and state hospitals, and Chapter 5 has examined the new custodial private sector of nursing homes, boarding homes, and single-room occupancies. Discussion of the specialty private psychiatric sector of private psychiatric hospitals and general hospital psychiatric units has been postponed in order now to examine the new alliance of public and private psychiatric facilities. This important new phenomenon is largely the result of the structural forces already discussed in Chapters 3 through 5 — efforts to transfer care and responsibility, the growth of private and public reimbursement practices, and the power and ability of private facilities to garner public funding. In this process, the traditions of the last two centuries of psychiatric care have been significantly altered.

ALTERATIONS IN THE TWO-CLASS SYSTEM OF CARE

In the early nineteenth century, private psychiatric care was the sole form of care until the proliferation of state hospitals in the 1830s. While the original conception of the state hospitals was for a short-term, more well-to-do clientele, the patient population quickly became working-class, immigrant, and chronic. Those able to afford care sought private hospitals, and state asylums became backward institutions of last resort. Localities no longer subsidized a certain proportion of poor patients in the private hospitals, since state facilities grew rapidly in number and size. By the middle of the nineteenth century the division of mental care into two spheres was complete. In the twentieth century, particularly in the first two post-World War II decades, the private sector grew further, as mental health care became more developed, available, and in demand. Advances in dynamic therapeutic methods benefited the private sector patients, while public patients remained in custodial asylums.

Two decades ago, when the CMHC program was just beginning, it was possible to clearly demarcate a public and a private mental health sector. Public sector patients were cared for in state hospitals, in some psychiatric wards of municipal hospitals, and in the remnants of the few urban psychopathic hospitals. Private sector patients were cared for in private psychiatric hospitals and a very few general hospital psychiatric units; those not requiring hospitalization were seen as outpatients in office psychiatry. A patient could either afford private care, or was forced to rely on low-cost or free public care. Health insurance was not generally available for psychiatric coverage, and federal reimbursements were not yet in place. Little, if any, crossover existed between the public and private sectors. Class differentials which had been thoroughly studied by Hollingshead and Redlich (1958) polarized the type and quality of care available to the mentally ill. This situation was obviously a 'two-class system,' as the Joint Commission noted, a system which federal planners and forward-looking professionals sought to rectify.

Both consciously and inadvertently, mental health practices in the last two decades have greatly altered the public-private separation, creating a complex public-private mix. In this new system, private facilities tend to care for the acutely ill and public facilities for the chronically ill. The private sector is no longer composed primarily of more well-to-do persons. This is a result of insurance reimbursements, Medicare and Medicaid reimbursements, CMHCs' collaborative structures, and most recently state hospital/general hospital 'trade-offs' to deal with state hospital deinstitutionalization and general hospital overbedding in medical/surgical units. While these factors have increased the number of private facilities, they have also boosted utilization of these private facilities by the less well-to-do. When one looks at the overall national cost of psychiatric care, it is evident that public expenditures have not declined, but that they have shifted the range of public and private facilities which they support. Further, the new types of publicly supported facilities generally do not serve ex patients who were former residents of state hospitals (Goldman, Adams, and Taube, 1983).

RECENT GROWTH OF FACILITIES IN THE PUBLIC-PRIVATE ALLIED SECTOR

As with nursing homes, reimbursement mechanisms were responsible for the initial development of other private psychiatric care. But while mental health planners may shy away from planned reliance on nursing homes, due to general displeasure with their care level, they very consciously plan for greater utilization of private psychiatric settings. Looking first at the role of reimbursement biases in the unplanned expansion of private psychiatric facilities, we recall that Medicaid excludes CMHCs and many mental health clinic services. Further, for recipients between 21 and 65 Medicaid covers care in private general hospital psychiatric units but not in private psychiatric hospitals. Similarly, Medicare limits psychiatric hospital inpatient care to a lifetime maximum of 190 days, but covers 90 days for each illness in a general hospital service. Again, no CMHC outpatient or partial treatment is covered. Thus, the two major federal health programs favor general hospital psychiatric wards. Private commercial and Blue Cross insurance favor both private psychiatric hospitals and general hospital psychiatric wards (Comptroller General, 1977; President's Commission on Mental Health, 1978; Sharfstein, 1978).

To see how these practices have favored the growth of the private sector, it is necessary to look at recent increases in those facilities. From 1968 to 1972 the only private psychiatric hospitals that opened were for-profit institutions, which increased by 34 per cent, while nonprofit hospitals declined by 3 per cent. Of the 42 new profit-making facilities, all but one were corporate (as opposed to individual/partnership structure) and half of those were part of multihospital chains (Taube and Redick, 1975). As Table 6.1 shows, for the period 1970-1980, the total of private hospitals rose from 150 to 184, an increase of 22 per cent (NIMH, 1982b). As Table 6.2 shows, these hospitals' inpatient admissions rose from 92,056 to 140,831 over approximately the same period, 1969-1979, increasing their share of all inpatient additions from 7.2 per cent to 9.1 per cent (NIMH, 1982c). General hospital psychiatric wards have increased markedly during the community mental health era. From 1964 to 1970 they increased from 538 to 766 wards nationwide, a 42.4 per cent increase. From 1970 to 1980 they grew to 923 wards, a slower increase of 19 per cent (NIMH 1972; 1982b). As seen in Table 6.2, these units' additions grew from 478,000 to 551,190 in 1979. Other categories of psychiatric facilities, many of which are private, include psychiatric halfway houses, whose 7,089 beds served 10,917 persons in 1973 (Lerman, 1982: 42) and residential treatment facilities for children (RTCs) with a 1975 daily census of 16,307 and

Table 6.1 Number of Psychiatric Facilities in the Public-Private Allied Sector, by Type, Selected Years 1970-1980

	1970	1972	1974	1976	1978	1980
General Hospital Psychiatric Unit	776	770	796	870	923	923*
Private Psychiatric Hospital	150	156	180	182	188	184
Residential Treatment Centers	261	344	340	331	375	368
Freestanding Outpatient	1,109	1,123	1,092	1,076	1,160	1,053
CMHC	196	287	391	517	555	691

Source: NIMH 1972; 1982b

*No accurate data for that year: estimate is from previous entry

a total population served of 28,199 (Witkin, 1977). Combined, these account for under 2 per cent of patient care episodes.

INCREASING ROLE OF GENERAL HOSPITAL PSYCHIATRY

The role of the general hospital psychiatric unit has been increasingly determined by patterns of state hospital depopulation and by Community Mental Health Center structure. In 1955, the rate of inpatient episodes in state hospitals (502 per 100,000) was three times that of general hospitals (163 per 100,000), but in 1977 the rate of both was nearly identical (265 per 100,000), and more than twice the rate of CMHCs (125 per 100,000) (Bachrach, 1981). Table 6.3 shows a slight decline in their per cent of all inpatient additions over this period. This must be qualified by three important points.

First, many of the CMHC inpatient units, the category with the largest per cent distribution increase, are in fact general hospital units. The collaborative structure of most CMHCs is such that they often utilize pre-existing facilities for part or all of their range of services. In 1972, 162 general hospital units are excluded from general hospital statistics in

Table 6.2 Number of Inpatient Additions to Psychiatric Facilities in the Public-Private Allied Sector, by Type, Selected Years 1969-1979

	1969	1971	1973	1975	1977	1979
General Hospital Psychiatric Unit	478,000	519,926	468,415	543,731	551,190	551,190*
Private Psychiatric Hospital	92,056	87,106	109,516	125,529	138,151	140,831
Residential Treatment Centers	7,596	11,148	12,179	12,022	15,152	15,453
CMHC	59,730	75,900	183,026	236,226	257,347	246,409

Source: NIMH 1982c

*No accurate data for that year; estimate is from previous entry

NIMH data. CMHCs have been central to the expansion of these general hospital psychiatric wards, since these units are the primary source of intensive care for acute patients and for short-term hospitalization of chronic patients. Nor are inpatient psychiatric wards in VA hospitals included in the NIMH tally of general hospitals. The American Hospital Association's 1978 survey showed 1,010 general hospital psychiatric units, with a total of 32,422 beds (Flamm, 1981). This is slightly less than the total of VA, CMHC, and hospital units, perhaps due to confusion about some of CMHC units actually being regular general hospital units that also have CMHC affiliations.

Second, the data showing slight decline in general hospital ward additions as percentage of total inpatient additions mask an important aspect of the public-private split. Virtually all of their growth from 1964 to 1970 was in private general hospitals, whose wards increased 71.9 per cent compared to a 2.2 per cent increase in public units. As Table 3.2 (p. 53) in Chapter 3 indicates, from 1971 to 1977 inpatient additions in private hospitals jumped 36.8 per cent while they fell 37.0 per cent in public ones. In 1977 there were nearly three times as many inpatients in private general hospital psychiatric wards as in public ones, almost double the public-private ratio in 1971 (NIMH, 1972; Witkin, 1981b). Thus, even if general hospital psychiatric wards have remained stable as a percentage of all additons, there has been a dramatic shift from public to private sponsorship.

Table 6.3 Percent Distribution of Inpatient Additions to Psychiatric Facilities in the Public-Private Allied Sector, by Type, Selected Years 1969-1979

	1969	1971	1973	1975	1977	1979
General Hospital Psychiatric Unit	37.3	38.9	33.1	34.9	34.8	34.8*
Private Psychiatric Hospital	7.2	6.5	7.7	8.1	8.7	9.1
Residential Treatment Centers	0.6	0.8	0.9	0.8	1.0	1.0
CMHC	4.7	5.7	12.9	15.2	16.2	16.0

Source: NIMH 1982c

*No accurate data for that year: estimate is from previous entry

Third, most of the patients treated in general hospitals are cared for in hospitals without separate psychiatric units. This is a rapidly growing location of mental health care in recent years (Kiesler and Sibulkin, 1982).

The Massachusetts Hospital Association reported that 26 of 119 short-term general hospitals in the state had psychiatric wards as of July 1, 1976. Eight of them had been opened in the previous year, and fourteen had been operating fewer than four years (Massachusetts DMH, 1977: 36). The basis for this phenomenon is found in the growth of facilities and patient loads, and also in the proportion of expenses covered by third party payers. Combined, commercial and Blue Cross/Blue Shield insurance programs in 1975 paid the fees of 60 per cent of private general hospital psychiatric unit patients and 68 per cent of private psychiatric hospital patients. That same year, Medicare and Medicaid paid for 26 per cent of private general hospital patients, and Medicare for 11 per cent of private psychiatric hospital patients (NIMH, 1976; 1977a; 1977c).

Apart from CMHC affiliations for their own inpatient care, the early growth of general hospital psychiatry appears to have been planned by general hospitals more than by mental health planners. Then, mental health administrators were often confronted with the fact that these private institutions provided more reliable care without many of the bureaucratic entanglements of the public system. The state officials began to look at private facilities as services with which to contract for state-paid services. This enabled the state mental health departments to provide certain programs without having to start them from scratch, a strategy well in place from years of CMHC affiliation agreements. State governments also were attracted by the opportunity to reduce the state's permanent payroll and its future pension costs, and to deal with what are in many states largely non-union private facilities.

Proponents of general hospital psychiatric units point out that the general hospital is extremely accessible since it is the community's basic inpatient health facility. It is open twenty-four hours a day and is more familiar than other facilities; many studies have found that neighborhood residents are unaware of the existence or extent of services of nearby CMHCs. Additionally, many mental health facilities exclude certain types of patients, such as substance abusers. The general hospital is considered to deliver better services due to its medical support systems which help minimize overlooking organic causes. Related to this, proponents hold that the return to a biochemical model provides for more rigorous diagnosis and treatment (this issue will be explored in the next chapter). At their most optimistic, these proponents claim that the general hospital can meet all twelve of the required CMHC services. Advocates also argue that psychiatric liaison services to medical-surgical staff will increase and improve, leading to broadened training for all physicians which will prompt reduction in inappropriate medical-surgical services and curtailment of length of stay (Flamm, 1981; Keill, 1981).

The greater accessibility of the general hospital is a benefit, but the medical environment does not necessarily offer advantages. A more powerful, if unspoken, impetus toward the growth of general hospital psychiatric units is the professional transformation of psychiatry. Many psychiatrists are attracted by the better income and the professional medical legitimacy and the academic connection of the general hospital; this is more an issue of status than of biochemical benefits. For practitioners as well as patients, there is also less stigma attached to a short stay general hospital than to inpatient care in a state hospital, freestanding CMHC inpatient unit, or even a private psychiatric facility.

General hospital units can deliver better service since they are small units with more pleasant surroundings than many other psychiatric institutions. The units are generally newer, and are thus able to develop effective routines, methods, and staffing patterns without involvement of cumbersome and inefficient state bureaucracies. Financial resources are larger than in state hospitals, since patients are usually only kept as long as they can provide personal or third party payment. Further, as will be mentioned later in specific cases, general hospitals can select their patient populations with more certainty than can other facilities, thus yielding an easier group with which to work.

Another factor in the expansion of private psychiatric facility use by state DMHs is the crisis in general hospital overbedding. As health policy analysts have understood for some time, hospital competition for physicians and patients has resulted in overbedding. State 'determination of need' programs came too late and could only stem future bed expansion. In Massachusetts in 1979 there were 3,500 to 5,000 surplus acute medical-surgical beds, yet approximately 800 beds in psychiatric units of thirty-six general hospitals and 770 beds in seven psychiatric hospitals had long waiting lists. It was, therefore, advisable to convert the excess medical beds into psychiatric ones. The first trial was planned for Central Hospital, a poorly reputed private hospital in Somerville, a city in the Boston metropolitan area. The hospital would take patients who would otherwise go to Westboro State Hospital, which serves the Cambridge-Somerville catchment area. Unlike past policy towards general hospitals, involuntary commitments would be allowed and the state would guarantee payment (Dietz, 1979a; 1979b).

Such involuntary admissions to general hospitals have aroused opposition, since hospital staff will be compelled to admit 'undesirable' patients committed from other sources. Leeman (1980) summarizes the major reasons why many general hospital psychiatrists oppose involuntaries. Good treatment, they argue, depends on a hospital's patient selection. This includes avoiding patients with poor impulse control who would endanger other patients and staff. To admit such persons would require locked wards and the use of seclusion rooms, thus placing more restrictions on all patients in the unit. More effort would go into containment of disruptive patients, taking time away from milieu treatment. Secure treatment is costlier in daily staff time and also due to the fact that involuntary patients tend to have longer stays. Longer stays would also prevent the unit from serving a larger number of patients. Further, chronic psychotic patients, who would be the typical involuntary admissions, have fewer resources for payment. Similarly, Medicaid and Medicare pay very low reimbursements to individual psychiatrists who provide consultations. Since discharge planning is seen as central to general hospital psychiatry, these patients would present a problem since they have few or no support systems, and there are few adequate agencies for such people. In sum, Leeman notes, compulsory admission of these involuntary patients would lead to a lowest common denominator of care, thus mirroring the state hospital system of the past.

If private general hospitals get their way, such involuntary patients, as well as voluntary chronics, will be shunted to public general hospitals. Professional and institutional autonomy will face a test in the coming battles over the extent to which health planning officials and other administrators can exert control over these facilities. This is a critical issue, since general hospitals must serve a diverse population, including the new young adult chronics who have not typically had careers in state hospitals. These are patients who would have been state hospital patients prior to deinstitutionalization, but who now receive most of their care in short-term inpatient or outpatient treatment. The baby boom of 1946-61 produced a disproportionate number of persons now aged 20-35, thus adding to the higher number of persons at risk (Bachrach, 1981).

But the state government, concerned by rapid cost increases in general hospitals, has used cost-containment laws to curb those increases. Newton-Wellesley Hospital in Masschusetts opened a forty-five-bed psychiatric unit in 1982 after seven years of planning. The unit was to admit part of its population from persons who would have gone to Medfield State Hospital. State Medicaid reimbursement was set at what Newton-Wellesley considered too low a level, and later the same year the hospital announced it might close the new wing due to a projected loss of $800,000 out of the Psychiatry Department's $3 million annual budget (Dietz, 1982).

Reimbursement issues are not the only obstacle to a successful public-private mix. Professionalist issues also play an important role. In 1979, the University of Massachusetts Medical Center (UMMC) was able to open a twenty-bed inpatient psychiatric unit in exchange for the closing of forty beds at Worcester State Hospital. The Medical Center, however, 'creamed' the preferred patients (depressed, acute), leaving the schizophrenic, chronic patients to the state hospital. This was in accordance with the Medical Center's Utilization Review Committee's desire for short-stay patients and its attempt to provide newly recruited staff with a dynamic, interesting unit. Further, economic constraints meant that people without personal resources or third-party payers would be unlikely to be admitted to UMMC. The few that were admitted were seen by residents rather than by staff psychiatrists (Morrissey and Goldman, 1980b).

Even with current alterations in the mental health system, public general hospitals have poorer, more disturbed patients, with an evenly distributed male-female ratio, and paid for largely by Medicare and Medicaid. Private general hospitals, however, serve less disturbed, more well-off persons, with a higher proportion of women, and largely paid by Blue Cross and commercial insurance (Heiman, 1980; Bachrach, 1981).

The alliance of public and private sectors in general hospital psychiatric wards allows for some indigent, working-class and lower-middle-class persons to benefit from the more dynamic treatments offered in private general hospitals. But the public general hospitals remain overcrowded with poorer elements of the society, many of whom are recent state hospital dischargees. New York City has been particularly hard hit in this fashion. A 1977 agreement between city and state officials and private voluntary hospitals sought to make the voluntaries responsible for local mental health care in similar manner to their responsibility for physical health. Impetus for this plan came from state investigations into patient deaths resulting from negligence at one state hospital in the city, and by loss of accreditation of Kings County Psychiatric Hospital, a municipal facility. But the voluntaries have shied away from this role, some due to their own overcrowding and some to low Medicaid rates. Public general hospitals have absorbed most of the burden. In November, 1980 the majority of New York City's municipal psychiatric units were operating at 100 per cent or greater occupancy, while also containing many mental patients in emergency rooms awaiting disposition (Sullivan, 1977; *New York Times*, 1980). As a result of this overcrowding and the large amount of resultant publicity, New York City's Health and Hospitals Corporation convinced the New York State Office of Mental Health to allow the city's ten municipal psychiatric emergency rooms to send patients directly to state hospitals, even if for only two days. In the first several months of that practice, overcrowding in municipal hospital psychiatric units was reduced to under the full occupancy rate (Marcos and Gil, 1983).

State utilization of private psychiatric hospitals has also begun. A Providence, Rhode Island CMHC contracts for inpatient care at Butler Hospital. Massachusetts plans call for providing involuntary and secure facilities at Fuller and Maclean Hospitals (Dietz, 1981a).

PUBLIC-PRIVATE CONNECTIONS IN MENTAL HEALTH TRAINING

Another important way in which public funds support the private sector is in training mental health professionals, mainly psychiatrists and clinical psychologists. NIMH funds had played a major role in professional training in the 1960s and early 1970s, providing 7,690 training grants and 6,600 fellowships through 1972. Federal CMHC planners had originally sought $190 million annually in training expenditures by 1970, but by 1969 funds had only reached $120 million. Cutbacks began at that point, and by 1976 funds were down to $85.1 million, a 52 per cent cut figuring for inflation (Foley, 1975: 42-43; B. Brown, 1977). These public funds have been instrumental in the production of a greatly expanded mental health professional cadre, many of whom later entered private practice and/or private facilities.

Talbott (1979) notes that psychiatrists' flight from the public sector has many causes. Increased public funding of private facilities makes those facilities more able to support training programs and to provide better clinical working conditions. The blurring of the distinction between the state hospital and general hospital client population also makes it possible for clinicians who wish to serve the chronic and underserved population to do this in the private facility. Talbott also notes the many constraints on performance in the public sector: custodial practices, state mental health department bureaucracy, underfunding, judicial and regulatory interference, public advocate inputs, public scrutiny, civil service and union protection, increased clinical responsibility of nonprofessionals, and lack of control over admission and discharge due to deinstitutionalization policies. The integration of private facilities with medical empires also attracts psychiatrists since they can obtain a social support network through medical schools and nonpsychiatric physicians. Light (1980) points out that psychiatrists generally feel stigmatized by their medical colleagues, a stigmatization partly due to not being located in the same hospital or hospital network. The community mental health orientation had placed psychiatrists too close to psychologists and social workers, whose proportion of CMHC professional staff grew as that of psychiatrists fell. Community mental health perspectives, by somewhat demedicalizing mental illness, threatened the specialty medical position of psychiatrists. Declining funding for community mental health added to that threat. A major response of psychiatrists was to leave the community ideology and revive biopsychiatry.

Common belief has stated that the large public infusion of training funds has not resulted in increased public sector service after training, since staff gravitate to the private sector. Chu and Trotter (1974: 61) calculated that one-half of psychiatrists supported by NIMH residency funding leave after training to work primarily or exclusively in private practice. Light (1980: 319-322) considers this to be a false argument, since the public and private sectors have intermingled so much. Further, psychiatrists often work in a combination of settings, and over time there has been an increase in the per cent of public-based trainees who spend at least part of their work time in a public facility. Light also points out that while studies have examined subsequent work location for public-trained psychiatrists, there have been no studies of matched samples trained without public funds.

What is clear is that mental health planning has not succeeded in redistributing psychiatrists. Albee's (1959) monograph for the Joint Commission found that psychiatrists were geographically maldistributed and that there were very few of them to serve minorities, children, the elderly, and poor people. In a re-study two decades later, Albee (1979) found the same problems. Of course there are other professionals, but since the prevailing opinion was to equalize psychiatrists' distribution, that goal should be taken into account. The number of psychiatrists on staff is quite relevant in terms of facility accreditation, higher reimbursement, rate, and public perception of quality.

PSYCHIATRIC CARE OUTSIDE REGULAR PSYCHIATRIC FACILITIES

The discussion so far has focused on the more commonly identifiable inpatient mental health facilities; however, these represent only a minority of all mental health services. As Figure 3.1 (p. 48) shows, inpatient care has diminished from 77 per cent of all episodes in 1955 to 27 per cent in 1977, while outpatient visits increased from 23 per cent to 70 per cent over that period. This is a statistical artifact, since inpatient care has risen absolutely, even if outpatient treatment has expanded faster. These data are for mental health facilities only, yet many mentally ill persons are seen outside the usual psychiatric facilities. Regier et al. (1978) divide all episodes into four sectors: specialty mental health (SMH), general hospital inpatient/nursing home (GHI/NH), primary care/outpatient medical (PC/OPM), and not in treatment/other human services (NT/OHS). In 1975 the specialty mental health sector accounted for only 21 per cent of the mentally ill persons, estimated at 31,955,000 (15 per cent of the US population) in 1975. The general hospital inpatient/nursing home sector accounted for only 3.4 per cent of the mentally ill, most of these being persons treated as general hospital inpatients, but not in psychiatric wards. Regier and his colleagues admit that they have grossly underspecified the number of mentally ill in nursing homes due to reliance on primary diagnosis alone. As various estimates presented in Chapter 5 demonstrate, there are far more mentally ill persons in nursing homes. The bulk of mentaily ill persons — 60 per cent — are seen in the primary care/outpatient medical sector, most of them by office-based nonpsychiatrist physicians and in outpatient clinics and emergency rooms of general hospitals. Only one-tenth of this 60 per cent are *also* seen in the specialty mental health sector. The not in treatment/other human services sector contains 21.5 per cent of all mentally ill persons.

Given the huge number of psychiatric episodes seen outside regular psychiatric facilities, the public-private mix is even more salient. Third-party payments to the general medical sector by Medicare, Medicaid, and by local, state, and federal employees' insurance plans play a major role in the expansion of treatment in nonpsychiatric facilities. Further, as political-economic analysts of the health care system have pointed out, it is difficult to make public-private distinctions. For instance, many municipal hospitals are affiliated with voluntary hospitals, and often share staff and facilities. That sharing allows the voluntary hospitals to utilize portions of the public resources (Health Policy Advisory Center, 1972). This is one example of the labyrinthine public-private mixture witnessed in medical empires. This phenomenon is defined by Kotelchuck (1976):

> *privately controlled medical complexes, usually but not always organized with a medical school at the hub. Radiating out from these centers like spokes on a wheel are a network of affiliations to smaller private hospitals, city hospitals, state mental hospitals, neighborhood health centers and subspecialty programs in areas such as alcoholism, rehabilitation or prison health.*

The expansion of medical empires is funded by private insurance and government reimbursements, and linked to drug manufacturers, medical supply companies, construction firms, real estate interests, and banks. This larger structure is the medical-industrial complex (Ehrenreich and Ehrenreich, 1970; Kotelchuck, 1976; Navarro, 1976).

By employing a political-economic analysis to the health care system, it is most logical to consider the entire health care system as very tied to public expenditures. It is expected that virtually all of public hospitals' funds would come from public sources. More importantly, however, a large portion of private hospitals' revenue also are publicly financed. Woolhandler et al. (1983) observe that public financing of private facilities can be considered as having three direct public sources: third party payments, savings due to tax exemption (e.g. property tax), and grants or subsidies from various levels of government. In calculating these costs for private hospitals in Oakland and Berkeley, California, Woolhandler et al. found that public funds provide 65.9 per cent of the revenue for those private hospitals. Other public subsidies of private health care which cannot be calculated for specific hospitals are also important, such as deductions on personal income tax for health costs, and deductions on personal and corporate taxes for health philanthropy. Taking all the public support into account, they conclude that public funds are central to private sector hospitals. The result is a public-private alliance, often with hazy demarcations between the two components. In such a combined system, there may be discriminatory services since private hospitals can choose patients more than public facilities. They can avoid reponsibility to their local communities, and can build additions and start services based on profitability rather than need. Thus, maldistribution of health resources can be perpetuated by such financing mechanisms.

Tax-exempt bonds for hospital construction and renovation play an increasingly important role. Up until the mid-1960s, philanthropic contributions were the largest source of hospital capital. In 1962 only 17.5 per cent of capital funds came from borrowing. This rose to 70 per cent by 1975, due to changes in Internal Revenue Service codes. Hill-Burton and Federal Housing Authority funds declined from 15.2 per cent of all 1976 community hospital construction to only 1.5 per cent in 1979. By 1981 tax-exempt bonds financed over half of all community hospital construction and renovation, totalling $5.4 billion. The importance of these hospital bonds is observed in that they make up 16.7 per cent of the total U.S. tax-exempt bond market. The benefits of raising such funds are not reserved for private non-profit facilities; for-profit hospitals can float up to $10 million in such bonds. The high costs of debt repayment are then added to Medicare, Medicaid, Blue Cross, and commercial insurance reimbursements (Wilson et al., 1982).

Trustees of the bond issue (usually a bank) have the power to prevent hospital closings or mergers, and can take possession of a defaulted hospital. In order to prevent default, hospitals are pressured into extracting maximum surplus, which often results in curtailment of those services which do not generate surplus (this would be termed profit in a for-profit enterprise). Hospitals also limit services to Medicare and Medicaid patients for whom payments are often problematic. Public dollars thus support the private facilities both in income tax losses and in higher pass-through reimbursement costs (Wilson et al., 1982).

Among private hospitals, for-profit ones have fared better than non-profit facilities. The non-profit voluntaries, generally older, face higher operating costs and higher wages to unionized workers. They are often tied to costly service relationships with other hospitals and public agencies. The new profit-making hospitals are chain operations, such as Hospital Corporation of America, with 102 hospitals, over 16,000 beds, and assets of over $2 billion. These chains benefit from large discount purchasing, non-union labor, and other cost savings, such as the ability to recruit low wage nurses in bulk in the Philippines. These hospitals lure physicians with free or low cost office space, though requiring them to maintain certain bed capacities and cost-effective treatment. As a result of all these practices, Hospital Corporation of America has cut labor expenses to 39 per cent of costs, as against 50-60 per cent for the industry as a whole, and has achieved an average charge per admission which is 13 per cent lower than the national hospital average (L. Kennedy, 1981).

While public funds have aided private facilities to survive and even expand, cutbacks in direct public provision of service have been severe. In recent years large numbers of public general hospitals have closed. California's county hospital system shrank from 66 hospitals in 49 counties in 1950 to 38 hospitals in 29 counties in 1980. Philadelphia General Hospital closed in 1977, leaving that major city without a public hospital. New York City's large public hospital system has closed several of its units in the last few years. Other cities have done likewise. Public hospitals were largely dependent on direct funding from their local governments, and the fiscal crisis beginning in the 1970s lowered those budgets. Since these public hospitals serve so many uninsured persons who have no resources for personal payment, they have a smaller revenue base. They also provide ambulatory care to many persons unable to obtain it in private office practice; the ratio of outpatient to inpatient visits is 29 per cent higher in public than in private hospitals. These outpatient visits are reimbursed at far less than actual costs, compared to inpatient episodes (E. Brown, 1980).

Since funding for public hospitals is a city and county matter, localized economic shortages can result in shutdowns and cutbacks. Public funding for private hospitals, however, is a result of national policies and often nationally floated bonds, thus making it easier to avoid local economic troubles. In sum, then, public funding accounts for hospital financing in both private and public facilities; at the same time that this system allows public hospitals to go under, it provides structural support for private facilities.

This structural fabric of the general medical sector is particularly important since so many psychiatric cases are seen in that sector. For instance, general hospitals *without* psychiatric wards serve twice as many inpatients as general hospitals *with* psychiatric units (Regier et al., 1978). Seen in different form, in 1978, there were 1,613,000 inpatient admissions to general hospitals with primary diagnosis of mental illness. Of these, only 552,437 (34 per cent) went to designated psychiatric units (Bachrach, 1981). This is almost entirely the result of unplanned policy, in that these patients were sent to medical units due to overcrowding on the psychiatric units or due to misdiagnosis. As a planned policy, such admissions to non-psychiatric settings have some conscious advocates. Markoff et al., (1981) implemented a mixed medical-psychiatric ward, which they consider to be a model for future practice. They believe that medical patients serve as a 'normalizing' influence on mental patients, thus minimizing aberrant behavior. Further, the researchers argue, such a mixed unit reduces stigma for the psychiatric patients and allows the referring family physician to have more continuous contact with the patient. This reasoning is similar to the arguments for general hospital psychiatric units as noted earlier. The prevalence of emotional problems in general medical practice of approximately 15 per cent is well-known, and has prompted NIMH to offer training grants to teach rudimentary psychiatric knowledge to general practitioners.

General hospital emergency rooms are also taking on a significant psychiatric burden. Bassuk (1980) reported that for the period 1972-1976, 3.9 per cent of all emergency visits to a major university-affiliated general hospital were psychiatric. Of these patients, 31 per cent were referred to outpatient care, 22 per cent returned to their current therapist, 17 per cent sent home, and 27 per cent hospitalized (only 6 per cent in the receiving hospital). There are important trends over time. From 1972 to 1975 the patient characteristics and disposition were stable, but 1976 showed a marked change. In the earlier period, only 19 per cent had prior hospitalization, but in 1976 this climbed to 31 per cent. In the 1972-1975 period, 23 per cent were chronic psychotics, compared to 35 per cent in 1976. And while only 13 per cent were hospitalized in private facilities in 1972-1975, that increased to 30 per cent in 1976. Bassuk suggests the possibility that there was a time lag where patient support networks dissolved. Further, CMHCs and other facilities had become saturated by 1976, leaving general hospitals as a major location of emergency care.

Not only have public funds promoted the growth of facilities such as nursing and boarding homes, but increasingly state and federal health regulation policies have cemented the public-private allied sector. The bed trade-offs mentioned earlier are practices which result from regulatory agencies and practices such as Health Systems Agency (HSA) planning, determination of need, and Offices of State Health Planning. Health services are far too costly and important to allow a purported free market to have complete freedom. The demands of a complex health delivery system require more integrated planning, as opposed to the more individualistic style exhibited by most physicians and hospitals. Yet health regulation presents a contradictory set of problems. On the one hand there are many flaws. For instance, hospitals often have the power to influence state health planners on issues such as determination of need for capital expansion. In Massachusetts this is common, but even when a determination of need has been turned down, hospitals have gone directly to the state legislature for special bills to permit hospital expansion. On a deeper level, health planning and regulation basically remain within the accepted parameters of a curative, high-technology medical establishment. Regulators accept much of the system as a given, and try to make it work more smoothly. Truly redistributive planning and regulation is usually absent from official actions. Even if some state or federal planners move in a more radical direction, they will likely be blocked by the legislative or the executive. Such obstacles are likely to result from the influential lobbying of the medical-industrial complex's various components. At any rate, those components are more powerful than the cumbersome wheels of government regulation.

On the other hand, when health planning and regulation do appear to provide curbs on unnecessary expansion, the health care industry seeks deregulation. It finds an ally in the Reagan Administration, which has already cut down on the extent of government regulation, and seeks to further diminish regulation.

Health planning and regulation have had far less impact on mental health than on medical services. Until recently, mental health services were not so directly tied to the medical sector. Also, many mentally ill persons are cared for in nursing and boarding homes and welfare hotels, which fall under social welfare agencies. Mental health planning has been weak itself, and has been poorly integrated with health planning. And compared to health services, it is difficult to 'cost out' psychiatric services. This especially holds true for chronic patients who move between many medical, psychiatric, and social service agencies, as well as urban jails.

There have been attempts to integrate medical and mental health services. NIMH has funded training programs to teach basic psychiatry to general practitioners, since they see many emotionally disturbed people. Probably the largest attempt at integration is the provision of psychiatric services in prepaid health plans (especially health maintenance organizations) in order to reduce medical utilization. These plans can provide cheaper mental health care since staff are usually salaried and have no vested interest in continued treatment, management can force professionals to ration care, treatment goals are oriented to 'return to function' rather than 'personality reconstruction', many non-medical staff are used, much group therapy is used, and management can make plans based on the relatively known homogeneity of the group plan's population (McGuire, 1981). While HMOs have proven that they can reduce medical utilization, it is not yet clear if their low-cost mental health services still cost less than the medical care which would otherwise be provided. A positive cost 'offset' has been found for certain chronic medical conditions in the Blue Cross Blue Shield Federal Employees Plan. Mental health care of seven to twenty visits reduced the amount and cost of medical care to persons with airflow limitation disease, diabetes, ischemic heart disease, and hypertension by the third year following diagnosis (Schlesinger et al., 1983). Above all, it is not clear how altruistic such motives are. HMOs are commonly understood to limit access to care in order to spend less of their capitation premiums. They may be limiting services to people who really need care, and therefore working against better mental health.

For psychiatric services, in sum, the public-private mix may be beneficial to acute patients who previously might have lacked resources for more intensive care. But for the growing number of chronics, the public-private allied sector has not performed well. The new public-private allied sector has definitely changed the organizational picture of the mental health system, creating a blurred separation of public and private facilities due to the role of public funding regulations. We are only just beginning to understand the functioning of this new sector, and much more remains to be examined.

One aspect of the transfer of care to general hospitals is the greater emphasis on situating psychiatry within medicine. This direction will be likely to intensify the centrality of the biochemical perspective. This matter is taken up in the following chapter, which begins the section on Social Aspects of Mental Health Practices.

PART III

Social Aspects of Mental Health Practices

CHAPTER 7

Effects of Deinstitutionalization on Public Attitudes and on the Work Force

For most of the history of public mental health care, the actual effects of psychiatric treatment were felt primarily by the patients and their caregivers. To be sure, other parties were involved: state legislatures and executives planned and financed state hospitals, psychiatric facilities provided training grounds for psychiatrists and other professionals, families were relieved of real and perceived burdens, and local economies benefited from payroll and sales taxes, employment, and purchasing. But generally, the effects of treatment were confined to the hospitals and their immediate surroundings. The mentally ill, in the perception of most of the society, were 'out of sight, out of mind.' Even the innovations ideas of the 1950s — milieu therapy, group therapy, and psychoactive drug treatment — were not well known outside of a knowledgeable circle.

Deinstitutionalization has altered the secluded nature of mental health treatment, making it far more visible, both in its planning and its outcomes. To the extent that deinstitutionalization has been the primary outcome of recent policies, both justified and unjustified public attention has been widespread. Previous chapters have examined the effects of recent mental health policy in terms of the institutional arrangements, ranging from psychiatric facilities to nursing homes. This chapter will discuss various effects which are not so readily apparent. I begin with a discussion of public attitudes toward mental illness in general, and opposition toward deinstitutionalization in particular. This involves general public attitudes, specific burdens on communities and other social institutions, ex-patient crime, and economic loss to communities. Next I address alterations in the lower levels of the work force, particularly psychiatric aides.

PUBLIC ATTITUDES TOWARD MENTALLY ILL PERSONS

Mentally ill persons have historically been a stigmatized and brutalized population. In Medieval and early modern Europe (Foucault, 1971; Rosen, 1968; Szasz, 1970), in the early American republic (Rothman, 1971; Grob, 1973), and into the twentieth century (Deutsch, 1948) mentally ill persons and persons falsely labeled as such have been scapegoats for many private and public fears. Their incarceration, maltreatment, and even murder would not have been possible without a prevailing stigma widely disseminated in the general culture. Despite large-scale attempts in recent decades to reverse public antagonism in order to effect greater community care and social rehabilitation, dislike and fear of mental patients has continued. Deinstitutionalization has brought the mentally ill in closer proximity with the general public than ever before, thus increasing social fears and hostility, despite concerted attempts to allay such attitudes.

Social science research in the last several decades has described such attitudes through survey research and general observation. Cumming and Cumming's (1957) Canadian investigation was one of the earliest major studies. It showed that the general community exhibited 'closed ranks' towards emotionally disturbed persons. Over two decades later D'Arcy and Brockman (1977) restudied the same communities and found that there were no major differences over time in stigma towards mental illness. This finding supports what Rabkin (1980) termed the 'pessimistic' school rather than the 'optimistic' school. The optimists have argued that recent attention to public mental health education and the increase in all forms of treatment would diminish public stigma. Yet precisely the same expansion of psychiatry may have made more people aware of what was previously hidden in the faraway state hospitals.

Scheff (1966) stressed the important role played by the broadcast media in portraying patients and ex-patients as essentially aggressive and violent, and as clearly physically distinguishable from all others. Print media join in this stigmatization by emphasizing the offender's status in crimes committed by ex-patients. Scheff further showed that stereotypes of mental illness are learned by children through comic books and cartoons. Ex-patients are also discriminated against in employment on the basis that their past or present condition prevents them from playing any productive social role. The combination of all these stigma and prejudices makes mentally ill persons a particularly disliked group. Tringo (1970) found that of twenty-one disability groups, mentally ill persons were the least preferred, even when compared with ex-convicts and alcoholics.

Some public fears which in the past may have seemed unfounded, are now based on actual circumstances. For instance, Nunnally's (1961) important research determined that unpredictable behavior — especially violence — was a key element of stigma and fear. Mental health providers and sociologists countered such fears by statistically showing that ex-patients had lower crime rates than the general population. By the mid-1940s, however, research showed that this relationship no longer held, and ex-patients generally had higher crime rates than the general population (Zitrin et al., 1976). Surprisingly, many mental health educators remained unaware of this transformation as late as the the early 1980s. This development will be briefly addressed here; more detailed discussion can be found elsewhere (Steadman, 1981; Rabkin and Zitrin, 1982; P. Brown, 1983).

Criminal behavior and arrests of ex-patients

Studies in New York State in 1922, 1930, and 1938 showed that mentally ill persons had lower arrest rates than the general population. A 1945 Connecticut study agreed, finding a felony arrest rate of 4.2 per 1000 for ex-patients as compared to a population rate of 27 per 1000. After this point, however, there were changes (Zitrin et al., 1976). Brill and Malzberg's (1962) five-year longitudinal study of 10,247 men released from New York mental hospitals between 1946 and 1948 showed that the ex-patients had 12.2 total arrests per 1000, one fourth the population rate of 49.1. But for felonies, ex-patients were arrested at the rate of 5.47 while the general population was apprehended at the rate of 3.28. Rappeport and Lassen (1965) compared the arrest records for five years before and after hospitalization of all men discharged from Maryland mental hospitals in 1947 (N=708) and 1957 (N=2,152). For serious personal crime, ex-patients were arrested at higher rates in both time periods. The researchers found similarity in higher arrest records for women in both periods for aggravated assault (Rappeport and Lassen, 1966). Giovannoni and Gurel's (1967) four-year follow-up of 1,142 male psychotic patients released from twelve VA psychiatric hospitals found that these persons exceeded the general population's arrest rate for homicide, aggravated assault, and robbery, but were below the general population rate for rape, larceny, burglary, and auto theft.

Zitrin et al. (1976) examined a sample of those patients admitted to New York City's Bellevue Hospital psychiatric service from Bellevue's local catchment area. These 867 people were compared to a control group of

977 patients from the catchment area who were screened but not admitted. In the two years prior to and after hospital admission, 202 of the sample (23.2 per cent) had been arrested; 117 of them for violent and 85 for nonviolent crimes. The violent patients were more likely to be between thirty and forty, and half were schizophrenic, while the nonviolent offenders tended to be between twenty and thirty, of which only 38 per cent were schizophrenic, and to have a large number of alcoholic persons. Interestingly, only 10 per cent of all schizophrenics in the sample were arrested for violent crime, while 16 per cent of all alcoholic patients were.

For all patients, arrests for bodily violence were more likely to occur after admission, while nonviolent crimes and violent crimes with potential for bodily harm occurred equally before and after. While rates for murder, rape, robbery, assault, and burglary are all higher in the sample than in the U.S. population, when compared to the catchment area population, murder and robbery were lower while rape, assault, and burglary were higher.

Sosowsky (1978) utilized Zitrin et al.'s (1976) categories in a study of all persons admitted to California's Napa State Hospital during a nineteen-month period, June 1972 to December 1973, from community mental health programs in the San Mateo County catchment area. Arrest and conviction rates were studied for the longer period of January 1966 to March 1974, providing 3 1/2 years prior to and 4 1/2 years subsequent to the implementation of the restrictive Lanterman-Petris-Short Act. One hundred and forty-two ex-patients (47.2 per cent) were arrested, distributed equally into violent and nonviolent crimes. As in Zitrin and his associates' New York City study, violent arrestees were more likely than nonviolent ones to be schizophrenic. Arrests for violent offenses involving bodily harm increased approximately 3 1/2 times in the post-LPS period; for violent offenses with potential for harm they increased 1 1/2 times, and for nonviolent crimes about 3 times. In that post-reform period, patients were arrested for violent crimes at 9 times more than the countywide rate. For aggravated assault, the cohort had 26.6 arrests per 1,000, compared to 0.93 for the county and 1.55 for all U.S. cities. Unlike Steadman, Cocozza and Melick's (1978) New York data, Sosowsky's study group showed arrest rates for released patients with no prior arrest to be more than five times that of the population. Monahan and Steadman (1983) argue that this results from an inaccurate selection of a general population for comparison. Sosowsky's general population is San Mateo County, where Napa State Hosptial is located, but the Napa State catchment area includes San Francisco and Oakland, cities located in counties which have double the arrest rate of San Mateo County. Further, San Francisco and Alameda counties send more than ten times as many people to Napa State as does San Mateo. Thus the comparison to the general population erroneously shows a higher arrest record.

Although we usually think of males as the more violent, in Sosowsky's cohort, women patients exceeded the female population thirteen-fold, while the corresponding magnitude for men was ten. Interestingly, the female patient violence was highest in the 50+ age group, while male violence was concentrated in the typical 20-29 group. This interesting difference is not mentioned by Sosowsky. It indicates that while the new chronic violent male patient is young, and usually not a veteran of long-term state hospital care, the new chronic female patient is such a veteran, and has probably been deprived of social skills to a greater extent than the younger males.

Durbin et al. (1977) sought to determine if these higher arrest rates were restricted to the coastal industrialized states. Their study of Wyoming compared arrest rates of all 1969 state hospital admissions with the general state population, 1964-1973. The male arrest rate of 33.1 per 1000 compared to the general rate of 28.7 for all state arrests — not such a large difference. But for the violent crimes of murder, rape, robbery, and aggravated assault, the patient rate was three times higher.

Steadman, Cocozza, and Melick (1978) acknowledged that the Zitrin et al. and Durbin et al. studies were important, yet only dealt with one point in time. They therefore sought to compare arrest rates of New York State patients released at two different periods of time, random samples of 1,920 patients released in 1973 and 1,930 released in 1968. While 131 (6.9 per cent) of the 1968 group were arrested for all offenses within a nineteen-month follow-up period, 183 (9.4 per cent) of the 1975 cohort were arrested. Looking at only murder, manslaughter, and assault, 17 (0.9 per cent) of the earlier cohort was arrested, compared to 33 (1.9 per cent) of the later one. The researchers emphasize the small absolute numbers involved, and warn that 'Too often the infrequency of such events is forgotten in the heat of the particularly bizarre or violent behavior of a former patient, which is given considerable media coverage.' Still, the rates of these arrests are higher than the general population, 2.7 times as high for the 1968 cohort and 3 times as high for the 1975 group. For the three violent crimes of murder, manslaughter, and assault, the 1975 patient rate was 12.03 per 1000, compared to the population rate of 3.62.

The three most important factors influencing arrest are, in order of strength, prior arrests, age, and admitting diagnosis. While 97.1 per cent of the 1975 cohort with no prior arrests were not subsequently arrested, this declined as the person had more arrests, so that of those with three or more prior arrests, only 63.7 per cent were never apprehended. As for age, the average age of ex-patients who were arrested was thirty-five, ten years younger than ex-patients who were not later arrested. Substance abuse and personality disorders were the largest diagnostic categories providing arrestees, as was the case in the Durbin and associates study.

Since prior arrest was the strongest predictor, Steadman, Cocozza and Melick concentrated further analysis on that area, calculating arrest rates for patients based on the numbers of prior arrests. They found that, with the exception of property crimes, ex-patients who had never been arrested had lower subsequent arrest records than the general population. The overall rate also held to this relationship, with a 22.1 per 1000 arrest rate with no prior arrest, compared to 32.5 for the general population. For violent crimes, the never-arrested patients had a subsequent rate of 2.2 while the population rate was 3.6. But as soon as they looked at patients with even one prior arrest, the researchers found a rate higher than the general population. Steadman et al. noted that the 1974 study by Brill and Malzberg that found lower patients rates than population rates, also found large differences in later arrests based on prior arrest. Further, by observing the increase over time in the number of patients with prior arrests, an interesting phenomenon appeared. In the 1947 study, only 15 per cent of male patients had arrest histories, but in the 1968 group it rose to 32 per cent and in 1975 to 40 per cent. Thus, the researchers conclude that this increase in patients with prior arrest histories accounts for the change over time from lower-than-population arrest rates to higher-than-population arrest rates.

Police discretion plays an important role in apprehension of mentally impaired persons. Lamb and Grant (1982) note that

> *If the person is thought to have committed a serious crime, the police and the criminal justice system generally do not want to leave this person in the hands of a psychiatric hospital where security may be lax, where the offense may be seen as secondary to the patient's illness, and where the person may be released by the hospital back to the community after relatively short periods of time.*

On the misdemeanors, however, law officers may be unable to determine if the person is in fact mentally ill, especially if drunk or under the influence of drugs. Given a certain amount of police discretion, officers prefer to make choices which minimize their work. For instance, they dislike long waits at emergency rooms which sometimes end in their being told that there is no psychiatric bed after all.

As Bonovitz and Bonovitz (1981) found in their study of suburban Upper Darby, Pennsylvania, mental illness-related incidents coming to police attention increased 227.6 per cent from 1975 to 1979. For a five-month period in 1979 they studied in detail all 214 such cases. Of the 100 potential arrests (based on legal grounds) the city's 133 officers arrested only 13 people. Based on this figure, on interviews, and on personal observation in accompanying police on patrol, Bonovitz and Bonovitz wrote that:

> *The data do not support the hypothesis that the noncommittable mentally ill are being arrested and jailed as an expedient means of removing them from the community. On the contrary, the police officers we interviewed firmly believe that mentally ill individuals should not be held responsible for minor criminal offenses.*

How can we account for the changes in ex-patient crime since 1965? Abramson (1972), writing shortly after the passage of California's Lanterman-Petris-Short Act (LPS), argued that stringent commitment statutes left the criminal justice system as the only option for social control of these marginal persons. Zitrin et al. (1976), Durbin et al. (1977), and Lamb and Grant (1982) share this 'criminalization/diversion' perspective as well. The argument holds that since these criminally-involved, mentally ill persons are only in inpatient treatment for brief episodes, they are on the streets and therefore more likely to commit crimes than those held continuously in jail. Sosowsky (1978) agrees in part with this viewpoint and in part with the other leading explanation, the 'at risk' approach, which holds that a greater number of mentally ill persons now exist in the community who are at risk for commiting crimes.

This latter perspective is mostly identified with the work of Steadman and his colleagues. The earlier study (Steadman, Cocozza, and Melick, 1978) showed the important fact that ex-patients with no prior arrests had a lower arrest rate than the general population for total arrests and for each category of arrests except property crime. Further, a greater number of ex-patients at present have arrest records than did earlier cohorts. In a later comment Steadman (1981) noted that released patients are younger. Even in the short interval between 1968 and 1975 the median discharge age of all New York state hospital inpatients fell from 38.2 to 33.2 years. Since there is a well known linear relationship between age and crime up until age 40, the rise in ex-patient crime is more understandable. In addition to a greater discharge of ex-patients with longer arrest records, Steadman notes that we are seeing an increased recognition of mental illness in jailed populations, rather than an increase in that sector as well. Further, as Bonovitz and Bonovitz (1981) found, police are not so likely to take control of mentally ill persons. In addition to these data, other data suggest that arrest records of patients may be underestimates of actual criminal behavior. Studies of re-hospitalization show high rates of violent acts which precipitate readmission (up to 36 per cent), but very low rates of prosecution (2.6 per cent in the same study) (Lagos et al., 1977). Felony rates may be further underestimated since charges are sometimes reduced to misdemeanors in states which do not permit felony arrestees to be held for lengthy periods for determination of competency to stand trial (Rabkin and Zitrin, 1982).

A further point made by adherents of the 'criminalization' theory is that more mental illness is now found among general jail populations. Prison officials have begun to claim that they are being saturated with new mentally ill populations for which they are unprepared. Swank and Winer (1976) found a 14 per cent rate of prior inpatient care among inmates of the Denver County Jail, and considered this to be a high degree of mentally ill people in a jail population. Steadman and Ribner (1980) looked historically at the problem and evaluated it differently. They examined all persons released to Albany County, NY from state prisons and the local county jail, for both 1968 and 1975. From the earlier to the later time, the per cent of ex-offenders from state prisons who had prior psychiatric hospitalization dropped from 19 per cent to 13 per cent. Ex-offenders from county jails increased, from 9 per cent prior hospitalization in 1968 to 12 per cent in 1975. Given these mixed findings, the researchers conclude that there is no significant trend overall in the increase of mentally ill persons in jail settings, though there is a very modest support for this thesis at the county jail level. However, they caution, this is not at all of the magnitude which penal officials and others are pressing.

If we look at a select sample of repeat criminal offenders with mental illness, there are some interesting differences according to offense. Lamb and Grant (1982) studied 102 men screened at the Forensic Mental Health Unit of the Los Angeles County Central Men's Jail. Of the misdemeanor arrestees about half lived in the most marginal settings (street, beach, mission, cheap hotel) and about half in more regular settings (e.g., own or other's apartment). Of the felony arrestees, over three-fourths lived in more regular settings and slightly under one-fourth in the more marginal locations. Lamb and Grant interpreted this as follows:

> *It is possible that the less serious misdemeanor offense is frequently a way of asking for help. Still another factor may be that many of this group of uncared-for mentally ill persons are being arrested for minor criminal acts that are really manifestations of their illness, lack of treatment, and lack of structure in their lives.*

One could also argue that the most severely impaired were incapable of committing the more serious acts.

The 'criminalization' perspective is sometimes put forth in terms of a 'hydraulic theory.' Steadman et al. (1983) note that Penrose's hydraulic theory shows a high correlation of r = -.87 between state hospital census and state prison population for the decade 1968-1978. But this is not, they argue, a direct balance between the two populations. Steadman and his colleagues chose six states which were representative of the U.S. on geographical and urban-rural dimensions. Over the decade, the percentage of state prison admissions with prior hospitalization did increase, from 7.9 per cent of all prison admissions in 1968 to 10.4 per cent of all 1978 incarcerations. But at the same time, all prison admissions rose by 42.4 per cent, creating a higher absolute number of prisoners with prior hospitalization. To analyze the changes in actual numbers of prisoners with prior hospitalization, the researchers compared those numbers with what would have been expected by an increase in total prison admission alone, holding constant the 1968 proportions of prisoners with prior treatment. One should find that the number of prison admissions with prior hospitalization should change by the same amount as the changes in the general prison rate. But for half of the states, the actual number was less than what would have been expected.

Turning to the other side — mental hospital patients with prior criminal histories — Steadman and his associates found a significant increase in the percentage of patients with at least one prior arrest. For the six states, this percentage increased from 38.2 per cent to 55.5 per cent over the decade. There were also increases in the percent of hospital admissions with multiple prior arrests, with prior imprisonment, and for serious crimes. As with the prison populations, these figures were evaluated by comparing actual numbers with what would be expected based on the 1968 rate. For multiple arrests there was an increase in all but one state, though the comparison was less clear with prior imprisonment. Thus the prison population was not more mentally ill than ten years previously, though the hospital census did have more patients with criminal records. As opposed to the hydraulic theory, Steadman et al. propose a 'buffer' theory. This holds that a change in size of both state prison and state hospital populations is buffered by an intermediate population of people, many of whom are housed in short-term county jails. This may occur through an indirect action whereby released patients affect other social groups, leading to prison incarceration of parts of this buffer group.

Answers to this question of 'criminalization' or 'at risk/recognition' are not so clear cut. There certainly are forces at work presently which suggest an impatience and distrust with 'medicalization,' a prominent approach of the mid-1960s and 1970s which placed in the hands of medical professionals and institutions the responsibility for a large number of non-medical forms of deviance (Conrad and Schneider, 1980). This impatience and distrust derives from medical inability to handle the wide variety of social problems we expect it to (Illich, 1976; Starr, 1983). It also follows from a growing general social conservatism and its 'law-and-order' component, a factor which has undoubtedly increased in the 'post-Hinckley period when many states are drastically curtailing the insanity defense in response to John Hinckley's attempted assassination of Ronald Reagan.

Another argument against the 'criminalization' theory is that state hospitals tend to admit mostly violent and potentially violent persons, not to divert them to the police apparatus. More stringent dangerousness criteria for involuntary commitment yield a hospital population of more violent patients who most likely have prior arrest records (Rabkin and Zitrin, 1982). Since prior arrest is the best predictor of future arrest (Steadman, Cocozza, and Melick (1978), this would leave us a more 'at risk' mental hospital population.

Ex-patient criminality may be largely a response to the criminal behavior of boarding home operators and SRO landlords, neighborhood opposition to their presence in the community, and to the high rate of victimization of ex-patients by local criminals (Zitrin et al., 1976; Cohen, 1980). Ex-patient crime is clearly higher than that of the general population in many cases, though not always higher than in the particularly poor areas where ex-patients congregate. But as discussed above, higher absolute numbers are as important as proportions when it come to public fear and perceived threats. Further, in the areas which host 'psychiatric ghettos' are also found many ex-offenders as well as other socially marginal people who may not have prior incarcerations in either the criminal justice or mental health systems, but nevertheless exhibit bizarre behavior. These deviant groups may be perceived as a congealed whole, through a process of *deviant-lumping* (more will be said on this in the final chapter). Since deinstitutionalization is so public a policy and so prominently a failure, it is easy to consider the average bizarre street person as an ex-patient and lay the blame for their disruption of local life at the door of the mental health authorities.

Other burdens on the community

Deinstitutionalization has produced other real and perceived burdens to neighborhoods. In the psychiatric ghettos of the major cities, tens of thousands of ex-patients may be found in nursing homes, boarding homes, SROs, and on the street. Neighborhood residents often feel that these persons are intrusive or dangerous, that they make the neighborhood less pleasant an environment, and that they diminish property values. As mentioned earlier, the criminal dangerousness concern is mainly a justifiable one. But property values are not affected by ex-patient concentrations (Dear, 1977), partly because such concentrations are found in already rundown districts and partly because housing shortages in the cities are so severe that even adjacent undesirable facilities do not reduce the bloated rents and prices of real estate.

Much opposition has been found toward placement of halfway houses and other group living situations, even in areas where there are no concentrations of ex-patients. Despite the fact that mental health planners usually screen out clients with violent or sexual offense histories, there is much fear of such facilities. Parents particularly worry about their children being bothered, and dislike the presence of retarded or emotionally disturbed persons in their suburban or urban neighborhoods. While there may be some discomfort, it is useful to situate such opposition in the context of a broader community opposition to integrated housing, low-income housing, and restrictive zoning against non-married individuals living together. Such conservative notions of 'community' seem more at fault than the small number of halfway houses.

Urban areas with high ex-patient concentrations do have legitimate complaints as a result of unplanned discharge without adequate follow-up and intensive community care. Further, other areas of the city have been burdened with problems which are difficult to deal with. For instance, the New York City public library system has had to endure troublesome patients hanging out in branch libraries, and to spend scarce funds on extra security. Parks, transportation terminals, and other public spaces have become less comfortable as a result of patient loiterers, many of them among the growing numbers of the urban homeless.

Economic loss also occurs when state hospitals are depopulated or closed. Morrissey et al. (1980) emphasize that one of the enduring functions of the asylum is to provide local economic support, particularly in rural areas. This occurs in the form of jobs, supply businesses, local tax revenue, and the range of regular commercial enterprises which thrive on the expanded economic base. Moore (1981) studied the potential impact of the merging of two New York state hospitals, Utica and Marcy Psychiatric Centers. The former is the state's oldest facility, and located 7 1/2 miles from the latter. It was estimated that the merger would save the state $8 million in capital renovation costs alone for the Utica hospital. However, the two-county area (Utica-Rome SMSA) is one of the state's most depressed areas, and the two facilities have accounted for 2 1/2 per cent of the entire work force. Taking into account a large number of factors, an economic multiplier model estimated that Utica's closing would produce a $1.8 million direct loss annually, with an additional $4.8 million annual loss due to regional economic multipliers.

The situation is similar to factory closings, which are so common at present: in a more equitable society, relocation would only be made if it was necessary when taking into account the balance of specific productivity and local economic effects. The point is not to argue that the state mental health authorities have the responsibility to revive the sagging economy of the Utica-Rome, or any other area. Rather, it is to demonstrate that in the absence of rational and equitable social planning, social policies have dramatic effects far beyond the scope and intentions of their planners. Let us now move to the direct and immediate impact of deinstitutionalization on the large number of people who work in the affected institutions.

ALTERATIONS IN THE LOWER LEVELS OF THE MENTAL HEALTH WORKFORCE

Any major change in production or service work functions will entail changes in the work force. Given the magnitude of institutional alterations in the mental health field during the past several decades, it is obvious that large personnel transformations would occur in the field. In the 1950s and 1960s a number of important clinicians and administrators conducted research which demonstrated that the custodial attitudes of mental health staff increased as one went down the occupational ladder. It was felt that significant reform would be impossible unless major changes were made in the work force (Gilbert and Levinson, 1957a;

1957b; Baker and Schulberg, 1967). In one sense, the stigmatizing attitudes and frequently brutal behavior of aides and attendants was to be expected, given their low wages, poor working conditions, and recruitment from uneducated strata. In another sense, however, the conservative and custodial notions of these workers were a reflection of the repressive and hopeless environment of the institutions. While field studies of state hospitals in the 1950s suggested that institutions had a life of their own — especially at the lower levels — the nature of that staff milieu was probably due to institutional structures more than to innate custodialism among aides.

When professionals began altering mental health care, they generally did not retrain lower level staff for the new approaches. Rather, they sought aides and attendants from higher class positions, often college educated young adults who would continue in some professional training after a short period of psychiatric institutional work. At the same time, large numbers of the traditionally working-class aides would retire and/or be dismissed in state hospital closings and retrenchments. Further, there would be larger numbers of new professionals — particularly psychologists and social workers — who would improve the staffing ratios of the asylums. Also, more volunteers would be attracted to a new, improved mental health system. Lastly, in the CMHCs particularly, paraprofessionals were recruited and trained to perform various work functions that might have been allocated to retrained aides.

The extent of state hospital deinstitutionalization described in previous chapters indicates the magnitude of personnel changes. In this process, lower level workers have been especially hard hit. From 1967 to 1972, New York's budget for state hospitals increased 71 per cent (from $226.9 million to $388.1 million), but the number of employees grew less than 4 per cent (from 36,115 to 37,540) (Lander, 1975). In 1971, 1200 workers were laid off in one budget cut (Cumming and Markson, 1975). From 1972 to 1976, full-time equivalent staff (FTE) for all mental health facilities increased 42 per cent for professionals, but only 4 per cent for non-professionals (American Federation of State, County, and Municipal Employees, 1977b ('Full-time equivalent' is defined as the total hours worked by fulltime employees, part-time employees, and trainees, divided by 40 hours). Most of the affected employees were in either front-line patient care or hospital maintenance.

From 1970 to 1976, FTEs of licensed practical nurses (LPNs) and mental health workers per CMHC declined 15 per cent while FTEs of professionals (excluding administrators) increased 17 per cent. While non-professionals constituted 37 per cent of CMHC direct care staff in 1970, by 1976 they were down to 30 per cent. Much of this decline was due to the bias in clinical training funds, which provided money primarily for professional staff while ignoring the need to retrain non-professionals for community mental health work (American Federation of State, County, and Municipal Employees 1977a; 1977b). In just one year at the height of deinstitutionalization, 1974-1975, state hospital closings across the country accounted for a decline of 3,755 FTE staff (Meyer, 1976).

The lack of attention to lower level workers is to be expected. Throughout the society, service workers and manual production laborers have suffered high rates of unemployment due to economic crisis and technological and policy changes. The massive unemployment of the late 1970s and early 1980s, so noticeable in the industrial heartland, has pointed out important structural flaws in the nation's economy. A greedy profit motive has led large firms to seek short-term gain without regard to long range effects. Outdated factories were depleted, while funds which could have modernized the old plants went instead to corporate takeovers or to investment in speculative credit markets. Wasteful and inefficient practices used up energy resources. Reckless lending, in search of higher return, placed banks in precarious liquidity crises. Chauvinistic attitudes of corporate and financial leaders led to their failure to evaluate the importance of foreign competition. And a lack of social planning by government and capital led to disregard for the impact of these economic troubles on the public. It is ironic that layoffs of mental health workers contribute to the increasingly more apparent psychological damage attributed to unemployment (c.f. Brenner, 1973).

When California's DeWitt State Hospital was closed in 1971, about 600 workers were affected. About half were over fifty years old, and most had only a high school education. These people were mainly long-term workers at the hospital; 40 per cent had worked there for ten years or more. A survey of the displaced workers (70 per cent responded) one year after DeWitt's closing showed that only 73 per cent were employed. Of these, 24 per cent felt that their new job was better, but 39 per cent thought it was worse. Only two-thirds of the hospital workers had been transferred to another state health facility. Many women were reported as having 'dropped out of the labor market' (Weiner et al., 1973). The DeWitt workers reported insecurity, loss of income, and less time spent with their families (since many had to travel long distances to their new jobs). Thirty percent of the interviewed workers were patient care professionals, 25 per cent were service workers, and 45 per cent were psychiatric technicians (aides). The psychiatric technician is a job category specific to California public mental hospitals. Begun in 1952, technician training provides 300 hours of classroom study and ward supervision over a 13-month period, in preparation for routine aides' work (Weiner et al., 1973). Precisely because that position is specific to California, technicians will have great difficulty in getting jobs at non-public California facilities, which would prefer college graduates, or at other states' psychiatric facilities, which would prefer not to have workers with a history of strong unionization, higher salaries, and sense of professionalism.

Mental health researchers have offered worker guidelines which usually propose much more than state officials can or will provide. One study of hospital closings proposes that workers receive the following rights: continuity of employment by transfer, retention of seniority rights in their new position, involvement of workers and their unions in plannings for closings, relocation allowances, and retraining opportunities. In practice, the picture is mixed. When Cleveland State Hospital closed, two-thirds of its workers were transferred within the state system; at Massachusetts' Grafton State three-quarters were transferred; and at Illinois's Peoria State only 35 per cent were that fortunate (Greenblatt and Glazier, 1975).

In 1974, the Massachusetts Mental Health Planning Project (1974: 85-87) admitted that provisions for displaced workers were not very thorough, and that the widely touted retraining was hardly put into practice. They agreed that a 'small residual proportion' of workers would have to be laid off, and they withheld criticism of the state's current hiring freeze which left a 20-22 per cent vacancy rate for funded positions. The following year, a state task force put it more bluntly: 'The problem of anachronistic personnel practices and policies is accentuated and made even more profound by necessary commitments to current state employees' (Task Force, 1975: 8). This was clearly directed at the aides, nurses, and maintenance and housekeeping staffs, since those are the workers whose unions and associations have been outspokenly critical of deinstitutionalization. Further, psychiatrists, psychologists, and administrators are rarely called 'anachronistic' since they always have the feasible option of developing new programs or finding employment elsewhere.

Retraining of state hospital workers for community mental health programs is very scarce, despite several pieces of legislation which call for retraining. Section 314d of the Public Health Service Act (PL 94-63), Section 796 of the Public Health Service Act (PL 94-484), and the Developmental Disabilities Services and Facilities Construction Act (PL 94-103) all provide for retraining as part of workers' protection, but the actual amount of money and effort put into retraining has been small. NIMH's Paraprofessional Manpower Development Branch, the office in charge of training and retraining lower level direct service staff, received only $2 million (2 1/2 per cent) out of a 1977 clinical training budget of $80 million, even though non-professionals make up one-half of direct care workers. Only $800,000 was available for grants at any one time, and given the past (and extremely low) expenditure of $1000 per person, only 0.5 per cent of all non-professionals could be retrained or upgraded in any one year. Further, of the $3.1 million appropriated for NIMH's new Community Support Program, $1.5 million came from these retraining funds. The American Federation of State, County, and Municipal Employees (AFSCME), which represents over 100,000 mental health workers in 33 states and the District of Columbia, most of them aides, was sensibly skeptical that retaining funds would be applied to worker retraining programs (American Federation of State, County, and Municipal Employees, 1977a; 1977b).

State hospital workers have opposed this neglect of attention to their plight, and have been the principal opponents of hospital closings. Following Governor Richard Thornburgh's 1980 announcement that he would close Retreat State Hospital, AFSCME persuaded the Pennsylvania legislature to pass a bill requiring legislative approval for any state hospital cut in beds or staff exceeding 5 per cent; the governor's veto of the bill was, however, upheld. California workers have been more successful. In 1974 they won legislation to limit the governor's power to close state hospitals (Frank and Welch, 1982). The California State Employees Association (CSEA), which represents psychiatric technicians and some professionals, sponsored legislation to increase hospital staffing, particularly for 1,000 vacancies in funded positions. Governor Jerry Brown in 1975 and 1976 vetoed bills which sought to establish by 1980 standards which were promulgated in 1973 (such standards, however, would still be lower than the minimal standards set by courts in right to treatments cases such as *Wyatt v. Stickney*). Union and other pressures forced Brown to back down and agree to an administrative increase of 1000 positions within a year and a half (by June 30, 1977). Brown had other pressures besides those of the union. Suspicious deaths of 139 state hospital patients over a three year period had drawn much public and professional attention, and prompted the Governor to set up an investigatory panel. The panel was headed by Brown's newly-appointed chief health administrator, Raymond Procunier. The day after Procunier's commission reported that the deaths were 'highly questionable', Brown announced his staffing increase. One of Brown's stated reasons was what he termed a new confidence in Procunier and other newly appointed administrators (Sacramento *Bee*, 1976; Bathen, 1976).

Brown's new confidence in Procunier was alarming in light of Procunier's earlier work as head of the Department of Corrections. In that position in 1971, Procunier proposed a stepped up program of psychosurgery, aversion therapy, and electroshock at the much-criticized Vacaville prison/hospital. Prisoners from California penitentiaries who were considered political, sexual, or behavioral deviants were the target (Liberation News Service, 1972a, 1972b), but lobbying, demonstrations, and other pressure defeated many of those plans.

Even with Brown's agreement to fill the vacant positions, the CSEA had doubts about his sincerity, partly since the governor had called for an increasing use of volunteers in state hospitals. To protect their members, the union had the original jobs bill reintroduced. Brown signed the passed legislation on May 24, 1977, providing for 2,300 new patient care positions, mostly psychiatric technicians, by June 30, 1980 (the new slots would require a slightly longer apprenticeship period).

The situation of mental health workers parallels that of health care workers in general. Despite the importance of increases in provider fees, drug and supply costs, insurance premium hikes, and duplication of services, low level staff have borne an excessive amount of blame for rising health costs. Health workers have been subjected to heavier work loads, lay-offs, cuts in real wages, union-busting, devaluation of credentials, and an ideological offensive which claims that they are not that important to patient care (Navarro, 1976).

Such attitudes have not been aimed at the professionals in the system. Further, among the professional levels, psychiatrists, psychologists, and administrators have had far less trouble in the shifting mental health scene. In fact, as pointed out in Chapter 5, many psychiatrists have already begun a shift from public service to private facilities. At the nursing level — a juncture of professional and non-professional layers — registered nurses without baccalaureates and licensed practical nurses can be expected to fare poorly, given the already sharp devaluation of their positions. Degree RNs have more job flexibility, due to the demand for their services throughout the health care system. They exhibit a high degree of turnover in the state hospital system because that system has failed to improve their wages and clinical responsibillty (Melick, 1982), despite the fact that it would be eminently sensible to increase their role in dynamic treatment methods.

While the above material has noted a callous attitude on the part of some officials, it is important to observe that much of the dislocation of lower level mental health staff is a function of the political-economic forces at work within the larger society. Although this means that officials and planners do not bear all the responsibility, it does not imply that such effects on the work force should be ignored. It is crucial to understand that deinstitutionalization, despite any person's or agency's intention, has a profoundly detrimental impact on lower level workers. This impact is indeed one of the major social implications of deinstitutionalization.

Deinstitutionalization, community mental health, and the totality of recent mental health practices have had some even larger effects on the whole society. The issues discussed in this chapter are large-scale, but still involve a limited number of sectors of the society. Also, they are mainly attributed to deinstitutionalizaton. In the following chapter, we will turn our attention to issues which do not necessarily flow from deinstitutionalization. These issues — psychoactive drugs and the new biologism — have serious ramifications for larger numbers of people than are affected by the specific mental health policies addressed here.

CHAPTER 8

Psychoactive Drugs, Psychotechnology, and the New Biologism

As has been pointed out throughout this book, cycles of institutional change and reform have been common. At times, the mental health field has shown an optimistic view of treatment and prevention. While this does not hold true for the entire field, significant developments have often permeated many areas of the professions. Although this does not mean that the whole mental health field will turn in a reform direction, such an optimistic framework is necessary if even a small part of the field is to seek reforms. The last era of general optimism was the community mental health period, roughly located in the decade and-a-half from 1960 to 1975. As earlier chapters have shown, many of the great promises of this approach were not met. In this failure we can locate the preconditions for the rise of a new biologism, a more strictly biomedical and asocial view of mental health and illness. This new biologism did not appear full-blown. First of all, psychiatry always had a high degree of biomedical inclinations which were merely offset or tempered by community mental health methods. Second, community psychiatry itself was predicated on biochemical methods in that psychoactive drugs have been considered a chief means of deinstitutionalization and community treatment.

The new biologism is characterized by several aspects, some of which have already been addressed. Psychiatric training and practice have become more biochemical and more opposed to community psychiatry, largely as a result of the ability of drugs to control psychiatric symptoms. Renewed biologism also stems from psychiatry's attempt to protect both its public image and its reputation within the medical community. Such protection in part reflects the loss of optimism concerning social treatments, a paradigm shift similar to the mid-nineteenth-century retreat from the cult of curability to the cult of incurability. NIMH research and training funds, which were central to community orientations, have been drastically curtailed, and funding now emphasizes biochemical modes. Psychology and psychiatry therefore are unable to support graduate and professional training in social psychiatry, thus cutting off that option for many practitioners. Research in mental illness, particularly in the psychoses, has gone in a more biochemical direction, since both physician and non-physician researchers consider chemical intervention to be more reliable than other treatments.

The most dramatic development is the huge expansion of psychoactive drugs in mental health institutions, other institutions for mentally ill persons, institutions such as prisons and reformatories, and among the general public. Another important phenomenon is the retention of harmful procedures — psychosurgery, electroshock, and aversive conditioning. While these procedures are not necessarily increasing, they might be expected to have declined in a period of socially directed mental health practice. In fact, aversive conditioning and certain applications of psychosurgery were developed in the period of community mental health. This chapter will focus on the matters of drugs, ECT, and psychosurgery, primarily on the first.

THE GROWTH AND IMPORTANCE OF PSYCHOACTIVE DRUGS

Psychotropic drugs have become central to mental health care inside and outside of institutions. They have become so commonplace that more than one-fifth of the *non*-institutionalized population receives at least one prescription annually (Gottlieb, Nappi, and Strain, 1978). In 1977, expenditures on such drugs totalled $850 million, more than was spent on all CMHCs (President's Commission on Mental Health, 1977, Vol. 2: 530). Until recently Valium (diazepam) and Librium (chlordiazepoxide), anti-anxiety drugs produced by Hoffman-LaRoche, were the world's first and third largest selling prescription drugs. In 1974, 3 billion Valium and 1 billion Librium tablets were sold in the U.S. by over 70 million prescriptions. Those prescriptions represented about one-half of all psychotropic drug prescriptions in the country. The two drugs accounted for over one-half of Hoffman-LaRoche's $1.9 billion annual gross sales worldwide in 1974 (half of that is in the U.S.) and for $100 million in profits. In 1974 England's Monopolies and Mergers Commission ordered 75 per cent and 60 per cent price reductions, respectively, when it was discovered that Roche's British affiliate paid the parent firm over 40 times more for the ingredients than they cost in Italy, where the absence of drug patent laws creates more competition. The Commission also ordered a $30 million refund for past overcharges. U.S. buyers are paying from 700 to 1000 per cent more than English buyers. One hundred 5-mg. tablets of Valium cost 24 cents to produce, package, and distribute; those pills wholesale for $7.25 and retail for $14. Much of the surplus goes to promotion — one-fifth of Roche's gross goes to drug ads, free samples, and detail men (the detail men are the drug industry's high-powered salesmen who, according to American Medical Association polls, are often physicians' main source of drug knowledge (Waldron, 1977)). When Smith, Kline, and French introduced Thorazine, that drug increased the company's total sales volume by one-third within a year. The manufacturer added a special task force of fifty detail men to sell Thorazine to state hospitals (Scull, 1977b: 80-81).

The rapid application of psychotropic drugs was not appropriately monitored by drug firms, the Food and Drug Administration (FDA), or by the psychiatric professionals and institutions. In 1953, just five months before SKF was to market Thorazine, it had only been tested on 104 patients. Yet thirteen months later, it was being administered to an estimated 2 million patients (Scull, 1977b: 80). Antidepressants, likewise, were rarely tested, and were marketed with FDA backing even though that agency was aware of many dangers. Parnate (tranylcypromine), an antidepressant introduced by SKF in 1961, was found to cause hypertension, frequently resulting in strokes which were sometimes fatal. Yet the FDA only kept 'watch,' preferring not to hold hearings until 1964. When the FDA finally decided to hold hearings, high levels of protest mail from psychiatrists and the refusal of the American Psychiatric Association to testify, led the FDA to cancel the hearings and to merely require minor changes in package insert labeling (Mintz, 1967: 199-213).

Like most regulatory agencies, the FDA has close relationships with the industry which it is supposed to regulate. FDA officials have received income from the drug industry. Industry lobbyists regularly spend time at FDA headquarters to push for their products' acceptance. Further, the FDA does not wish to hurt the drug industry by excessive regulation. And, since it accepts so much of medical ideology, the FDA rarely listens to public outcry to remove drugs from the market. As early as 1963, when over 200 psychiatric drugs were being discussed at Senate hearings, Dr. Fritz A. Freyhan of NIMH's Clinical Neuropharmacology Research Center testified that 'relatively few' drugs had been 'demonstrated to be potent and effective,' and that many patients had increased anxiety with tranquilizers (Mintz, 1967).

Miltown (meprobamate), introduced in the late 1950s as an anti-anxiety medication, had no more effect than placebos. In 1957 FDA investigator Dr. Barbara Moulton told FDA medical director Dr. Albert H. Holland, Jr. about meprobamate's addictive qualities, and he responded by telling her to do nothing, because 'I will not have my policy of friendliness with industry interfered with.' Two years later Holland resigned and began working for American Home Products Corporation, whose Wyeth Laboratories division manufactured meprobamate under the trade name Equanil. Shortly, however, meprobamate was withdrawn and replaced largely by Valium and Librium, which have come to approach addictive levels (Mintz, 1967: 193-195; Scheff, 1976). Valium was long considered to be free from most soporific and addictive effects which had been common in earlier minor tranquilizers. Yet recent research has shown a high degree of addiction, as well as dangerous withdrawal symptoms, including psychotic breaks (Koumjian, 1981). Barbara Gordon's autobiographical *I'm Dancing As Fast As I Can* (1979) popularized this problem of psychotic breaks upon withdrawal. When the film version was produced, Roche Laboratories (1982) mailed a letter to all physicians in the nation, arguing that Gordon's personal misuse of Valium was the problem. Roche believed that 'The film may generate serious, unjustified concern and disrupt doctor/patient relationships.' Gordon in fact sought without success a psychiatrist who would provide a positive relationship, but was continually confronted with psychiatrists who relied on drugs, often switching inappropriately from one to another.

Overdosing of patients with psychoactive medication is common, and even at regular doses these drugs have long-lasting side-effects. Parkinsonism (also called pseudo-Parkinsonism) is one of the best known, and when frequently accompanied by akinesia, produces physical immobility. Emotional indifference also is common, and these combined symptoms are often misdiagnosed as psychomotor retardation (Crane, 1973). In discussing such effects, Crane suggests that 'Some clinicians may even consider it a desirable effect because it helps control unruly behavior.' Scheff (1976) is even stronger: 'Like lobotomy, the phenothiazines may cause permanent irreversible brain damage,' as well as many other serious conditions. A short list of those other effects includes: hypertension, jaundice, photosensitivity, impotence, excessive weight gain, lupus, edema, breast engorgement, fainting, dizziness, EKG abnormalities, convulsive seizures, amenorrhea, corneal deposits, blindness from retinitis, and even 'sudden death.' These, and many more, may be read off of any number of drug ads, which themselves already minimize the dangers. Nevertheless, manufacturers and doctors continue to protest further such listings (Crane, 1973).

Tardive dyskinesia (TD) is perhaps the most serious and most notable condition. This illness was actually noticed within a few years of the widespread administration of phenothiazines in the early 1950s. Tardive dyskinesia is irreversible, and cannot even be cured by removal from phenothiazines. Crane (1973) describes the 'slow, rhythmical movements in the region of the mouth, with protrusion of the tongue, smacking of the lips, blowing of the cheeks, and side-to-side movement of the chin, as well as other bizarre muscular activity.' All parts of the body may display motor disorder. 'Overextension of the spine and neck, shifting of weight from foot to foot, and other abnormal postures indicated that the coordination of the various segments of the axial musculature was also affected.' In the early 1970s psychiatrists claimed that only 2-3 per cent of all mental hospital patients had this disease, but more recent studies have established that as many as 62 per cent of inpatients have tardive dyskinesia. Outpatients as well are prone to this illness — some 43 per cent of outpatients on phenothiazines for more than a year have dyskinesia (Asnis et al., 1977; Smith et al., 1979). Smith et al. (1979) showed that reported prevalence of TD in inpatients varied from 62.2 per cent to 6.9 per cent, depending on the criteria chosen to define the condition. When psychiatrists insist upon higher severity of symptoms to diagnose TD, their defensive definition yields very low prevalence rates (Brown and Funk, 1984). Interestingly these criteria are usually unstated; a major review of thirty-six studies (Jeste and Wyatt, 1981) found that only seven mentioned the severity used to establish the diagnosis.

Through the 1970s the drug industry, and the psychiatric profession were not very concerned about problem of tardive dyskinesia, even though it had become common, and more than 100 scientific papers on the subject were published between 1967 and 1972. Before 1971 package inserts provided only one sentence on tardive dyskinesia, and noted its rarity. Psychiatric literature before the early 1970s often argued that TD was not a side effect of antipsychotic medication, that it was not persistent, and that symptoms attributed to TD were due to other disorders. The literature also minimized predisposing factors to TD, such as prior brain damage from electroshock, insulin shock, and psychosurgery (Brown and Funk, 1984). Reports since the early 1970s have retreated from these positions. More recently, psychiatric literature has 'discovered' this serious condition, but too late for the many patients already afflicted. Further, a large number of recent studies which do recognize the dangerous symptoms of tardive dyskinesia merely try to counter them with other drugs (Crane, 1973), thus perpetuating polypharmacy. Some clinicians have even employed electroshock to treat TD (Price and Levin, 1978), despite the fact that ECT predisposes patients to TD in the first place.

Doctors know surprisingly little about the psychoactive drugs which they more and more commonly prescribe. One study of the adoption of a new drug reported that drug company detail men were the first source of information for about half of the doctors, and drug company mailings and periodicals for another quarter. Journal ads and the drug industry's *Physicians' Desk Reference* (PDR), which downplay negative effects, are also widely used. An investigation of the 177 references given by one drug ad showed that 160 of those references were to articles having nothing to do with the ad's recommended usage (Waldron, 1977); the manufacturer was using unrelated medical research to convince psychiatrists to use the drug.

Gottlieb, Nappi, and Strain (1978) reported on a survey of doctors' knowledge of key psychoactive drugs. They administered a twenty-two-item questionnaire at the Bronx's Montefiore Hospital to test basic knowledge of diazepam (Valium), imiprimane (Tofranil, etc.), and amitriptyline (Elavil, etc.) (the latter two are tricyclics used as antidepressants). Knowledge was tested in the areas of clinical indications for use, basic pharmacology and physiology, and toxicities and side effects. Three groups were tested: medical interns and residents; psychiatric residents, fellows, and attending staff; and medical students on their psychiatric rotation. On the use of diazepam for anxiety, all three groups were comparable on clinical diagnosis (ranging from 72-82 per cent correct response) and on phar macology and physiology (with a very low range of 33-39 per cent), but the medical students did significantly better on side-effects. 'Only 20 per cent of the medical and psychiatric staff were able to relate their knowledge of the metabolism and duration of action of diazepam to the clinical task of devising a pharmacologically rational dosage schedule.' Further, 'Ten per cent of the medical house staff and 23 per cent of the psychiatric staff failed to recognize that diazepam may occasionally precipitate hostility, rage, or even physical violence.' While psychiatrists did significantly better on the use of tricyclics in depression, their ability in all areas of study for the three drugs yielded only a 70 per cent correct response rate.

The researchers concluded that 'neither the trainee in internal medicine nor the psychiatrist (at any level of training) is sufficiently informed about the diagnosis and psychotropic drug treatment of anxiety states and depression syndromes.' Yet, these investigators are very favorable toward drug treatment, pressing for further training of all physicians, and emphasizing that psychiatrists have a 'unique role' in patient care due to their knowledge of and skills with psychoactive drugs. Actually, the results of this study are alarming, given the length of time during which these drugs have existed and the great frequency with which they are used. Presently, 40 per cent of U.S. psychotropic prescriptions are written by general practitioners, 18 per cent by internists, and 10 per cent by osteopaths. This increase in non-psychiatrists prescribing psychiatric drugs, for such reasons as obtaining 'a less demanding and complaining patient' (Waldron, 1977), is testimony to the impact of these drugs on the general medical scene in this country, and a reflection of the flaws in psychiatric practice.

A glance at the drug advertisements in psychiatric and medical journals easily show the medical ideology promoted by the drug manufacturers, a viewpoint one assumes is not lost on its professional audience. The ads promise male physicians relief from pesty or depressed women, such as the housewife 'with too little time to pursue a vocation for which she has spent many years in training' or the new college student whose 'newly stimulated intellectual curiosity may make her more sensitive to and apprehensive about unstable national and world conditions' (Waldron, 1977). Ads favor the use of drugs to keep people in placid states, and extol the cost-saving resulting from lessened staffing needs.

Psychiatric drugs have expanded to other institutions, the result of an expanding biologistic model. Prisoners are often given such medication (Spiegelman, 1977; Diamond et al., 1981). In one New Jersey reformatory, 76 per cent of teenage girls received one or more sedating or tranquilizing drugs daily (Lerman, 1982: 56). These criminological applications of psychotechnology cannot be considered as anything more than social control and institutional preservation. This separates such treatment from the psychiatric perspective where it can clearly be argued that when not abused, psychoactive drugs can be of certain value in calming psychotic symptoms in order to facilitate treatment. In prisons and reformatories, such medical/psychological treatment simply is not an issue.

In the non-institutionalized population, more than one-fifth of whom received at least one psychoactive prescription annually, psychoactive drugs are part of a mechanical model of psychological distress. Koumjian (1981) argues that anti-anxiety drugs are considered a treatment of choice since anxiety has been redefined on an 'objective' scale which focuses attention on individual symptoms rather than social causes. This redefinition sees anxiety in a broad non-specific sense, without regard to the variety of physical, emotional, and combined problems of which anxiety is a manifestation. It also allows physicians in various practices to curtail time spent in patient visits and to offer a tangible treatment. The expanding non-specific application of anti-anxiety drugs produces an interesting situation in which their somatic prescription as muscle relaxants can lead to their psychological continuance. Cooperstock and Lennard (1979) conducted sixty-eight interviews and twenty-four lengthy mail questionnaires with Valium and Librium users. Fifty-eight per cent claimed their use began as a response to a somatic disorder but that they continued to use the drugs, a majority of them recognizing that such continued use reflected a response to role strains. For women, who were twice as likely as men to be given such a prescription, such strains usually involved stress associated with traditional wife, mother, and housekeeper roles. For men, work roles were typically the recognized reason.

By defining psychological issues as medical problems — mostly to be treated by drugs, which only a physician may prescribe — the medical profession guarantees medical dominance over the mental health field. Scheff (1976) argues that 'present mental health laws, which establish medical dominance in the mental health field, are costly and probably unwise. These laws encourage treatment policies and practices which overemphasize chemotherapy and underemphasize sociopsychological treatment.' The laws to which Scheff refers are those which require psychiatrists on staff in certain numbers and in the dominant positions. Yet those psychiatrists are rarely in direct patient care; most of the front-line work is performed by aides and nurses. The institutional and ideological dominance of psychiatrists, combined with the overwork of the nurses and aides, often leads the lower levels of staff to accept the psychiatric profession's over-drugging.

Many mental health professionals argue that the side-effects of these drugs are outweighed by their benefits in reducing the worst symptoms of psychosis. For many symptoms such reduction in severity is very positive. The complaint concerning psychoactive drugs is their global, indiscriminate use. Psychiatry has often argued that psychoactive drugs allow for greater amounts of therapy and other forms of patient care. Crane (1973), in a major review article, dismissed that claim. He explains that the extensive use of drugs has in fact prevented federal, state, and local agencies from providing adequate staff and better facilities due to the automatic assumption that great improvements were already occurring. Crane wrote that 'Anyone who has had experience with the institutional atmosphere before and after the introduction of drugs knows that the understaffing, insufficient funds, poor housing, marginal food, and improper maintenance of patients' quarters are as great now as they were in the immediate postwar period.'

In a number of cases, drugs have had negative effects on patients, including longer hospitalization, higher recidivism, and less remission of symptoms. Scheff (1976) cited several studies which show that drugs provide hardly better than a placebo effect (10-15 per cent) over a one-year period, and in a long run study with three-year follow-up, placebo patients showed better adjustment. Gunderson (1977) began an important review article by noting that:

> *When one of the early studies of psychotherapy of schizophrenia was begun, it was considered unethical to have a control group which received drugs without psychotherapy. Ten years later...it was stated that it would be unethical to conduct research on treatment of schizophrenia with patients who were given psychotherapy without drugs.*

Gunderson criticized this drug orientation. In discussing a number of recent studies, including one noted by Scheff, he found that placebos did better over time, even in one investigation where the placebo group had more mentally ill fathers than the drug group. In another study, drugs produced no significant difference when psychotherapy was given. In another experiment, chronic schizophrenics (with an average hospitalization of seventeen years) were transferred into an active milieu ward; non-drug patients had higher discharge rates, less readmission, and better symptom remission. While Gunderson's review shows that psychosocial treatment by milieu therapy, individual therapy, group therapy, or family therapy may be more effective for some groups of schizophrenics, 'The most surprising results have come from those reports which suggest that the drugs can be deleterious to the effectiveness of psychosocial treatments.' As Gunderson added, 'Hawthorne effects' in such research are common: psychopharmacologists find greater efficacy of drugs, while psychosocial treatment professionals find better results with their techniques. Further, the motivation, attitude, and egalitarianism of treatment staff is more important to outcome than is the specific model of treatment.

One mental health clinic which strove to spend more therapeutic time with patients and to lessen drug use reported reductions from 40 per cent to 90 per cent in use of various tranquilizers (Waldron, 1977). Kupers

(1982) has had success in relatively rapid dosage reduction, and sometimes discontinuation, in a community mental health center where he offers social treatment, including a special emphasis on advocacy for a broad range of issues affecting patients' social and economic well-being. Some psychiatrists have estimated that as many as 50 per cent of medicated chronic schizophrenics seen as outpatients would do as well without drugs. Various studies have shown that even placebo replacement yields improvement. In consideration of such knowledge Kurucz and Fallon (1980) discontinued the medication of fifteen chronic schizophrenics on a thirty-bed inpatient ward in a New York state hospital. At six-month follow-up, two patients were well enough for discharge, and altogether seven of the fifteen were off medication. At one-year follow-up, another patient was well enough for discharge, and 30 per cent of the patients remained drug-free. These results prompted a hospital-wide trial. Ninety days after beginning, 31 per cent of 944 patients involved were no longer on antipsychotics. The best success was in one of the geriatric wards. The researchers believe that more widespread application of such dosage reduction techniques is hindered by psychiatrists' opposition to intervention in personal treatment choices, non-medical staff fear of more responsibility, and patient and family anxiety.

The indiscriminate use of psychotropic drugs, with hardly any concern for their utility and/or effects, is one of the chief outgrowths of post-World War II mental health policy. Deinstitutionalization has proceeded on the technical basis of psychoactive drugs, which mask or decrease many symptoms. While early deinstitutionalization preceded widespread introduction of psychoactive drugs, without those drugs state authorities would never have entertained discharging tens of thousands of back-ward patients. Additionally, CMHCs, designed as an alternative type of facility, have used drugs widely. Outpatient treatment has also brought psychoactive drugs to a large number of less seriously disturbed people. And, as noted above, one-half of the country's prescribed psychoactive drugs are written by non-psychiatrists. While some people may partly benefit from some use of these chemicals, the routine usage and overdosing of mental patients has obscured most positive applications. Since tardive dyskinesia takes several years to appear, we will be seeing countless more cases over the next decade or so. One reason for this expected increase is that nursing homes are rapidly adding phenothiazines as part of their low-cost custodial maintenance efforts. And, as shown earlier, nursing and boarding homes are the fastest growing and largest source of mental health care in the U.S.

INTRUSIVE PSYCHIATRIC PROCEDURES: ELECTROSHOCK, PSYCHOSURGERY AND AVERSIVE CONDITIONING

Prior to the development of psychoactive drugs and the sociological critique of total institutions, psychosurgery and electronconvulsive therapy (ECT) were frequently used for custodial maintenance and for punitive reasons. It is important to note that these are psychiatric procedures, since their use in non-therapeutic fashion constitutes a specific application of psychiatric power in the production of social control. Further, their origin in the psychiatric armamentarium justified them as acceptable, due to their medical form. Aversive conditioning and certain applications of psychosurgery developed alongside the community mental health approaches, and electroshock was often advocated by community psychiatry proponents. There was little attempt by community mental health advocates to stem the use of these intrusive procedures. This shortcoming facilitates the potential growth of these methods in the post-community psychiatry period. Similar to the appeal of psychopharmacology, these somatic procedures are attractive in the current period when medical, governmental, and public opinion calls for treatments with measurable effects. For this reason, these procedures require some discussion.

Electroshock treatment

Modern psychiatry has been very dependent on electroconvulsive therapy (ECT). As noted earlier, important community mental health planners, among them Milton Greenblatt, were avid proponents of ECT. This is curious, since as Breggin (1979: 136-140) notes, ECT is best viewed in context of the array of somatic treatments which were employed beginning in the 1930s as a result of vast overcrowding and atrocious state hospital conditions. ECT was one of a number of shock treatments, along with metrazol and insulin. In addition, other 'heroic' methods included blows to the head, snake bites, bromide intoxication, cyanide poisoning, induction of anoxia (lack of oxygen) by forced breathing of nitrogen, and hypothermia coma induced by lowering the body temperature by as much as twenty degrees.

In a 1942 survey, 93.8 per cent of state hospitals sampled used ECT, as did 79.4 per cent of federal hospitals and 74 per cent of private psychiatric facilities (Breggin, 1979: 152). Even according to many physicians who supported ECT, it was frequently used as punishment for ward rule infractions, with no therapeutic intent at all. The advent of psychotropic drugs in the mid-1950s obviated the need for large-scale administration of ECT in state hospitals, and from that point on the treatment has been used primarily in private psychiatric hospitals and general hospital psychiatric wards. This is one reason why ECT deserves discussion here, since Chapter 6 pointed out the importance of these types of institutions in current mental health care.

A 1975 NIMH survey found 60,000 persons receiving ECT. This is certainly a low count, since the study excluded treatments administered in private offices and in outpatient clinics. Reponse bias, particularly from for-profit hospitals was a problem, since their responses indicated that only 7.5 per cent of patients in such facilities received ECT. This figure is far out of line with two more systematic local studies, which found corresponding rates of 21 per cent and 25 per cent. Using various studies, Breggin extrapolated a 1975 national figure of 100,000 patients (Breggin, 1979: 3).

Massachusetts data for 1973-1974 showed an annual total of 2,441 patients in the state receiving ECT in VA, state, and private mental hospitals (general hospitals were excluded from the study). Of all ECT cases, 90 per cent took place in private hospitals, 6 per cent in state hospitals, and 4 per cent in VA facilities. Five of the eleven private hospitals reported giving ECT to 33 per cent or more of all patients, two of those asylums giving the treatment to 50 per cent or more (Grosser et al., 1975). A study of New York City and three suburban counties found ECT employed in thirty of thirty-six hospitals sampled (83.6 per cent). City, state, and VA facilities gave shock treatment to 1 per cent of inpatients, nonprofit and university hospitals to 5.2-5.3 per cent, and for-profit facilities to 21.3 per cent of patients. Four of the proprietary hospitals gave shock to from 16 to 40 per cent of all patients (Asnis et al., 1978). In both the Massachusetts and New York City data, profit-making private hospitals employed shock treatment on twenty times as many patients as did public institutions. In New York State, 84 of 121 responding hospitals (69 per cent) reported ECT administration in the period 1972-1977. State hospitals accounted for 11.7 per cent of all treatments (individual treatments, rather than patients), general hospitals for 3 per cent, and private psychiatric facilities for 86 per cent (Morrissey et al., 1979). The New York researchers did not find a difference between private non-profit and private for-profit facilities, a distinction which Asnis et al. (1978) did find. However, when looking at changes over a five year period, the New York State researchers found for-profit general hospitals to stand out. From 1972 to 1977, the statewide number of treatments fell by 49 per cent, with the largest decline in state hospitals (64 per cent). Profit-making general hospitals declined only 2.8 per cent. Third party reimbursement plays a key role in the employment of ECT. Private general hospitals, both for-profit and non-profit, have grown noticeably in their share of total ECT treatments. This fits with the discussion in Chapter 6 of the growing importance of private sector institutions which become more linked to public planning and funding. It is conceivable that despite reductions in ECT usage in all facilities, the growing importance of third party payments will combine with renewed biochemical approaches to maintain or even increase ECT utilization. Private psychiatric hospitals which sometimes treat 70 per cent of all patients with ECT have earned much money from reimbursements. These 'shock shops,' as they have been termed, consider ECT their treatment of choice (Paige, 1972a; 1972b). The 1982 referendum victory against ECT (subsequently ruled invalid by a court) in Berkeley was largely directed at a single such hospital — Herrick Hospital.

Although space does not permit lengthy discussion of the effects of ECT, some brief attention is necessary due to the intense debate over this mode of treatment. Proponents of ECT have claimed success in treating depression, although they have generally downplayed the costs of such success, i.e., the other effects of ECT. Electroshock produces brain hemorrhage, cerebral edema, and toxic effects resulting from the brain's being exposed to chemicals in the blood that it was ordinarily protected from by the blood-brain barrier. All of this leads to death of brain cells, which results in memory loss, often of a severe and long-term nature. ECT also causes changes in the brain chemicals used to synthesize protein and RNA. Cerebral disrhythmia, a slowing of the EEG waves, also occurs; it is long-lasting and possibly permanent. Brain damage, organic psychosis, epilepsy and even death by cardiac arrest also result from ECT. Breggin calculates an overall death rate of 1:1000, and a rate of 1:200 for persons over sixty. Autopsy studies have demonstrated brain damage, as well as its increase with increase in number of ECT treatments (Sterling, 1976; Breggin, 1979). Memory loss is the most common result. Most studies have ignored this problem through focusing on periods of only several post-ECT days, using recently learned material, and failing to employ a control group.

Irving Janis in the 1950s conducted a series of studies with ECT patients and matched patients treated with psychotherapy. Follow-up was several months, and memory was tested before and after in terms of basic life history such as schooling, job history, family relations, and childhood experiences. Pre-treatment ECT patients often gave long, complex answers to single questions, whereas their post-treatment responses to the same material were brief and required many further questions. This phenomenon was not observed in non-ECT patients. Memory loss is so well-known an effect, that many consent forms include a waiver of responsibility for it (Sterling, 1979).

ECT administration is often haphazard. Even proponents of the treatment (e.g., Asnis et al., 1977) remark that there is a problem in the variety of practices in terms of concurrent drug therapy. Also problematic is the limited amount of training and record-keeping. Further, memory loss has been shown to be less with unilateral ECT applied to the non-dominant side of the brain. Nevertheless, bilateral ECT remains the typical mode; in the New York City area study, of the thirty facilities giving ECT, twenty-five used bilateral treatments exclusively (Asnis et al., 1977). Critics of ECT (c.f. Breggin, 1979) note that consent procedures are very weak.

Given the increasing importance of public funding in private practice, mental health policy makers could exert more controls on ECT practices in private institutions. There is much precedent for federal policy applications in private institutions — for instance, determination of need procedures. In a conservative vein, the Department of Health and Human Services recently prohibited any staff or facility sharing of federally-funded family planning with hospital-specific abortion services. Yet even if there were progressive directions in terms of treatment forms, this might be cancelled out by recent emphasis on cost-effective treatment methods, of which ECT promises to be an example.

Psychosurgery

Psychosurgery is the surgical alteration of brain tissue for reasons of behavior control, rather than for intractable pain or lesions. It is the most invasive, irreversible, and destructive psychiatric procedure, and one which many persons might expect to be abolished in an era of mental health reform. Yet psychosurgery continued into the recent period, at times with HEW and NIMH support. Further, as will be mentioned below, the punitive and social control aims of psychosurgery became more central in the 1960s and 1970s.

From 1936 to 1955, 40,000 to 50,000 psychosurgical operations were performed in the U.S., mostly lobotomies. Lobotomy was so widely used on World War II veterans that the VA set up crash programs to train surgeons in the procedure. A leading proponent of psychosurgery, Walter Freeman, noted that lobotomy in this period resulted in epilepsy in 30 per cent of patients, and 1-3 per cent died from cerebral hemorrhage (Chorover, 1979: 154; Chavkin, 1978: 23-24). Most patients were turned into vegetables, with little imagination, emotion, or capacity for future planning. Lobotomy declined in the 1950s due to its negative reputation and the introduction of psychotropic drugs. But in the mid-1960s, psychosurgery was revived. Breggin (1977) estimated that by the mid-1970s approximately 600 operations were performed annually in the U.S. While some lobotomies are still performed, at present, the operations are more sophisticated than the early lobotomies; cingulotomies, amygdalotomies, thalamotomies, and hypothalamotomies involve laser beams burning out parts of the brain which are held to be responsible for certain undesirable behaviors. In some cases, strings of electrodes are laid across the brain to allow remote control of patient behavior (Breggin, 1977; Chavkin, 1978; Chorover, 1979).

One of the main purposes of psychosurgery is social control. Following the 1967 Detroit riots, Harvard doctors Vernon H. Mark and Frank R. Ervin wrote in the *Journal of the American Medical Association* and in their book, *Violence on the Brain* (1970) that the unrest in Detroit was caused by individuals with 'episodic dyscontrol syndrome', rather than by hunger, poor housing, high unemployment, police brutality, and other aspects of racism. The doctors' solution was large-scale screening of ghetto residents to find these 'violence-prone' people and to perform preventive psychosurgery. Mark and Ervin teamed up with William H. Sweet, chief of neurosurgery at Massachusetts General Hospital, to obtain $500,000 from NIMH and $100,000 from the Justice Department's Law Enforcement Assistance Administration to develop these ideas in the Boston-based Neuro-Research Foundation (B. Brown et al., 1973; Chorover, 1979).

Similarly, California Governor Ronald Reagan sought a $1.5 million center which would be operated by the University of California at Los Angeles and the Neuropsychiatric Institute, to initiate a program such as Mark, Ervin, and Sweet suggested. In light of psychosurgery and aversion therapy programs already being conducted at California's Vacaville prison/hospital, Reagan's proposal raised great fears of massive psychosurgery under the cover of scientific medicine. Prison files showed that officials had listed as psychosurgery candidates a number of politically active prisoners. Protests by civil liberties, political, and professional organizations forced a cancellation of the project (Klein, 1974; P. Brown, 1977; Coles, 1977; Chorover, 1979: 195-196).

Besides prisoners, women are another target of psychosurgery, consitituting over 70 per cent of the patients. Leading psychosurgeon Walter Freeman openly claims that the procedure makes for better housewives, and the literature abounds in similar claims. Psychosurgery is promoted for 'promiscuity' in women, 'hyperactivity' in children, and for homosexuals (Roberts, 1972; Breggin, 1973; Chorover, 1979). Breggin (1977) remarks that 'One finds the patients [after psychosurgery] less able to feel intensely and subtly, and less able to handle multiple alternatives and choices.' Psychosurgery is surely the most destructive and dehumanizing technique which is considered to be ethical medical practice. Proponents of psychosurgery hold to their claims that the techniques reduce violence, but make no comment as to why their target populations are women, prisoners, activists, and homosexuals.

Despite these avowed social control intentions, an American Psychiatric Association task force concluded that there was no such purpose in psychosurgery, that the 1,039 operations performed from 1971 to 1973 were an insignificant number, and that the practice of psychosurgery was not a major problem (Donnelly, 1978). In responding to opponents' criticism of psychosurgery for its destruction of cognitive processes, one study which resulted in HEW's recent clearance for psychosurgery claimed that such cognitive destruction 'may be a necessary condition for psychosurgery to be effective. Too much thinking can cause emotional distress' (Coles, 1977). HEW's 1977 guidelines recommended psychosurgery as a valid therapeutic tool which had gone beyond the 'experimental' stage, and essentially placed the guidelines in the hands of those who would perform the operations, while shortcircuiting patients' safeguards by providing for psychosurgery by a guardian's informed consent. The document even cited Mark and Ervin's book, without mentioning its proposals for preventive psychosurgery (Coles, 1977).

As mentioned above, NIMH has directly funded some psychosurgery. In response to criticism, an NIMH publication (B. Brown et al., 1973: 2) stated:

> *Although it is easy from our current vantage point to condemn the 'lobotomists,' it should be pointed out that they were dedicated and genuinely concerned professionals who were trying to help patients suffering from a devastingly serious psychiatric disease. Their view that it was ethical and reasonable to change an immobile, uncommunicative, or destructively hyperactive patient into a placid 'homemaker' by psychosurgery is not entirely*

> *without merit. The most extreme symptoms of mental disease which they were faced with on a daily basis might have made the most ethically concerned and moralistic of us resort to desperate measures.*

It is thus evident that psychosurgery's resurgence in the 1960s and 1970s was not an aberrant phenomenon, nor a matter unconnected with other NIMH policy.

Behavior modification and aversive conditioning

During the period when psychosurgery was being revived in new forms, other psychotechnologies were being developed, the result of the application of psychological and psychiatric methods to social problems. The growth of the mental health field, and its promise of a variety of general social problem solutions, contributed to these retrograde applications. Abuses of behavior modification and aversion therapy have often been aimed at homosexual and uncooperative prisoners. Combination mental hospital/prison facilities like Massachusetts' Bridgewater State Hospital, California's Atascadero State Hospital, Maryland's Patuxent Institution, and New York's Dannemora State Hospital, as well as several federal penitentiaries, have submitted prisoners to a wide variety of such procedures. The least dangerous of these are the non-drug behavior modification programs where a strict reward and punishment system is established, aided by attempts to coerce prisoners into informing on each other. Popular therapies like transactional analysis are often employed (*Rough Times*, 1973a; *Liberation News Service*, 1973a). The more extreme activities involve forced human experimentation to test out new psychiatric drugs, aversion therapy with shock treatment (one form of which involves giving homosexuals shocks to the penis for having an erection in response to a slide or photo of a naked man), and aversion therapy with anectine (a procedure in which anectine is injected into the person, slowing their heartbeat and respiratory functions; this produces a fear of imminent death, at which point clinicians give suggestions for appropriate behavior) (*Rough Times*, 1973b; Chavkin, 1978; Chorover, 1979).

Implications of psychotechnology for future biomedical directions

As mentioned above, the application of psychiatric and psychological procedures to prisoners and various non-institutionalized persons is not an isolated phenomenon. Rather, it occurred as part of the expansion of the mental health fields into a range of non-psychiatric arenas. Mental health planners and practitioners urged expansion into other fields, the criminal justice field being a key sector. While only a minority of mental health professionals were involved in the abusive psychotechnologies, these modes were supported in part by NIMH, and they enjoyed at least tolerance on the part of many professionals. More importantly, few mental health professionals were willing to publicly criticize these abuses.

It should be remembered that such activities were made possible by the rightist government policies of the Nixon period, characterized by domestic espionage, international destabilization and support of reactionary coups, and disruption of liberal and radical groups involved in antiwar, civil rights, and feminist activities. Current rightward trends in the 1980s could potentiate a renewed interest in a wide range of authoritarian responses, including psychotechnology. Apart from such applications, mental health professionals need also to be aware of the individual levels of violence involved in psychotechnological approaches. Psychosurgery, electroshock, aversive conditioning, and uncontrolled utilization of psychotropic drugs run contrary to the humanitarian impulse found in so many mental health professionals and staff. This necessitates reconsideration of support of, or tolerance of these phenomena, if mental health practice is to be a healing process. As was discussed in Chapter 2, psychiatric expansionism always had tendencies to apply narrow perspectives to larger social problems, and to ignore real and potential fears on the part of target populations and other critics. Thus a good number of mental health professionals, whether intentionally or inadvertently, worked in the service of conservative social control functions.

The most vocal source of criticism of psychiatric social control has come from the patients' rights movement and the larger body of antipsychiatry of which that movement is a part. This response, as well as its impact on the mental health system, is the topic of the following chapter.

CHAPTER 9

Antipsychiatry and Mental Patients' Rights — Their Impact on Mental Health Care

Some pressure for mental health reform and restructuring came from the mental health system and from the state and federal governments which were responsible for the system. This part of mental health reform has been touched on already, in particular the critique of custodialism and the role of financial considerations. Yet there have been other significant inputs from outside the regular channels. These are collectively termed as antipsychiatry. Antipsychiatry certainly includes the theory and practice of R.D. Laing, David Cooper, and their associates, who coined the term. It also includes the mental patients' rights movement, efforts against psychotechnological abuses such as psychosurgery, aversive conditioning, and electroshock, Marxist and radical critiques of mainstream psychiatric practices, feminist therapy theory and practice, and gay therapy. Antipsychiatry, defined in this broad manner, has had a tremendous impact on popular perceptions of the mental health system and on theoretical and clinical advances.

ANTIPSYCHIATRY

A proper treatment of antipsychiatry requires more space than I devote to it here; more detailed analysis can be found in Castel et al. (1982) and P. Brown (1984). I will provide here a brief discussion of antipsychiatry since the patients' rights movement is a part of that larger critique of psychology and psychiatry. In this book I am more concerned with the patients' rights movement because it has had a significant impact on institutional mental health practices. Other components of antipsychiatry have left their mark more on private practice psychotherapy, other psychological practices, and on general conceptions of mental health.

Laing and the original antipsychiatrists produced a major break with much of existing psychiatric theory, and to a lesser extent, practice. Laingian thought criticized the organic psychiatry founded on Krapelin's mechanistic typologies and perpetuated by a largely physio-chemical approach which relies on medication and institutional management. These British radicals also opposed behaviorist models which applied a highly reductionist model of stimulus-response conditioning and learning, a model full of narrow, empirical observations but with little sense of the social whole. Early antipsychiatry further broke with many of its own psychoanalytic predecessors. While Freudian thought provided a basis for an analytical depth psychology which grasped human development and biography, it also included a rigid theory of instincts and intrapsychic determinism which Laingians rejected. Laing's application of psychoanalytic theory derived mainly from Ludwig Binswanger's (1963) existential-phenomenological psychoanalysis. This existential view shared with psychoanalysis a pessimistic deterministic view of the human condition, though not one based largely on drives or instincts. Yet it also took the individual more seriously and sympathetically than did psychoanalysis, focusing on the specific development of each human being rather than fitting that person's life into rigid developmental schema. Contrary to the impersonality, detachment, elitism, and intellectualism of psychoanalysis, existential-phenomenology understood mental illness as referring to real relationships. It sought to make sense out of symptoms rather than to follow the Freudian method interpreting those symptoms as part of a predefined logic of universal development.

Laing's *The Divided Self* (1959) and Laing and Esterson's *Sanity, Madness, and the Family* (1965) provided crucial foundations for roots of mental breakdown and the role of the labeled schizophrenic as a scapegoat for family disorganization. In that book, in Laing's *The Self and Others* (1963), and in Morton Schatzman's, *Soul Murder* (1973), antipsychiatrists developed the theory of collusion. Family members ally with a psychiatrist in protecting themselves; they project their own disturbances onto another and then this abdication of responsibility is stamped with scientific approval.

Laing's *The Politics of Experience* (1967) and David Cooper's *Psychiatry and Antipsychiatry* (1967) posed antipsychiatry as a political critique of capitalism's effects on human life. Here we see the Laingian paradigmatic question: who is crazier, the schizophrenic who believes they have a nuclear bomb inside their disembodied self, or the well-adjusted military man with the capability of dropping that bomb? Thus, antipsychiatry shifted the questions — a mentally and physically destructive society was seen as more in need of analysis than were its victims. But this political perspective was often personalistic, naive, and undeveloped. This weakness allowed antipsychiatry to degenerate into a glorification of insanity and into an extreme idealism which could de-emphasize the pain and misery experienced by many patients. For instance, in *The Leaves of Spring* (1970) Esterson pursued one of the cases in *Sanity, Madness, and the Family*. In the same work in which he attempted a Marxist philosophical foundation for psychiatry, he also attributed the family's psychotic constellation primarily to anal development. In Laing's, *The Facts of Life* (1976) the leader of antipsychiatry actually gave up the materialist basis of antipsychiatry, and posited that the fundamentals of human development occur in the transit of the fertilized ovum in the Fallopian tube and its experience of uterine implantation.

Apart from those later problems, there were important clinical applications of antipsychiatry. Laing's and his associates' radical therapeutic community style was best displayed in Kingsley Hall. There, a small group of professionals and patients endeavored to overcome the traditional staff-inmate distinctions in order to offer a retreat where people could review and relive their madness and its formative stages (Berke and Barnes, 1972). Though shortlived, Kingsley Hall and the later Arbours Housing Association served as models throughout the world of a democratic therapeutic community. Similarly, Cooper's (1967) shortlived Villa 21 experiment in a public mental hospital provided ideas for sympathetic mental health workers seeking to reform from within by breaking down the arbitrary hierarchies and rigid, distancing structures of the eternal asylum. Laing and colleagues prepared much of the way for more incisive critiques which developed more specifically activist solutions.

In the 1960s and 1970s a revolt against traditional psychology and psychiatry took place. This revolt was largely influenced by Laingian antipsychiatry, though it had roots in early American academic work (Bramel and Friend, 1982). Activist scholars argued against the myth of scientific neutrality and objectivity, the manner of looking at isolated variables rather than the totality, the prevalence of ahistorical theories, and the notion that all the world's social facts are already 'out there' waiting to be discovered by increasingly sophisticated methods and statistical techniques in the absence of expanded social knowledge and consciousness. This activist scholarship was a logical component of the student movement of the time which criticized the 'multiversity' for its support of the military-industrial complex, its lack of sensitivity to social problems, and its failure to provide relevance in education.

Outside of academia, activist antipsychiatry also took firm root. In the late 1960s, Psychologists for a Democratic Society (PDS) was formed, an offshoot of Students for a Democratic Society (SDS), a leading radical group of the time. PDS published a magazine, organized New York City school psychologists to counter their use against student activism in the schools, agitated on campuses for relevant psychology courses, held public forums on issues of politics involving psychology, and organized psychologists and students to participate in the contemporary anti-war movement. And, like many other radical groupings in the professions, PDS performed agitprop and guerrilla theater skits at professional association meetings, questioning political uses of psychology such as psychologizing student activism. For instance, PDS members would ask panelists why they investigated why *some* people were antiwar activists instead of why couldn't we get *more* people in the streets to stop the war against Vietnam.

Soon thereafter, the *Radical Therapist* magazine was begun. It published from 1970 to 1980, under several name changes *(Rough Times, RT,* and finally *State and Mind*). *RT*, as it was often known (regardless of name changes), was involved in a wide range of activities: criticizing the conservative elements of psychotherapy, protesting against psychosurgery and aversive conditioning in prisons, working with mental patients groups and mental health workers groups in organizing drives, serving as a nationwide network center for such activities, and sponsoring educational conferences and workshops. Alternative radical therapies developed in this period, including the Radical Psychiatry group which originated in Berkeley. Many of the free clinics of the 1960s also provided alternative counseling services to clients who found that most mainstream providers were unable to understand the contemporary social ferment.

Feminist therapy has also been a major force in the revolt against psychiatry. Part of the revival of the women's movement in the late 1960s was a critique of sex role socialization and of the sexist roles played by social institutions such as the mental health establishment. This movement held that psychiatry and psychology provided pseudo-scientific justification for institutionalized sexism, and for enforcing many of those institutional barriers to equality. This struggle took place on a number of fronts. Within professional psychology the Association for Women in Psychology worked to oppose psychological sexism in general, and that of the American Psychological Association in particular. Psychologists such as Naomi Weisstein (1972) and Phyllis Chesler (1973) produced early critiques which spurred a whole new field of criticism and study, and led to the development of a strong feminist psychology curriculum. Feminist therapy collectives and centers were founded to provide nonsexist therapy in an environment which was supportive of women's experiences.

Donovan and Littenberg's (1982) analysis of feminist therapy argues that 'Feminist therapy is better defined by the political awareness and social commitment on the part of the therapist than by the particular set of techniques she uses.' The authors believe that the women's movement critique of therapy was the inevitable result of two factors. First, therapy is concerned with those areas of experience assigned to and carried by women in our culture — relationships and emotions. Second, psychology has been widely used as a justification for women's subordinate role. The first task — of individual and interpersonal change — is unattainable without first correcting the second factor — psychology as social control. Therefore, Donovan and Littenberg continue, feminist therapy contains 'analysis of the forms of social, economic, and political oppression that affect women individually as well as a group. This analysis informs the therapist's understanding of how women develop and function in our society, and how change may occur.' As a result, feminist therapy is much more involved in the outside, social world than is most other therapeutic practice. Thus, 'the feminist therapist actively struggles with forces of sexism, racism, and class which affect her own attitudes and values.' She also encourages social, rather than solely individual change.

In its comprehensive nature, feminist therapy as conceptualized by Donovan and Littenberg yields a comprehensive alternative to traditional practices. First, it provides a valuable critique of psychological/psychiatric theory. Second, feminist therapy addresses practical political problems in its treatment and its political involvement: violence against women (rape, battery, incest, sexual harrassment), substance abuse, compulsive eating and dieting, and sexuality. Third, feminist therapy restructures the clinician's work relationship by building a collective work situation where the practitioners have a great amount of control over their work, as well as space for integrating political activism, therapeutic practice, and feminist analysis.

Gay therapy has similar features to those of feminist therapy. In fact, much of lesbian-oriented therapy is similar to feminist therapy. Therapy oriented towards both gay men and women deals with ways in which mental health professionals have stigmatized homosexuality and frequently attempted to make gay people give up their sexual preferences. Separate gay therapy centers were often a necessity, due to the checkered past of most mental health professionals. Much of the gay alternative involves dealing with the difficulties of growing up 'in the closet' and with the choice of whether or not to 'come out' (Castel et al., 1982: 241-247).

These various forms of antipsychiatry provided a very broad critique of psychiatry and psychology, and offered valuable alternative services. These parts of the antipsychiatric movement mainly affected private practice psychotherapy for relatively undisturbed people, and became part of a general progressive social and cultural awareness. By this influence, antipsychiatry paved the way for acceptance of the mental patients' rights movement by more sectors than might otherwise be supportive of the movement. The criticisms leveled by the ex-patient activists were quite similar to those of the rest of antipsychiatry, as detailed above. Thus, the non-institutional transformations aided the institutional reforms pursued by patients' rights organizers. Still, these two major segments were often unconnected. This is in contrast to Western Europe, especially Italy, where institutional reform has been much more integrated with non-institutional antipsychiatry (this will be explored in the final chapter on future directions). Since this book is mainly concerned with institutional developments, the patients' rights movement receives the largest share of the discussion of antipsychiatry.

MENTAL PATIENTS' RIGHTS: THE CONJUNCTURE WITH INSTITUTIONAL REFORM AND ECONOMICS

Mental patients' rights issues have been extremely important in recent mental health practices and policy, although this role has not been well understood. From one perspective, mainstream policy makers and clinicians have overemphasized this role by claiming that they have generously expanded patients' rights in a campaign to reform the system. As a corollary such arguments cite the flaws in allowing patients the right to refuse treatment, which they consider to be an obstacle to implementing other rights, especially the right to treatment. From another perspective, certain political-economic analyses (e.g. Scull, 1977) hold that the patients' rights explanation is essentially ideological, with its purpose to mask the central financial aspect of current policy.

The mainstream perspective errs in overemphasizing a deep benevolent interest. Humanitarian impulses were not in fact as central as has often been claimed. They were certainly not nearly as important as were economic motivations. From the other side, the denial of any role to patients' rights does a disservice to the patients, ex-patients, and their advocates who pursued such rights. It also ignores the impact of humanitarian concerns on the part of some mental health professionals. A more sensible understanding of the role of patients' rights must take into account the junction of economics, libertarian attitudes, and institutional structures, and must examine how different parties take divergent approaches to defining and implementing patients' rights.

Patients' rights and institutional change posed a complex mixture of social forces. This resulted from the rising costs of state hospital care, the general increase in civil liberties efforts during the 1960s and 1970s throughout the society, and from the specific efforts of patients and their advocates. The decaying physical plants and understaffing of state hospitals had begun to be insufferable. Renovation and higher staffing standards were imperative for reasons of safety, certification, and human rights. Yet the costs of such change were too high. Thus, states preferred to rid themselves of the burden of state hospitals. In this sense, patients' rights led to deinstitutionalization. At the same time, professionals who criticized custodialism were given broader support by an expanded set of parties with interests in patients' rights: patients' rights groups, civil libertarian attorneys, mental health planners and officials, lay advocates, sympathetic judges, and fiscally cautious legislatures and governors. These groups shared in one form or another the critique of custodial mental health care, a perspective discussed in Chapter 1. This critique was not new to the recent period, but had been put forward over a century earlier. However, that nineteenth-century critique was very limited and held by very few people, whereas recently it has become a major tenet in mental health policy. Further, the financial necessity to curtail hospitalization was far less serious in the past century than at present. Anticustodialism was so strong that the Joint Commission for Mental Illness and Health lost its drive to obtain federal support for improving state hospitals, while the National Institute of Mental Health achieved its Community Mental Health Centers (CMHC) program which sought to avert hospitalization by prevention and early treatment. This led, unfortunately, to the separate development of the state hospital and CMHC sectors, without sufficient attention paid to discharged chronic residents. As discussed throughout the book, massive state hospital discharges took place before adequate community treatment was available. Further, follow-up and continuity of care were difficult due to lack of coordination between mental health sectors, and poor quality nursing homes rapidly took on a major role in warehousing the discharged patients. Anticustodialism remains a powerful attitude, both in terms of the remaining state hospital residents, and in terms of the many ex-state hospital patients living in nursing and boarding homes, welfare hotels, and single-room occupancies. To the extent that anticustodialism criticizes the abuses committed against individuals, it also emphasizes their human rights. In this sense, the critique of custodial institutionalization often leads to support of some degree of patients' rights. Patients' rights issues also raised the question of ordinary reform of the mental health system. Such reform and restructuring is often difficult to attain, given the plodding bureaucracy and archaic practices in many mental health departments. Legal attacks, combined with a burst of popular exposes and civil libertarian protest, provided a necessary impetus and a social justification for pursuing goals that might otherwise be challenged for being too innovative or experimental.

The intersection of forces and interests described above has led to many changes in the mental health system. This can be observed in the range of legislative, judicial, and administrative changes in patients' rights which have greatly affected recent psychiatric care. These include: due process in commitment hearings, a preference for voluntary rather than involuntary commitment (usually obtained by reform in commitment statutes), the attempt to provide treatment in the 'least restrictive environment,' the abolition of compulsory patient labor, the right to treatment (i.e., the state's responsibility to provide therapeutic and/or rehabilitative treatment, rather than merely custodial care), the right to refuse treatment (e.g., psychosurgery, electroshock therapy, chemotherapy, restraint, seclusion), various safeguards for hospital procedures, and granting of civil rights, such as the right to contract, vote, and hold licenses.

The mental patients' rights movement

Much of the success of patients' rights issues has been due to the organizational efforts of patients' rights groups. This impact has not been widely accepted by the mental health establishment, since the system wishes to preserve its self-proclaimed humanitarian impulses, a subject which will be discussed shortly. While individuals have previously conducted psychiatric reform campaigns (e.g., Elizabeth Packard in the mid- to late-nineteenth century), the mental patients liberation movement provided the first critique of psychiatry coming largely from the side of the patients. Small groups of ex-patients began to assert their anger at being committed for what they saw as minor deviant acts, and then being resocialized into an institutional life style. Groups with names such as Mental Patients Liberation Front made their initial appearance with angry denunciations of mental hospital abuses, and sometimes with 'jailbreaks' in which they attempted to release friends who had been involuntarily committed. They also organized through publications, news conferences, demonstrations, and forums to oppose psychosurgery, electroshock, aversion therapy, and prison behavior modification programs. Further targets of the movement included involuntary commitment laws, denial of civil rights to patients and ex-patients, and unwilling treatment such as physical restraints and chemotherapy. These groups also provided outlets for ex-patients to talk over their problems with others who would be sympathetic to them. From this consciousness raising and support group structure developed various forms of self-help organizations.

A key element of the patients' rights legacy is in the area of litigation. The early patients' rights litigation was not a direct result of the collective actions of patients' rights groups which did not yet exist. Even many of the cases in the 1970s were initiated by individuals and/or professional advocates. The early suits were partly a result of the general upsurge of civil liberties activism in the 1960s, largely prompted by the civil rights movement. This provided a backdrop for the formation of patients' rights groups. Some of the later court cases were spurred by the patients' movement, even if not initiated by them. And the movement's publicity, demonstrations, and other actions played important roles in the outcome of those suits and subsequent enforcement.

Patients' rights litigation

In studying the significance of patients' rights litigation, it is first useful to examine the right to treatment issue. In 1966 Judge David Bazelon ruled in *Rouse v. Cameron* that Washington, D.C. statutes provided for the right to treatment when confined to a mental hospital. Such rights could be derived from the U.S. Constitution's eighth amendment guarantee against cruel and unusual punishment, and fourteenth amendment guarantees of due process and equal rights under the law. Bazelon ruled that inadequacy of resources was an unacceptable reason for failing to provide treatment. If a person was deprived of liberty on the grounds that he or she needed treatment, such treatment had to be provided. The court made no specific ruling for remedies, but merely asked the hospital to make an honest effort. In 1968, a Massachusetts case supported the right to treatment for persons judged incompetent to stand trial by reason of insanity. Although these cases had little direct effect on mental health policy since they involved persons originally charged with crimes, they were important in the historical development of right to treatment litigation (Stone, 1975; Bernard, 1977).

Wyatt v. Stickney was the real landmark case in the right to treatment. In a 1971 ruling, U.S. District Court Judge Frank Johnson, Jr. held that 'involuntarily committed patients unquestionably have a constitutional right to receive such individual treatment as will give each of them a realistic opportunity to be cured or to improve his or her mental condition.' A 1972 decree followed, stating that the two mental hospitals and one facility for the retarded named in the case had failed to provide '(1) a humane psychological and physical environment, (2) qualified staff at numbers sufficient to administer adequate treatment, and (3) individualized treatment plans.' Unlike the 1966 *Rouse v. Cameron* case, *Wyatt v. Stickney* produced a definite set of specific standards. Patients were granted the right to privacy, mail, phone, and visitors. Concerning legal rights usually taken away from mental patients, the court ruled that 'No person shall be deemed incompetent to manage his affairs, to contract, to hold professional or occupational or vehicle operator's licenses, to register and vote, or to make a will, *solely* by reason of his admission or commitment to the hospital.' Patients were 'to be free from unrestricted or excessive medicine,' to receive weekly medication reviews from physicians, and medicine should not be used 'as a punishment, for the convenience of the staff, or as a substitute for programs, or in quantities that interfere with the patient's treatment program.' Physical restraint and isolation were restricted, and human experimentation limited to express consent. Therapeutic labor was strictly defined so that hospital maintenance work must be voluntary, and paid at minimum wages. Specific standards were promulgated on floor space, toilet doors, closets, nutrition, and other living arrangements. Rigid staffing minimums were prescribed, and each patient was to receive a detailed individual treatment plan within forty-eight hours of admission (P. Brown, 1972).

In the same vein as the *Wyatt* decision, the right to treatment was given strong support in a consent decree involving Massachusetts' Northampton State Hospital. The 1976 class action suit for all patients in the facility sought the least restrictive environment, and a phasedown from 475 to 50 patients by 1980. The Department of Mental Health consented to provide this, largely as a way to obtain legislative funds above the regular budget lines (Booth, 1979a; 1979b). Similar phenomena have occurred throughout the country.

Patient labor has been an important area of litigation, with a high degree of success. Such labor was previously a major source of free or extremely cheap labor for many state hospitals. It has now been outlawed, unless it is voluntary and is paid at minimum wages. In *Souder v. Brennan*, testimony disclosed that one patient worked twenty-nine days a month for thirty-three years at the rate of $10/month. The court ruled that patients should receive competitive wages, and that the Secretary of Labor should find ways to apply the Fair Labor Standards Act to patient employees. High costs of paying regular workers are often cited as one reason for closing the expensive to maintain asylums. At times, mental health planners complained about the high cost of non-patient labor, without comprehending the importance of ending asylum peonage. Yet here, too, the civil liberties issue raised another issue of psychiatric reform favored by most planners and providers — community care. Once the mental health professionals got over their initial outrage at patient labor litigation, they found that such decisions added to their reasons for pursuing community care. Several years after the *Souder* decision, the application of the Fair Labor Standards Act to state hospitals was found inapplicable, in *Usery v. League of Cities*. Despite this reversal, the forward motion of state hospitals' policies on patient labor was so well developed that no attempt was made to return to the prior status.

Another key issue is due process in commitment. In the 1972 case of *Lessard v. Schmidt*, a federal district court ruled that an allegedly dangerous patient had a right to a speedy hearing, with advance notice of what expert testimony would be heard. Further, dangerousness had to be proven beyond a reasonable doubt, and indefinite involuntary commitment was to be a last resort after a less restrictive environment was tried (Flaschner, 1975). In 1974 federal judges overturned commitment statutes in Alabama *(Lynch v. Baxley)* and Michigan *(Bell v. Wayne County General Hospital)* for failing to provide constitutional guarantees of notice of hearing, right to be present at hearing, and right to counsel. The court also held that the commitment laws were unjust in failing to provide for such due process and for permitting such patients to be given shock treatment and chemotherapy unwillingly (Kopolow et al., 1975).

But various states began to change their statutes without waiting for litigation. Massachusetts was one of the several states that changed commitment laws in the early 1970s so that involuntary commitment was technically made more difficult and less frequent. When the 1971 commitment law took effect, it increased the percentage of voluntary commitments from 27.9 per cent in 1971 to 62.9 per cent in 1972 (Massachusetts Department of Mental Health, *Annual Reports*). This drastic change was largely effected by pressuring involuntary patients to sign voluntary forms, and was therefore a technical, bureaucratic solution rather than a systemic change. By 1973 a more significant change took place when the revised code contained a more restrictive definition of probability of harm to self or others, rather than the previous code's wide range which included behavior 'which clearly violates the established laws, ordinances, conventions, or morals of the community.' Indefinite commitment has been abolished, with periodic reviews now required (Flaschner, 1975).

It is definitely a step forward to have abolished many of the arbitrary commitment procedures of the past. Yet humanitarian reasons for these reforms may not necessarily have been foremost. Psychiatric hospitals now cite legal reasons for refusing to admit persons in serious need. This is a type of 'defensive medicine,' which denies help for fear of legal consequences. Just as 'defensive medicine' is a type of backlash against growing criticism of the medical establishment, 'defensive psychiatry' may be a type of backlash against the patients' rights movement. It is also a rather callous method of cutting costs and shedding responsibilities. More recently, involuntary commitments have been rising again. This is partly a statistical artifact, since many voluntary patients are refused admission. Further, the 'new chronic' population of more aggressive and violent patients may require a greater reliance on involuntary commitment.

A landmark case in 1975, *Donaldson v. O'Connor*, questioned the hospital's right to hold a patient to whom they failed to provide treatment. The U.S. Supreme Court ruled that non-dangerous persons who were not receiving treatment should be released if they could survive outside of the hospital. Kenneth Donaldson was involuntarily committed to Florida's Chatahoochee State Hospital, where he spent fifteen years. Well educated in legal matters, he began in 1960 to fight his unjustified confinement. Donaldson was so well versed in patients' rights law that he published an article in the *Georgetown Law Review* while in the hospital. The hospital superintendent constantly blocked Donaldson's legal efforts, saying that Donaldson was uncooperative for denying his illness, refusing ECT, and for his legal battle for freedom (Greider, 1975; MacKenzie, 1975). However, the court failed to uphold a lower court's monetary award to Donaldson, thus partly taking pressure off mental health authorities (Stone, 1975) and probably defeating a significant precedent for malpractice suits.

Backlash against patients' rights

At present there is a cautious, yet not entirely negative attitude in the Supreme Court toward reform litigation. The 1979 ruling in *Addington v. Texas* allowed for commitment by 'clear and convincing evidence' of 75 per cent certainty, rather than the previously held 'beyond a reasonable doubt' evidentiary level of 90 per cent certainty. The criminal law burden of 'beyond a reasonable doubt' had been widely criticized as unrealistic. And in the *Parham v. J.L and J.R.* case and *Secretary of Public Welfare v. Institutionalized Juveniles* (originally *Bartley v. Kremens*) cases, the Court held that minors' due process rights in commitment were satisfied by 'independent professional review' of their parents' decision to commit them, rather than by formal judicial review (Tancredi, 1980).

On April 20, 1981 the Court reversed a federal court ruling which held 1,200 retarded patients at Pennsylvania's Pennhurst State School were being deprived of their rights to the least restrictive environment (Greenhouse, 1981). The lower court ruling involved a specific interpretation of a specific congressional act. In reversing that interpretation, the Court still left open the possibility that other rights violations existed on constitutional or statutory grounds. These recent Supreme Court decisions have neglected or narrowed lower court rulings which were considered patients' rights movement victories. However, many of those rights had already been ensconced in state codes (Weiner, 1982). Still, as Tancredi (1980) points out, the Supreme Court has retreated from its own early- and mid-1970s libertarianism in patients' rights, and this contributes to a lack of enthusiasm for large-scale institutional rights litigation.

A November 16, 1981 federal appellate ruling reversed court-ordered spending in the Northampton consent decree, as established in 1976. District Judge Frank Freedman had followed the 1976 ruling with an injunction to the state legislature not to reduce the hospital budget from $53 million to $48 million. The Appeals Court set aside that injunction (Doherty, 1981).

Patients' rights activists and their lawyer colleagues are certain that severe cutbacks and the threatened dismantling of the Federal Legal Services Corp. will have drastic effects on patients' rights litigation, since many state hospital patients and their families lack funds for private litigation (Schwartz, 1981). Parallel to this, we may expect the sharp federal cutbacks in human services to deeply affect areas such as NIMH's advocacy program which provides small grants to about a dozen local public interest groups and one patients' rights organization. The American Bar Association's *Mental Disability Law Reporter* (1983a) has predicted additional problems as well, such as removing the advocacy system from the Developmental Disabilities Act and declining to fund advocacy services under the Mental Health Systems Act. In addition, the wide use of block grants could exempt states and localities from specific advocacy provisions under current federal regulations.

Economic reasons are also significant factors in current retrenchment, since patients' rights are costly. Rubin (1978: 83-84) calculated that as of January 1975 nationwide implementation of staffing alone under *Wyatt v. Stickney* standards would cost between $139 million and $167 million. In real dollars this is equivalent to $83 to $94 million, yet it took eight years from 1967 to 1975 for state mental hospital expenditures to rise by $151 million in real dollars. Therefore the implementation of *Wyatt v. Stickney* standards is unlikely, especially since real mental health expenditures have been declining since 1973. Further, Rubin's estimates did not include physical plant improvements necessary to meet stringent standards. Looking at a single state hospital operating under court-monitored spending increases to secure the right to treatment in the least restrictive environment, Massachusetts' Northampton State Hospital required $10 million in extra legislative funds for its first three years under the consent decree (Dietz, 1981b). It is not surprising that financial considerations block the wide implementation of patients' rights decisions. After all, a good deal of the impetus for such reforms came from a desire to curtail mental hospitalization by making it too costly.

Recent 'aberrational cases', such as John Hinckley's attempted assassination of Ronald Reagan, have amplified existing backlash, most notably in the rash of state actions to abolish or curtail the insanity plea. Paschall and Eichler (1982) and Lamb (1981) see the patients' rights movement as itself a barrier to the effective growth of patients' rights in practice, due, respectively, to excess litigation and intervention in institutional life. Perhaps another backlash factor is the spread of patient activism in the area of the right to refuse treatment. This important issue has not yet been discussed so far due to its special status, which often sets it in seeming opposition to most of the other patients' rights.

THE RIGHT TO REFUSE TREATMENT

In many ways, the right to refuse treatment is a dividing line in the patients' rights arena. While the above-discussed intersection of various parties' interests allowed for an expansion of many patients' rights, most of those parties do not agree that psychiatric patients should have the right to refuse treatment. This applies particularly to psychoactive drugs, but also to seclusion and restraint. Refusal of ECT and psychosurgery is more accepted by mental health professionals. Ultimately, the right to treatment is merely an affirmation that state hospitals are supposed to heal patients, not simply warehouse them. Staffing, sanitary, dietary, and residency standards are not a guarantee that in fact humane treatment will occur. What is considered proper treatment in the eyes of a large number of mental health professionals may include psychosurgery, shock treatment, and abuse of psychiatric drugs and restraints. Expert testimony can often be marshalled by the administration and medical staff to prove dangerousness and thus circumvent present safeguards against forced treatment. Patient organizers and civil liberties activists thus believe that it would be shortsighted to remain content with a statutory right to treatment.

Some suits had already touched on the right to refuse treatment. The *Wyatt v. Stickney* ruling held that patients had the right to refuse ECT, aversive conditioning, psychosurgery, or other major surgery. Other cases established similar rights in terms of ECT and chemotherapy. In *Kaimowitz v. Department of Mental Health* a Michigan court held that an involuntarily committed patient's consent to psychosurgery was uninformed, and that no involuntary patient should be subject to psychosurgery (Ferleger, 1975).

Federal court rulings on treatment refusal for more typical treatments — especially drugs — have been mixed. In *Rennie v. Klein*, a New Jersey District Court granted patients a conditional right to refuse, contingent upon review by an independent psychiatrist. A 1981 Appellate decision, however, removed the requirement of outside review and patient advocacy. In *A.E. and R.R. v. Michell*, however, committed patients were found to have no right to refuse treatment since Utah law employed commitment for patients considered incompetent and since hospitalization was the least restrictive alternative under the circumstances (Mills et al., 1983).

The major right to refuse treatment suit is the *Callahan v. Rogers* (formerly *Rogers v. Okin*, case, involving Boston State Hospital patients' right to refuse chemotherapy, restraint, or seclusion. The plaintiffs won the case in 1979 in a lower court. It was particularly significant in that it was the result of several years of in-hospital organizing by the Boston Mental Patients Liberation Front. Several years before the suit was initiated, the organization started a discussion group in one of the hospital's wards. The group addressed general social and political topics, as well as patients' rights. Increasing attention to the latter topic generated staff opposition, which in turn, led to barring the activists from the ward. Following this, a number of past and present patients sued the hospital, the Department of Mental Health, and various individual psychiatrists. Federal District Judge Joseph Tauro granted the plaintiffs a temporary restraining order in early 1975, and on October 29, 1979 the judge issued a permanent order. The order granted patients the right to refuse seclusion or forcible medication, except with express consent by themselves or their guardian, or in the event of substantial likelihood of extreme violence, personal injury, or attempted suicide *(Mass. Psych. Wards*, 1979.)

Judge Tauro refused to order $1.2 million in damages from the psychiatrists named for assault and battery, infraction of civil rights, and malpractice. The court held that the doctors acted in 'good faith' and without attempt to deprive patients of their rights. Yet testimony from patients, lower level staff, and even some professional staff revealed that seclusion was not used for emergency situations, but rather as punishment for minor rule violations. The six-by-twelve foot seclusion room has nothing in it but a plastic covered mattress, and patients had been incarcerated in such rooms for months *(Mass. Psych. Wards*, 1979).

Mental Health Department officials and hospital staff defended themselves by claiming that a committed patient was de facto incompetent to decide on treatment issues. The defendants also testified that there had been no forcible medication at all, except in cases of psychiatric emergency. Further, they stated that neither a voluntary nor an involuntary patient had the right to refuse treatment whether in emergency or non-emergency situations; existing state law stated the opposite. The staff psychiatrists claimed that the temporary restraining order would encourage widespread refusal of medication, yet, in a twenty-five month period from the time of the temporary order, only 12 of 1000 patients refused medication over a prolonged period of time and most changed their minds in a few days *(Mass. Psych. Wards*, 1979). Despite the overwhelming evidence in favor of the litigants, the state filed an appeal on the grounds that the state has a responsibility to treat committed patients, and that Tauro's ruling prohibits necessary exceptions to the right to refuse treatment (Dietz, 1979).

An appeal by the state led to a partial reversal in November, 1980 of Tauro's ruling. Federal Appeals Court Judge Frank M. Coffin sent the case back to Judge Tauro, asking for 'deference to the professional judgement of the state doctors.' The Appeals Court held that Tauro too narrowly limited forced medication to cases where patients were either mentally incompetent or were prone to harm themselves or others. Coffin also struck down the lower court's strict guidelines for appointing guardians for incompetent persons, as well as the court's stringent definitions of emergency situations in which regular safeguards could be abrogated. Despite these reversals, Judge Tauro and the patients' attorney, Richard C. Cole, considered the appellate decision as upholding the essential rights of patients to refuse treatment in a wide range of situations (Dietz, 1981b). Yet in 1982, the Supreme Court returned the Boston State case to the First Circuit Court of Appeals for a redetermination, since Massachusetts law potentially provided a greater right to refuse treatment than did the U.S. Constitution (Mills et al., 1983). While this holds some potential for a positive outcome, it may indicate that the Court is unwilling to continue its pro-patients' rights stance. The Boston State case has heightened the existing friction between the mental health system and its challengers. Let us now turn to some larger issues in this conflict.

Law versus psychiatry in the right to refuse treatment

Prior to the emergence of the right to refuse treatment as a major factor, the mental health system shared certain agreement with patient activists. In the landmark right to treatment *Wyatt v. Stickney* case, mental health professional bodies and support groups filed *amicus* briefs (Ennis, 1975). However, when attorneys supported filing contempt of court citations against psychiatrists who administered electroshock, the American Psychiatric Association withdrew support for the case. In Massachusetts' Northampton State Hospital case, the DMH entered a consent decree to achieve increased legislative funds due to court order. The right to treatment was in the interests of mental health professionals and administrators, even if they were reluctant at first, since it might lead to increased funding. In particular, the *Wyatt* case was important in staving off dismissals of state hospital staff (Rubin, 1978). In some right to treatment and 'least restrictive environment' cases there was criticism of professional behavior and official policy, but as with the 1950s and 1960s exposes which criticized the state hospitals, such criticism helped to move the system forward. The right to refuse treatment, however, does not offer such leeway for negotiation. Freddolino (1982) found that while one-half and one-third of his sample of administrative and clinical staff in New York and California mental hospitals, respectively, agreed that patients should be informed of rights, including the right to refuse treatment, and three-fourths of the California respondents felt that institutions should provide advocacy services, only 27 per cent and 39 per cent supported the right to refuse treatment. My national survey (P. Brown, 1982b) found that the mental health establishment and patients' rights groups did not differ on perceived expansion of the right to treatment, but did differ on the right to refuse.

Professional attention has focused increasingly on the right to refuse. In 1980 there were three times as many articles on patients' rights indexed in *Index Medicus* as in the previous year. Much of this increase is attributable to the October 1979 ruling by Federal District Court Judge Joseph Tauro which granted a wide latitude of right to refuse treatment for Boston State Hospital inpatients. Many authors were aware of the case's progress, and by mid-1980 were often citing Tauro's final ruling (Brown, 1982b). Professionals commonly argue that the right to refuse would mean that patients would be deprived of the previously won right to treatment: patients would be in a mental hospital but would not receive benefits from psychiatric techniques. Perhaps the professionals holding such an opinion feared a great deal of exercise of the right to refuse. This might seem logical given the strength of the patients' rights movement, and given the ways in which other rights have been applied.

Patients have exercised, or indicated a desire to exercise, other rights. Wenger and Fletcher (1969) examined eighty-one commitment hearings on the grounds of a state hospital. They found that sixty-one of sixty-six unrepresented patients were committed, while only four of fifteen with legal counsel were committed. Even when the authors grouped the cases by legal criteria for commitment, legal counsel meant less likelihood of commitment. There are, however, flaws with this study, according to Gove (1970). Given the short time of commitment hearings (median length of hearing with counsel was ten minutes), it seems unlikely that lawyers would have the opportunity to influence the psychiatrists. Further, Gove continues, Wenger and Fletcher's controlling for severity was flawed by using non-psychiatric raters. Thus despite the positive relationship between legal counsel and release, Gove maintains it could be a spurious relationship based on the tendency of less disturbed persons to engage lawyers. Hiday (1977) found a higher rate of commitment when lawyers were passive towards damaging psychiatric testimony, with nearly twice the commitment rate as when lawyers challenged testimony. Even when patients are not actively exercising their rights, they desire the availability of those rights. Epstein and Lowinger (1975) interviewed fifty recent admissions to a Michigan state hospital and found that 20 per cent felt the need for legal assistance at the time of admission, and 44 per cent would want it in future court hearings. Desire for counsel was higher in involuntary patients and in those with previous hospitalization.

But if patients apply or wish to apply other rights, they do not apparently apply the right to refuse very widely. A look at Boston State Hospital is very useful since it is the locus of the primary right to refuse case in the United States. As mentioned a few pages ago, in a twenty-five month period from the time of the temporary order, only 12 of 1000 patients refused medication over prolonged periods of time, and most changed their minds in several days (Mass. Psych. Wards, 1979). This is particularly striking since large numbers of patients must have been aware of their right to refuse treatment due to public knowledge, activist organizing, and court-ordered notification.

Appelbaum and Gutheil (1980a) studied drug refusal over a three-month period in 1978 at the Massachusetts Mental Health Center. Twenty-three patients, accounting for seventy-two individual refusal episodes, refused medication in that interval, while there were fifty-six admissions, fifty-two discharges, and an average population of forty. For only one group of five patients was refusal considered clinically problematic, and of the rest, 84 per cent of the episode lasted one day or less and 93 per cent lasted two days or less. Despite the authors' strong opposition to the right to refuse treatment, they remark that drug refusal did not hinder treatment except for their five 'symptomatic refusers' whose actions were deemed a symptom of their illness. For the others, Appelbaum and Gutheil hint that refusal may be beneficial: 'Areas of concern and periods of stress were signaled nonverbally at times when direct communication may have been difficult, giving doctors an opportunity to explore material which might otherwise have remained buried. '

In a more general sense, Fanning et al. (1972) found that three-quarters of their sample of eighty-two CMHC inpatients wanted to share in treatment decisions, though they generally wanted to do this in conjunction with staff, and mainly at the time of admission. The researchers concluded that this should allay professionals' fears of patients' desire to be very involved in treatment issues.

While my own survey research (P. Brown, 1982b) has shown patients' rights organizations to be strenuously in favor of greatly expanded rights, other research has found different attitudes for individual patients. There is some evidence that large numbers of patients may be more accepting of traditional hospital relationships and less favorable to patients' rights. There are, however, different ways to interpret these findings. R. Weinstein (1981), for example, examined a large number of studies of patients' attitudes towards inpatient treatment. He found that they overwhelmingly were supportive of institutions and staff. From this Weinstein concluded that the sociological critique of custodialism had erred in a subjective perception that patients opposed the total institution. The implication in Weinstein's work, partly expressed in his conclusions, is that we should not accept the broadly agreed upon critique of custodialism and therefore not exert pressure on the system.

Perry's (1982) national survey included inpatients and outpatients among the groups he queried on patients' rights. Outpatients were always more favorable to patients' rights than were inpatients. Yet on some clusters of items both patient groups were somewhat unfavorable to rights. One of those two clusters, termed 'Freedom from restraint', included items on dangerousness criteria, the validity of involuntary confinement, and the use of physical restraints. The other cluster, 'Patient's role in treatment planning', included questions on outside consultation, right to refuse, and participation in treatment plans. On two other clusters, however, 'Protection of constitutional rights' and 'Protection of due process', patients ranked second in favoring patients' rights, after only the public defender respondents, who were in all cases the most pro-patients' rights. Perry reads these results as meaning that patients are willing to accept 'protective restraint, even if this means curtailment of their freedom', and that inpatients in particular accept a 'doctor knows best' attitude. Perry considers his findings to agree with Weinstein's opinions. Freddolino (1982), alternatively, interprets Perry's work differently:

> *It may be that assertive, self-protective behavior is impossible to achieve in an inpatient setting, given the role requirements for patients placed on them by staff — particularly by the administratively powerful psychiatrists and the practically powerful aides.*

Further, 'There is a strong indication that resistance to patients' rights may be structurally inherent in the system of inpatient mental health treatment,' whereas in a shift to outpatient care as the norm, staff would have less need to control patients in an all-encompassing manner (Freddolino, 1982). It is also necessary to point to a flaw in Perry's methodology. He mailed packets of questionnaires to state hospitals and CMHCs, entrusting directors with the task of allocating them to patients and staff. This may have allowed for considerable bias in selecting respondents who would hold less favorable attitudes toward patients' rights.

More important is the fact that even if larger numbers of patients were polled randomly, their potential opposition to or lukewarm support of certain rights should not be considered a reason to cease efforts at expanding patients' rights. One could picture a random sample of blacks in the 1960s which would show less than enthusiastic support for the civil rights movement, yet a strong civil rights movement was a necessity of blacks' social survival. Certainly one would not use such an attitude study to halt support of civil rights. Many populations have groups which may not be numerically representative in the sense of complete consensus but which ultimately are representative of long-term goals and interests.

If treatment refusal is uncommon, and potentially not likely to increase dramatically, why is there so much opposition to this right? First, professionals and institutions seek to defend professional and institutional autonomy against challenges to their clinical judgment from activists who dispute that psychiatry has patients' best interests at heart. Second, and related to the first reason, psychiatrists usually oppose legal interference in their work since this would infringe on their professional autonomy. Third, there is a long-standing debate over who is being protected, the patient or the community.

Research is needed on the types of patients who refuse. One earlier study by Jansen (1974) found that over a ten-month period in 1973, patients who visited a patients' rights office in a Minnesota hospital were more likely to be involuntarily committed patients with more psychopathology than those who did not visit. Similarly, Epstein and Lowinger (1975) found that desire for legal counsel was higher in involuntary patients and in those with previous hospitalization. Their research, and that of Jansen, hints that impaired patients might be more, rather than less likely to avail themselves of legal services. However, in Jansen's research it is not known what resulted from those visits to the patients' rights office. They may have been merely visits, with no subsequent complaint or action. And in Epstein and Lowinger's study it does not follow that expressed desire for legal aid would be matched by actual utilization. Further, both studies took place prior to significant pressures for the right to refuse. More recently, Marder et al., (1983) studied fifteen drug refusers, along with a matched control group of fifteen nonrefusers in the psychiatric unit of a VA hospital. When psychopathology was measured by the Brief Psychiatric Rating Scale (BPRS), refusers had higher ratings on a number of symptoms. Consenters were more likely to believe that they were ill and to have confidence in ward staff and drug therapy. The researchers believe that patients were confused by the consent form, leading to negativism on the part of some of them. Refusers were felt to be delusional in some cases, though a variety of reasons for refusal were recognized.

Even when informed consent procedures are invoked to allow patients to choose whether or not to accept drugs, patients may not be giving fully informed consent. Grossman and Summers (1980) read consent forms on a fictitious antipsychotic drug, Lamex, to twenty schizophrenic patients who had the consent form in front of them. When questioned on understanding, only three were deemed fully informed, nine partially informed, and eight not informed. All of the fully informed patients gave consent. Of the nine partially informed, six consented, one refused, and two were indecisive. Of the eight not informed patients, three consented, four refused, and one said both yes and no. The researchers conclude that the average patient understands only about one half of information presented to him or her, and is therefore not giving fully informed consent. Such findings can be interpreted in a variety of ways apart from the researchers' suggestion that true consent is not being provided. One could argue that the more fully informed patients are, the more likely they are to agree with psychiatric advice. Alternatively, one could argue that severely disturbed patients are unable to understand basic drug information, and that regular consent procedures are therefore inappropriate.

The first reason for psychiatric opposition to the right to refuse is that patients' rights issues, particularly the right to refuse, interferes with professional and institutional autonomy. This is manifested in challenges to many basic assumptions and habits of the mental health system. Most mental health caregivers assume that psychiatry basically has the patient's best interest at heart. This is one assumption challenged by advocates of the right to refuse (Chamberlin, 1978). Psychiatric sociologists have long studied the elements of professional self-interest that operate in the mental health system (Scheff, 1966; 1975), and many of those scholars would agree with rights advocates in positing that psychiatrists, psychologists, and others in the mental health system have not always placed patient interest in first place. But even if professionals attempted to place patients' interest in the primary position, there is a disparity between the system's ideals and its practical realities. This is witnessed in patients' rights by the important disparity between what the staff and professionals abstractly view as constitutional rights, and what they might consider as practical matters. Daugherty (1978) surveyed forty-three aides at a Montana state hospital and found a majority agreement on each of ten rights. However, aides agreed more with those rights 'dealing with abstract issues or basic human necessities' and less with 'those that might disrupt ward routine (potentially increasing the work of the ward staff) or that required the attribution of certain amounts of responsibility and judgment to the patient.' Thus, work habits and routines are important, even if they do not involve ideological or clinical values. Psychiatry, like the rest of medicine, is accustomed to a wide range of institutional and professional autonomy, and has frequently rejected 'external' inputs. Institutional psychiatry has had to accept a large degree of outside involvement in recent years, and the right to refuse is no doubt considered the ultimate potential loss of professional judgment and power. Further, treatment refusal holds the potential for disruption of various levels of the hospital's daily work routines and habits. This is therefore the point at which the greatest resistance is offered.

Psychiatry generally believes that the area of greatest tension in the right to refuse — psychotropic medication — is precisely the area where modern psychiatry has had the most success in relieving the symptoms of psychosis. Not only is professional autonomy at stake, but personal liability and blame are also present. While most cases name as defendants officials such as the Commissioner of Mental Health, the Boston State suit named individual psychiatrists. These physicians argued (and the court ultimately concurred) that they had acted in good faith because they were doing what was considered standard practice. Personal liability is very threatening, both legally and professionally, and engenders an air of personal animosity.

A second reason for mental health professionals' opposition to the right to refuse treatment is that they do not want involvement in their practice from lawyers or judges. This is actually a special subcase of the first reason which concerns professional and institutional autonomy in general. In this case, another powerful profession — law — challenges psychiatry; this brings forth a defense of professional dominance. Psychiatric antagonism to legal involvement has always existed. Lawyers and psychiatrists have disputed the criteria for the insanity plea since the M'Naghten case in 1843. In the nineteenth century Dorothea Dix's campaign for institutional reform, Elizabeth Packard's crusade for commitment safeguards, and other such reform efforts were invariably met with clinical arguments which supported psychiatrists' judgment against the public's rights (Chesler, 1973; Rothman, 1971; 1980; Grob, 1973). In Senator Ervin's 1961 and 1963 hearings on patients' rights this longstanding antagonism was publicly aired. Snooks (reported in Perry, 1982) surveyed sixty-six clinical social workers in five states and found that while 80 per cent favored patients' rights legislation, 70 per cent believed that attorneys intruded into mental health issues without sufficient knowledge. There is much concern that legal involvement in psychiatric issues is harmful to patients, for instance, by producing unnecessary stress due to public hearings. Szasz (1961) has responded to this point of view by observing that very little could be more stressful than losing one's liberty without due process and being confined for a long period in a custodial asylum.

In this light, it is surprising to note Kumasaka and Stokes' (1972) anomalous finding that the legal-psychiatric interaction was not so highly charged. Those researchers conducted structured interviews with thirty psychiatrists and twenty-six lawyers on the indispensability of involuntary hospitalization, the reasons given for hospitalization, the validity of dangerousness as a criterion for long-term hospitalization, and the definition of dangerousness. In comparing the respondents' attitudes with the actual number of involuntary commitments in their jurisdiction, Kumasaka and Stokes found that:

> *On the whole, the result is a sort of compromise by both psychiatrists and lawyers, both perhaps attempting to conform to societal expectations. The psychiatrist tries not to rely too heavily on his judgment alone, possibly in order to avoid criticism for railroading the mentally ill. The lawyer similarly tries to avoid being accused of preventing hospitalization of dangerous mentally ill patients. Thus, in spite of the problems of defining dangerousness of the mentally ill on the theoretical level, there is not much problem on the practical level, when lawyers are involved in the processs of involuntary hospitalization.*

Most research seems to indicate divergent perspectives, if not antagonism, between the two professions. This is evident in Perry's (1982) research. In all forty-one items of Perry's questionnaire, and in each of four clusters of items determined by cluster analysis, public defenders were the most supportive of patients' rights (though district attorneys were somewhat or very opposed to patients' rights); psychiatrists were always somewhat or very opposed, and psychologists were generally in a middle position. Kahle and Sales' (1980) national survey also discovered lawyers to be more supportive of rights than either psychiatrists or psychologists. Nevertheless, Kahle et al. (1978) concluded that psychiatrists are merely 'less emphatic in their support of rights' and that overall, psychiatrists have been erroneously stereotyped as opponents of patients' rights. This stereotype results, they believe, from the social psychological phenomenon of 'anchoring,' by which

> *Psychiatric opinions provide an anchor or endpoint on the anti-rights side of the continuum of commonly held positions about patients' rights in involuntary civil commitment, and this endpoint is frequently contrasted with other groups who support patients' rights even more strongly than psychiatrists.*

The legal and psychiatric professions' attitudes on these issues mirror their professional bases. Lawyers seek a high degree of proof that patients need to be committed, to be given certain treatment against their will, or to be deprived in any manner of their rights; the assumption is that retention of civil liberties is primary and that overwhelming proof must be brought to bear to justify deprivation of rights. Psychiatry, however, usually maintains that a person presented for commitment, or already in the hospital, is in need of treatment of the type that the doctor recommends; the assumption here is that civil liberties are merely a barrier to effective treatment. In this line of thought, the right to refuse treatment can be considered the 'right to rot' (Appelbaum and Gutheil, 1980b). Bloom and Asher (1982) discuss the notion of 'substitute judgments' which differentiates law and medicine. In medicine, such substitute judgments are typical for medical practitioners and their patients, but in lawyers' interactions with their clients such judgments are 'in theory contrary to the principle of legal advocacy.' Yet another difference, noted by Shwed (1980), is that law centers on rationality while psychiatry focuses on irrationality.

Psychiatrists' frequent opposition to legal involvement involves a critique of judges as well as of lawyers in terms of lack of psychiatric information. In the Boston State Hospital case, for example, Gutheil (1980) argued that Judge Tauro erroneously considered seclusion as a form of restraint rather than as 'a safe and effective treatment in its own right.' Appelbaum and Gutheil (1980b) wrote that the court held too stringent a definition of 'psychiatric emergency' in that it only included imminent harm to self or others, rather than the psychiatrists' broader definition which included 'property destruction, extreme anxiety or panic, bizarre behavior, illness severe enough to interfere with daily functioning, and situations in which a response is necessary to prevent or decrease the likelihood of further severe suffering or the rapid worsening of the patient's clinical state.' The authors also opposed the judge's conception of psychotropic drugs as being used for 'involuntary mind control.' In responding to Tauro's emphasis on antipsychotics' side effects, particularly tardive dyskinesia, Appelbaum and Gutheil commented:

> *We speculate the nonclinicians such as lawyers and jurists may be disproportionately attuned to the importance of side effects because, being physical, they are more concrete than the more abstract and imprecise mental phenomenon beneficially affected by medication.*

In a more negative vein, Shwed (1980) remarks that 'Mental health advocacy has provided a natural niche for socially minded young lawyers who have rejected traditional career tracks,' and who suffer the 'vagaries of the job market for law school graduates.' Further, Shwed writes, mental health lawyers are playing out what psychoanalysts consider a 'rescue fantasy.'

The third, and final reason that psychiatrists so strenuously oppose the right to refuse treatment concerns the longstanding question of who is being protected — the individual patient, or the family, community, or society. Perry (1982) concluded from his national survey that most respondents expressed the least agreement with issues related to freedom of restraint, 'suggesting that, when the issue comes down to the protection of the individual versus protection of the community, there was a shared willingness to sacrifice the rights of the individual.'

Historically, individual rights protection has most commonly been sacrificed, though it is not always clear that the community being protected was worthy of that protection. Medieval persecution of mentally ill persons by the Catholic Church's Inquisition was part of a general offensive against all social forces which threatened the religious/feudal hegemony (Foucault, 1971). Early twentieth-century state hospitalization was often directed at poor immigrants and natives alike, with the function of providing a form of social control over them (Scull, 1977a). Such control was not merely a monolithic control by the dominant classes, but was also desired and accepted by much of the public. As Scull writes:

> *Working people had little alternative but to make use of the asylum as a way of ridding themselves of what, in the context of nineteenth-century working class existence, was undoubtedly an intolerable burden: the caring for their sick, aged, decrepit, or otherwise incapacitated relatives. From the upper classes' perspective, the existence of asylums to 'treat' the insane at public expense could be invoked as a practical demonstration of their own humanitarian concern for the less fortunate.*

Similarly, Rachlin et al. (1975), in a very informal research design, found that patients' families and communities were less supportive of patients' rights regarding involuntary commitment than were mental health professionals. To the extent that mental health officials and practitioners accord protection to communities, then it is logical that they might oppose the right to refuse treatment since treatment refusal would be expected to yield disturbance to the community. This is catalyzed by a medical, and particularly psychiatric, sense of responsibility for larger social issues. One example is psychiatrists' prediction of dangerousness. The physicians seek to protect the outside world from the potential violence of various persons. But, as Steadman's (1980) important research on psychiatric prediction of dangerousness shows the high degree of inaccuracy in this area amounts to an abrogation of the 'right not to be a false positive' (in other words, the right of a non-violent person to not be falsely labeled as violent). Psychiatrists, and many courts hearing expert psychiatric testimony, are too often willing to accept a higher degree of false positives than in criminal proceedings. What psychiatric sociologists pointed out in the 1960s (Scheff, 1966) was apparently still true: there was more protection of the rights of accused criminals than of mental patients. That this condition might be due to mental health professionals' claim to be concerned with helping patients does not mitigate the resultant loss of rights.

Even clinicians and administrators at institutions for the criminally insane have been critical of dangerousness determinations. Hospital administrators at Massachusetts' Bridgewater State Hospital reported that about one-half the 1,100 patients sent there by courts in a one-year period did not belong there. Further, of the 75 transferred from regular state mental hospitals, only 10 required the high-security atmosphere of Bridgewater (Hutson, 1976). Despite poor prediction of dangerousness, professionals are aware of using rates of violence among discharged patients. They may believe that pressuring patients to accept treatment will alter this phenomenon.

PROFESSIONAL SELF-INTEREST, CO-OPTATION, AND REFORM

This sense of responsibility can be understood as part of the professional self-interest of the mental health professions. The more these providers can portray themselves as acting in patients' interests, the more they can insure and expand their social position in terms of status, wealth, and power. Likewise, mental health agencies and officials seek to protect their offices from external inputs and criticism. Even if outside influence is necessary to catalyze needed reform, the mental health system wishes to feel in control of that process. As discussed in Chapter 3, the psychiatric field has often portrayed itself as a social movement in its own right. Therefore it is difficult for the system to acknowledge the positive impact of advocates and activists. Thus, credit for the promotion of patients' rights usually is given to the benevolent conceptions of mental health professionals and institutions, and to a lesser degree to Mental Health Associations, parents/friends organizations, the mental disability public interest bar, a few sympathetic judges, and social science research on the problem of custodialism in asylums. While these other sources have been important, it is striking that the social movement so integral to this issue — the patients' rights movement — is neglected, slighted, or misperceived. Let us explore the reasons for these behaviors.

In a wide-ranging reading of literature in the patients' rights field, one finds little mention of patients' rights groups. In a rare number (e.g., Lamb, 1981) activists are indicted as completely irresponsible, based on two instances where their actions went against the perspective of providers. In other cases, activist demands are co-opted by elements of the psychiatric system. An example of this can be seen in the 1978 executive order by the Massachusetts Department of Mental Health which limited the use of seclusion, restraint, and excess medication (Bruzelius, 1978). These were the same issues currently being demanded by the Boston Mental Patients' Liberation Front through litigation and public pressure, yet the DMH presented the reform as purely an official decision. It appears that public support for the complainants was the catalyst for certain actions that the Department might have desired in part, but couldn't grant them as an explicit response to patient activists. Further, they were probably trying to limit the magnitude of the outcome.

Co-optation here refers to professionals usurping control of situations in order to achieve an outcome favorable to the professionals. It may be a purposeful subversion or minimalization, or may be an unintended consequence. Many hospitals began to post a 'Mental Patients Bill of Rights,' modeled after the original demands of the movement groups. Although enforcement of those rights was hardly guaranteed, the hospital could claim to be concerned with such rights. Most patients, however, are unaware of and/or unable to exercise their legal rights, even if there is a lawyer or law student in the hospital. In a sense, such recourse is available only *after* the fact of commitment, forced treatment, or other denial of rights. Encouraging hospitals to nominally grant patients rights in this fashion may therefore be an abdication of responsibility by the state hospital and Department of Mental Health, which should have prevented rights violations in the first place.

An interesting case of co-optation can be observed in a 1972 situation in which administrators at a state hospital in the Northeast organized a weekend of workshops and visits on patients' rights. Organizers came from New York City's Mental Patients Liberation Front, the Radical Therapist Collective, and Number Nine, a New Haven alternative free clinic. They worked with patients in the hospital who were seeking more rights and some control over treatment, such as a patient-run halfway house for predischarge patients. Some hospital staff who proposed the weekend activities were genuinely committed to these issues, but the administration was basically trying to co-opt the cutting edge of the patients' demands. They vetoed a number of plans, such as the patient-run halfway house, put forth by the patients and visiting advocates. Testimony at one large meeting showed that the hospital was particularly critical of some patient activists in community residences who were involved in demonstrations at the local trial of antiwar activists (P. Brown, 1972b). One could argue that such involvement in supporting antiwar activists could be a beneficial and therapeutic activity, but to the administration it was a sign of the patients' inability to adjust to social norms. They may have also seen it as a threat to the hospital, since the state government wouldn't feel comfortable with one of its state hospitals being an antiwar center.

Another form of governmental co-optation is the trend towards establishing state-run mental health advocacy offices (Brooks, 1977). Also, patients' rights activists increasingly appear on panels at professional meetings, and have been placed on advisory boards for mental health planning, including the President's Commission on Mental Health. This participation on the PCMH was different from most prior efforts, since the relevant task force adopted a pro-patients' rights stance far stronger than any other such body. According to the Task Panel on Legal and Ethical Issues:

> *While there is an understandable concern about balance and the danger of excess, the 'patients' rights' or advocacy movement is widely credited with producing the most significant reforms in the mental health system during the past ten years (President's Commission on Mental Health, 1978).*

Flowing from this report were a number of far-reaching recommendations: legislation for publicly funded legal advocacy for the disabled; Justice Department litigation on behalf of such persons; enforcement of existing advocacy requirements (as in the Education of All Handicapped Children Act); enforcement of antidiscrimination laws concerning mentally handicapped persons in the areas of employment, education, and housing; more protection for patients in guardianship procedures; safeguards on human experimentation; and further commitment reform. Implementation of these recommendations and of the 1980 Mental Health Systems Act, however, is unlikely, given the Reagan Administration's recent budget cuts which effectively repealed the Act.

The mental health establishment's resistance to crediting the patients' rights movement for advances in patients' rights can be explained by noting several points. First, activist groups are hostile to the mental health system. This makes it difficult for the system's components to acknowledge their positive role. Second, many professionals believe that rights groups employ irresponsible methods, even if some of their goals are acceptable. This makes it hard to credit the groups, since this might appear to be an acknowledgment of what are perceived as inappropriate methods. Third, to the extent that establishment figures seek to co-opt activists, as in the Massachusetts example above, they cannot credit the activists since they are taking responsibility for the reform themselves.

These issues bear on broader questions of reform movements in health care in general. The entire health field has been subject to intense criticism from clients, often organized in social movements. Yet the medical system at worst remains hostile to those movements and at best ignores the movements while implementing some of the reforms sought by activists. A good example is the women's health movement, which has pointed to abuses in contraception, sterilization, and obstetrical practices (Ruzek, 1978). An activist organization, the Committee for Abortion Rights and Against Sterilization Abuse, wrote guidelines for New York City sterilization procedures in order to prevent uninformed or coerced sterilization. These guidelines were accepted by the City, and later became important in producing federal HEW guidelines. Other organizations pressed for obstetrical reform such as alternative birthing rooms, presence of fathers at birth, and minimalization of medical/surgical intervention. Yet the movement is not credited with these advances, even when progressive obstetrics departments boast of their liberal policies.

As in the patients' rights issue, the above example shows how professional response to reform finds a way to ignore, downplay, or co-opt the reform movement. This is necessary for the retention of professional dominance and protection of the institutional structure. To admit that nonmedical persons, particularly those with a radical perspective, had a valid critique which dealt with fundamental issues would be to admit that the establishment was unable to adequately police and regulate itself and to acknowledge that some of the deeper elements of the critique were justified — for example, the well-documented sociological perspective of medicine used as an instrument of social control (e.g. Zola, 1972).

Professionals and institutions also find it hard to accept the input of organizations and movements who have a harsh and impolite attitude toward the system they are criticizing. In the case of the mental patients' rights movement, this is very noticeable. This hostility is often combined with a simplistic notion of mental illness — for instance, accusing professionals of 'mentalism' for believing that there is such a thing as mental illness (Chamberlin, 1978). Such a purist position argues that mental illness is a myth and that professional intervention must always unfairly label and stigmatize the person. While such attitudes may frustrate mental health professionals, those professionals need to understand the functional reasons for such exaggerations. One reason is that activist groups have far less power and influence, and therefore find it necessary to be sharper in their criticism in order to be heard. Another reason is that they may be aware of the possibilities of co-optation, and therefore assert a maximum position in order to be assured of winning a moderate degree of reform. Also, they may incorrectly view the mental health system as a monolithic entity which is uniformly opposed to patients' rights, and therefore assume a hostile attitude without discrimination. While it may be difficult for professionals to hear such views, if they understand the historical and structural underpinnings of those positions they can in fact be sympathetic to patients' rights and be supportive of winning and implementing those rights.

No doubt there are many providers and planners who sincerely seek to increase patients' rights, but are confounded by the contradictions involved in such efforts. Disputes within facilities and within governmental units prevent concerted action, and bureaucratic inertia contributes to the difficulties. Mental health professionals also face increasing legislative and public reaction to libertarian programs. And, they face the frequent opposition of mental health workers' unions. State hospital workers fear violence from patients, and believe that reduction of restraint, seclusion, and forced medication will increase that violence. Patient violence is a real fear, but dangerous behavior could best be reduced by overall structural reforms in the mental health system, not by maintaining the status quo. Yet one major labor organization, The California State Employees Association, greatly exaggerates the level of patient and ex-patient violence (Chase, 1973). That union's publications reinforce many conservative notions of patient care which would lead to renewed emphasis on custodial institutional care. Such opposition derives at least in part from the most sensible fear on the part of the mental hospital workers, that of job loss. As shown in Chapter 7, state hospital closings and patient population reductions have resulted in large layoffs, without significant retraining programs to prepare aides for community mental health care. Workers and their unions may feel that further implementation of patients rights would lead to further deinstitutionalization, and therefore to even more layoffs.

Thus, even sympathetic professionals encounter obstacles to the implementation of patients' rights. Of course, whether or not certain programs are co-optation or reform rests with the definition of social change, which in turn derives from one's position in the mental health system. It may be asked why reformers do not actually expect and desire co-optation, or at least institutional acceptance of reform goals. Certainly the activists shouldn't be surprised at institutional attempts to control the reform process. This question can be approached by looking at examples in state hospital reform. For some activists, the goal is patient-controlled facilities (Chamberlin, 1978). Therefore, any institutional acceptance of activist-initiated programs might be seen as co-optative, since it would enable the hospital to operate more effectively as a traditional, professional-dominated facility. But patient-run facilities are rare, and typically are new facilities established by patients, rather than institutions which patients gained control of. The Mental Patients Association in Vancouver, British Columbia is the classic model of a treatment center originated by patients and ex-patients. In other countries, attempts have been made to extend a large degree of patient control, though often propelled by professionals. Franco Basaglia's efforts in Italy (Ramon, 1983) and the Chinese psychiatric reforms (Sidel and Sidel, 1974) are cases of this type.

For professionals and others who support a wide application of patients' rights, total patient control is not usually the goal. Such people would seek reforms which diminished custodialism and hierarchy, increased patient involvement, and might strive for community placements in the resident-run halfway houses of the Mental Patients Association. In this sense, then, they would seek radical reforms which were not co-optative. These sympathetic professionals would share with the patient activists a pervasive critique of existing mental health facilities. And even if they did not adhere to a totally patient-run model of mental health treatment, these professionals would largely support the ex-patients' social movement in its other political goals.

Anspach (1979) terms as 'identity politics' the new movements of ex-patients and handicapped people who strive for not only social policy and institutional reform, but who also 'consciously endeavor to alter both the self-concepts and societal conceptions of their participants'. For these activists, both the goals and the participation in political action are important, for, as Anspach comments, purposive political action is a sign of health. Forceful co-optation attempts to break down the strong self-image of political activists, for such identity politics present a major challenge to mainstream institutional practices and ideologies and the power of the professional establishment. Support then may be distinguished from co-optation on the basis of whether or not the institution, agency, or professional accepts a significant level of ex-patients' identity politics. Such acceptance would be accompanied by reform work in the patients' and ex-patients' interest, and in particular would include the activists in that work. For instance, the Mental Patients Civil Liberties Project in Philadelphia is an advocacy group headed by an attorney, but it works closely with the local rights group, the Alliance for the Liberation of Mental Patients.

The criteria discussed here indicates that it is not the location of a service or facility that determines whether it is co-optative, but rather its orientation to dominant professional power. The determination must be made in each case for halfway houses, ex-patient clubs, advocacy services, and other mental health reform features. Of course it follows that the majority of professionally run services and facilities will fall short of acting in a pro-patient fashion (as defined by patient activists).

IMPLEMENTING PATIENTS' RIGHTS

In fact, it is somewhat unreasonable to assume that mental institutions would generally reorient themselves in such a fashion. Although some of the less seriously disturbed patient activists have demonstrated their ability to plan psychiatric services, such potential is not typically present. Further, there are some cases where forcible treatment may be necessary. It is reasonable to prevent people from harming themselves and others. The problem is how to gauge this potential dangerousness or to treat actual dangerousness. This has not been possible. Further, an initial finding of dangerousness should not imply the right of psychiatrists to have free rein over the patient (Ford, 1980). Also, the vestiges of custodial institutions, such as wide-scale restraint and seclusion, should not be touted as therapeutic when they are more likely to be used for staff ease or even for staff protection.

Stemming from this is a further issue of how to create a climate in which patients, both dangerous and nondangerous, would trust the institutional and staff judgments and best intentions, and thus accept their proffered treatment. This would involve a very drastic restructuring of the mental health system, a difficult task given its history of professionalism, relatively uncritical medical model, and institutional conservatism. Psychiatrists often argue that the nature of psychosis is such that patients are unable to make proper judgments and are often distrustful of all authority figures. Changing the environment, they argue, would not improve trust. This may be true for some patients, but clearly the traditional relations between patients and institutions have had detrimental effects which violate trust. In the absence of such fundamental change there will continue to be a need for patients' rights advocacy on various levels. Litigation by itself is insufficient. Like legislation and administrative decrees, it requires monitoring. Freddolino (1982) concluded from his survey research that mental health staff do not believe in present statutes which give the right to refuse to voluntary patients; thus laws alone will not affect ward life, since staff find ways to circumvent the law.

Part of the problem of poor implementation of rights is that mental health staff are often uninformed about patients' rights. Affleck et al. (1978) ascertained that psychiatrists in the District of Columbia and Connecticut were not thoroughly informed of legal statutes governing involuntary commitment. Many were aware of requirements of danger to self or others, but were still confused about commitment in that they incorrectly believed that certain diagnoses were in themselves certifiable. Additionally, virtually none of the psychiatrists knew of the patients' rights to be examined by a physician of their own choice.

Laves and Cohen (1973) conducted both mail questionnaires to psychiatrists, psychologists, and social workers, and hospital-administered questionnaires to those staff plus nurses and attendants. The researchers sought to examine knowledge of New Jersey law and attitudes towards patients' rights which were stipulated in the law. Nurses and psychiatrists in the hospital sample were the most knowledgeable, though their differences from each other were not statistically significant. Attendants were next, followed by social workers and psychologists, though there were not significant differences between any groups. In the mail sample, psychiatrists were the most informed, followed by psychologists and social workers. Psychiatrists differed significantly from each of those other groups in being more informed, but the psychologists and social workers did not differ from each other. When the mail and hospital samples were combined, nurses were the most knowledgeable, followed closely by psychiatrists; attendants were in a middle position, and the least informed were social workers and psychologists. Significant differences were observed between the high-scoring psychiatrists and nurses on one hand, and low-scoring social workers and psychologists on the other; attendants had no differences from either of the other groupings. Lack of rights information was also found in research by Peszke and Wintrob (1974) and Tancredi and Clark (1972). In an attempt to educate mental hospital professionals about recent legal developments, NIMH's St. Elizabeth's Hospital provides legal services to the staff. One interesting facet of this program is that some patient-psychiatrist disputes are handled by negotiations between lawyers for both parties (Steadman and Brooks, 1977).

Turning to attitudes of mental health professionals, Laves and Cohen (1973) determined that psychiatrists are the least favorable to rights and psychologists the most favorable. These findings hint that knowledge alone, as studied by Laves and Cohen, does not produce more positive attitudes. Overall, the researchers found that all professionals had somewhat favorable attitudes to rights. Kahle and Sales' (1980) findings for psychiatrists and psychologists were very similar. Like Kahle and Sales, Laves and Cohen find it encouraging that mental health staff are so favorable, and that the real problem is lack of education, which leads to a 'rent between knowledge and attitudes'. Their answer is more education. As a caution, the authors note that their small response rate of 27 per cent may indicate that the most favorably inclined personnel responded. Unlike most of other research (Rabkin, 1980; Cohen and Struening, 1962; Baker and Schulberg, 1967; Gilbert and Levinson, 1957; Freddolino, 1982), Laves and Cohen did not find more conservative opinions in lower level staff.

Practical access to the exercise of patients' rights is another obstacle. Paschall et al. (1983) found that despite legal requirements, an Ohio state hospital was quite derelict in informing patients of their rights and providing a way for them to exercise those rights. A lawyer (K.Kramer, 1974) who worked at a New York state hospital legal services office found 'subtle subversion' of patients' rights, such as posting written notice of rights, but not providing verbal information. Taking the above into account it is clear that a strategy for securing and enforcing patients' rights must have several components: legislation, litigation, public and staff education, monitoring safeguards for each institution, and statewide and national monitoring. Since the mental health system is often reluctant to reform itself, external advocacy is required. There is some small role for institution-based or state DMH-based advocacy services, but as Kemp (1978) and Paschall et al. (1983) found, such services do not adequately perform their task.

Patients' rights advocacy as a concept needs to be rescued from its overgeneralization, similar to that found for 'community mental health.' Bloom and Asher (1982) note the wide array of advocacy programs which includes: obtaining regular services for individual patients, institutionally-appointed social workers who investigate grievances as part of their regular jobs, state DMH-ordered ombudsperson for each facility, DMH contract with the state bar association to staff patients' rights offices in state hospitals, court-appointed attorneys for each patient committed, mental patient advocacy section of a statewide public advocate's office, and free-standing patient advocacy organizations which bring class action suits.

Freddolino (1983) counted 417 advocacy organizations and grouped them into five types: legal programs, patients and ex-patient groups, Mental Health Associations, parent/family groups, and internal programs. Using that typology, all but the patient and ex-patient groups and some legal programs can be considered as engaging in 'supportive advocacy,' that is, in improving services and generally protecting clients. The patients groups and certain legal programs can be viewed as 'representational advocacy' in that the group does whatever the client wishes. Those two categories are congruent with what Bloom and Asher (1982) discuss as 'operational' and 'legal' advocacy programs. Yet another way to distinguish advocacy programs is between case-by-case 'service' advocacy to individual patients and 'policy' advocacy for all patients or a class of patients. This latter category could overlap with the earlier ones, since, for example, an entire class of patients — say, involuntarily committed ones — could receive DMH-sponsored 'policy' advocacy which was 'representational.'

Wald and Friedman (1979) put forth a distinction between two main types of advocacy which they consider to be the leading tension in the entire advocacy system. The 'civil libertarian' advocates are most concerned with deprivation of liberty by commitment and intrusive procedures, while the 'services-oriented' advocates want the right to treatment expanded, and feel that commitment is all right if treatment is provided. It seems clear that 'supportive', 'operational', and 'service-oriented' advocacy procedures are suitable for the right to treatment, but it would be most unlikely to see them pursuing the right to refuse. Thus, the right to refuse treatment plays a crucial role in differentiating types of advocates. Adherents of the right to refuse, even if they have disagreements over exceptions to the right, generally would agree with Wald and Friedman (1979) that meaningful advocacy must challenge the mental health system, since otherwise advocacy would merely be channeled into the existing delivery system without fundamental change.

Suchotliff et al. (1970) described their experiences as professionals seeking significant reform in the hospital. They were poorly received by administrators in various ways: threats and small compromises, accusations of disloyalty to the 'team,' charges of using patients' rights concern for personal power and ambition, and being discredited for not using proper channels. When Suchotliff and his colleagues found their hospital to be violating existing rights, they provided patients with names of legal agencies such as the Legal Aid Society, mailed letters for patients whose mailing privileges had been suspended, and sought institutional change to prevent further violations. In response the administration asked for their resignations. The three psychologists agreed to work within the system and were allowed to stay, yet they soon found out that the facility's Hospital Advisory Committee would not act on valid complaints that were pursued within official channels. The psychologists later learned that psychiatrists testifying in commitment hearings were connected with the institution, contrary to state law. When they brought this to the attention of the superintendent, he told them to take it up with the relevant judge. Upon doing this they were once again asked to resign, and their research activities were sharply curtailed. Subsequent public exposes of the hospital's conditions, however, led to a state investigation and replacement of the superintendent.

In terms of strategy, Suchotliff and his colleagues wisely concluded that administrators only responded when staff were willing to apply pressure by going outside the system. Allies came from a broad range of outside forces: state and local MHAs, private citizens, other critical staff, patients, sympathetic professionals, legislators, the Civil Liberties Union, and the local newspaper. The main strategy for welding these forces together was to demonstrate the discrepancy between the humanistic ideas of the mental health system and its real effects. Professionals might find such a clash to be unacceptable professional conduct, but the authors believe that a true professional responsibility requires active advocacy. This is increasingly important as backlash of various kinds hits the patients' rights advances.

THE IMPACT OF PATIENTS' RIGHTS ON MENTAL HEALTH POLICY

This chapter has examined the impact of patients' rights with respect to the three main themes of the book: political-economy, professionalism, and institutional structure. Attention has been paid to the conjuncture of these forces. This avoids the most common error within the mental health system — the attribution of primarily humanitarian interest in the spread of patients' rights. It also avoids the less common error among some political-economic approaches which holds that there were no humanitarian goals, but merely a concern with cost-savings.

In fact, there has been a conjuncture of forces. Economic factors yielded a necessity to reduce state hospital populations and costs. Political factors centered on general civil libertarian developments and the development of a forceful patients' rights movement. Professional ideology included a contradictory humanitarianism, as well as a way to coax more funds from state legislators. Institutional reform and restructuring were prodded by the need to ascertain definite treatment goals for inpatients.

Almost as soon as these factors coalesced, problems developed. Despite some court-ordered funding increases, there were insufficient resources for a strong application of the right to treatment in the least restrictive environment. Also, backlash against such caregiving has increased due to excess rates of ex-patient violence, widespread social nuisance behavior, 'aberrational' cases, and generalized stigma and prejudice; and the largely unproven successes of the rights to treatment, due process, confidentiality, commitment safeguards, and other issues have brought forth the right to refuse treatment. The right to refuse also polarizes parties who might share agreement on other rights.

The strength of these problems is testimony to the important effects of patients' rights. The analysis presented here argues that such rights have been more important than is often believed. But even if one adheres to a mainstream mental health prespective, patients' rights have been crucial, even if they are now seen as very problematic. And even if one believes that concern for rights is an ideological cover for economic insolvency, that ideological content has been powerful in its own right. Certainly the political-economy of mental health care has contributed more than the other factors to the general policy directions of the last two decades. Yet despite this primacy, certain actors may feel more personally impelled by other issues. Even if it takes economic crisis to raise rights issues, once raised they become very significant forces. The long history of maltreatment of mentally ill persons has made such concern more salient, and by extension will make it harder to retract that concern.

At the same time, funding cutbacks and public backlash threaten the extension of more rights. Many rights have been largely implemented by state hospital discharge and commitment reform, thus allowing mental health officials and clinicians to claim credit. Extension of rights will likely be curtailed, however — particularly full implementation of the least restrictive environment and of the right to refuse treatment. Full implementation of the former is too costly in the present circumstances, and application of the latter is too threatening to the system.

Patients' rights activists have also had important effects on psychiatric issues beyond their own specific circumstances. Patients' rights groups have been among the most vocal opponents of psychosurgery, aversive conditioning, and other social control applications of psychotechnology. Their criticisms of psychiatric drugs also serve a more general interest in that they bring to light the increasing use of psychiatric drugs for non-institutionalized people. The activist critique of psychiatric ideology also aids people to better evaluate individual therapy, and puts pressure on therapists to rethink their approaches and orientation. Tied to this is a general change in public attitudes toward mental illness in that the ex-patient offers a new picture of the commonality of problems which many non-hospitalized people share to some degree. This structural understanding of 'symptom-as-protest' puts an appropriate level of blame on social forces, rather than seeing emotional distress as merely individual pathology.

But whatever specific paths are chosen, discussion and debate will continue to include patients' rights as a clear concern and focal point. The indirect influence of patients' rights issues is a generalized critique of many basic assumptions of psychiatric theory and practice. On a broader level, this general critique has been observed in the perspectives of the larger antipsychiatry movement. Antipsychiatry has affected many more people than the patients' rights movement since it has a larger audience. Also, antipsychiatry has wrought important changes in office-based therapy and other psychological services for the relatively 'healthy' segments of the client population. The next, and final chapter will explore how the influences of antipsychiatry and the lessons of the mainstream mental health sectors can lead to beneficial changes in the future.

PART IV

Conclusion

CHAPTER 10

Future Directions in Mental Health Care

This book has analyzed many problems in mental health services and policy. Now, in the concluding chapter, this analysis can be brought to bear on suggestions for change. Future directions for mental health care will involve several interrelated factors: changes and reforms in existing institutions, wider provision of alternative treatment forms, a fuller understanding of the long-term results of mental health policy, and a reconceptualization of deinstitutionalization and mental health policy in general.

The first two factors — change within institutions and increasing alternatives — are to some extent dealt with in the normal operations of the mental health system, though not always in a comprehensive fashion. Mental health planners and administrators often seek improvements in regular and alternative institutions, though these improvements are often flawed due to structural limitations and inadequate perception of the problems. Structural limitations, a theme throughout the book, include the political-economic structure, institutional inertia and obsolescence, and professionalism. These limitations prevent major restructuring, even if professions and organizations offer well-intentioned programs. Most people and agencies in the field, however, do not base their programs on an understanding of the underlying issues. More likely they are unable to perceive these various levels of problems. This is to be expected, since any professional group or social agency tends to defend its fundamental belief system, knowledge base, and professional practicc.

The result is that most change within the system — including alternate treatment modes — fails to break fully with out-of-date conceptions of mental health care. Figure 10.1 shows a highly schematic representation of how different approaches to mental health policy might address the three major areas dealt with in this book. Type I, the conservative approach within the mainstream mental health establishment, is not so common. While this was the more typical approach prior to the community mental health era, it remains in only a minority position among mental health professionals, though it may enjoy a resurgence as biologistic models replace social ones. This conservative approach is commonly found in state and federal officials at higher levels, and in state legislatures. The Type I conservative approach largely accepts professional expertise and the overall institutional framework of facilities as presently constituted. This approach may have some sense of political-economic factors, but only insofar as it seeks cost savings by budget cuts. Thus, the 'x' mark is in parentheses.

The Type II liberal reform approach within the mainstream mental health establishment is by far the most commonly occurring viewpoint. This approach emphasizes the realization and tackling of problems in internal institutional structures and interorganizational relations, but not of professionalist biases. Political-economy is again in parentheses, since the awareness of this factor is limited, even if those limitations are different than for the conservatives. Type II liberal perspectives often criticize reimbursement biases and even the profiteering of the nursing home industry, but they do not share an analysis of the ultimate determination of public policy by the society's political-economy (e.g., the centrality of the medical-industrial complex). Further, this liberal position often blames most failures on budget shortages when some of the blame should be placed on professional practice.

The Type III radical, structural reform approach is typically found outside the mental health system, although some persons within the system belong here as well. Adherents of this position are not at all a uniform group. They include patients' rights activists, some public interest attorneys, civil liberties groups, many social scientists, and a varied group of persons generally critical of the overall social welfare and health care systems. These persons hold to a radical, structural critique which seeks fundamental change in political-economic, institutional, and professionalist arenas. This radical viewpoint is presently a weak force, though it had a period of brief ascendancy in the late 1960s and early 1970s. Changes sought by those with this perspective would include large-scale economic redistribution, widespread application of consumer-oriented self-help services, and curbs on many traditional psychiatric practices. The discussion at the end of this chapter of Italian and Chinese

Figure 10.1 Typology of Perspectives on Mental Health Policy as Reflected in Their Position on the Three Themes of Political-Economy, Institutional Problems, and Professionalism

	Realization of and Attempted Solution to:		
	Political-Economic Factors	Institutional Factors	Professionalist Factors
TYPE I Mainstream mental health conservativism	(X)		
TYPE II Mainstream mental health liberalism	(X)	X	
TYPE III Largely external critique - radical, structural reform	X	X	X

X indicates presence of this position. X in parenthesis indicates incomplete presence.

psychiatric restructuring provide examples of such an approach. While such a viewpoint may seek reform in traditional and alternative institutions, it also believes that such change is unlikely to occur in great magnitude. Adherents of this worldview thus seek more general social change as well. In terms of studying mental health policy, the Type III radical perspective seeks a reconceptualization of community mental health, deinstitutionalization, and other elements of mental health policy. Some considerations for such a reconceptualization will be discussed at the end of this chapter. First, however, it is necessary to look at change and reform possibilities within the existing parameters. In doing so, the typology discussed here may be of some use in predicting where mental health professionals and interested laypersons may fall. The typology should not, though, be taken in any absolute sense. Typologies are useful in delineating broad categories which allow us to locate likely critical points of agreement and disagreement, and permit us to better define the margins of possibilities within a given perspective.

REFORM AND CHANGE WITHIN INSTITUTIONS

Institutional change and reform are far more complex at present than they were in the pre-community mental health, pre-deinstitutionalization era. Then, most change could be centered in the state hospitals. Now, however, state hospitals are joined by many other facility types in a multiplicity of structural problems in need of major attention.

As Chapters 3 and 6 show, the development of CMHCs and the growth of general hospital psychiatry units and private psychiatric hospitals has produced some positive effects in expanding the range of services and the range of clients. Yet those new facilities have had their own problems as well, while state hospital problems remained from the earlier period. NIMH's emphasis on CMHCs led to a low level of attention to state hospital improvement. The Institute believed that if CMHCs were to take over so many state hospital functions, then it would be unwise to bolster those institutions which were always so problematic. By the time large-scale deinstitutionalization was under way, state hospital improvement was clearly a low federal priority. Thus, while state hospitals no longer contain many thousands of patients, they still exhibit many of the same poor living conditions and non-therapeutic environments as in the past.

CMHCs and state hospitals failed to coordinate their efforts, as the centers sought out new client populations. Federal optimism about state, local, and private support for CMHCs failed to take into account the potential for centers to face financial crises. Although conceived of as responsive to local needs, CMHCs were hampered in catering to local needs by federal guidelines on types of services offered. Centers' community orientation was largely a geographic definition of catchment areas. At the same time, much of their specifically community orientation — e.g., consultation and education — was typically formalistic agency-to-agency contact rather than public health preventive work. And despite the federal initiative in CMHCs, federal Medicare and Medicaid biases prevented the centers from serving many people who needed service. As Chapter 8 added, psychotropic drugs became an overutilized mainstay of all elements of public mental health practice.

This brief summary of points made in earlier chapters serves to note areas where change is required. Let us begin with perhaps the easiest prescription: drastically increasing funding. Recent state and federal cutbacks have highlighted the need to expend significant resources on mental health care. Even in the late 1960s and early 1970s it was evident that there were not enough funds allocated for the tasks at hand. Much higher mental health funding clearly is needed, but it is erroneous to pose this as the chief solution. Agency and program structure, and professionalist practices must also be changed at the same time. An infusion of money into existing channels would do little to improve the situation. This in no fashion implies that it would be useless to pressure the federal government to reverse its aggressive military policy in favor of social programs. It does mean that the problems within agencies, organizations, facilities, and professionals must finally be faced.

Kupers (1982) has demonstrated that within the economic constraints of public mental health centers, clinicians could provide greatly improved services. The requirement for this was a confrontation with the professionalist notions by which providers and agencies restricted themselves to specific therapeutic interactions. Such narrowness prevents mental health professionals from addressing other issues such as work, unemployment, problems with police, and housing needs. Ultimately, Kupers is merely practicing the best elements of the original community mental health approach by being an active outside advocate for CMHC clients. In order to understand these needs, Kupers emphasizes a social context which situates patients' problems in terms of class, race, and gender stratification. Rose's (1982) work in community-based aftercare also revolves around the perspective that providers should pursue client-based advocacy functions.

Past and present practices have been wasteful as well as clinically deficient. Central here is the importance of wide-scale planning. After various federal bodies noted the uncoordinated nature of mental health policy, planners were urged to develop more comprehensive plans which would provide for the totality of patient needs — mental health care, medical care, rehabilitation, living skills, job placement, housing, and recreation. NIMH's Community Support Program (CSP) was a small-scale answer to this need. Rose (1982) notes, however, that CSP demonstration projects repeated past practices by contracting out to state mental health departments who had not previously shown themselves able to transcend their traditional institutionalism. Further, there is tension between state DMHs and local providers over a wide range of issues. And, CSP's support of patient advocacy fell short since it allocated that function to the same CSP agency which would administer the program, a conflict of interest which would minimize effective advocacy. At the same time, Rose continues, many local providers have had serious flaws which should not be tolerated in a new program, yet state planners emphasize higher degrees of coordination among existing agencies. In addition to general faults within existing agencies, Rose believes that community agencies often hold an overwhelmingly psychiatrized conception of ex-patients' needs, rather than a reconceptualization which understands their basic needs for income, housing, medical care, social interaction, and other routine aspects of social life.

The President's Commission, noting that NIMH had not moved rapidly enough in pursuing such community programs on a large scale, designed a more comprehensive approach in the Mental Health Systems Act. Significant funding was planned for community integration projects, which would receive priority over CMHC funding. While it is unclear if this new approach would remedy many past flaws, the Mental Health Systems Act was effectively repealed by the Reagan Administration when almost all of its sections were placed in one of the four block grants for health care. This reduced accountability to central planning, and also produced a funding reduction of 25 per cent by 1984. Thus any nationwide move to correct the path of uncoordinated deinstitutionalization remains unfulfilled.

While much of what must be done for patients requires posthospital planning and care, there are numerous factors in hospital life which can prepare patients for better outside life. This includes organization of hospital structure as well as discharge policies. Holland et al.'s (1981) study of twenty-two wards in three Ohio state hospitals found that patient functioning at intake was not a determinant of community adjustment potential. Rather, major factors in such adjustment potentials were individualized treatment plans, daily maintenance, and the participation of ward staff and patients in treatment decisions. These variables yielded more job satisfaction, which increased adjustment potential. In another case, a drug reduction program at a New York state hospital (discussed in Chapter 8) produced more appropriate and earlier discharge.

As considered in Chapters 3 and 4, hospitals' discharge policies were often unplanned dumping, with little or no follow-up. In one case when a state hospital (New York's Harlem Valley Psychiatric Center) was very consciously restructured to provide more active care and community treatment, no follow-up studies were conducted to measure the efficacy of community care (Levine, 1980). Clearly there is a great need for compelling state hospitals to have specific plans for each patient. This means more than specifying that the patient is suitable for discharge to a nursing home. It requires finding out more about individual needs and locating resources to meet those needs. This is not solely a responsibility of state hospitals, since CMHCs are also responsible for ex-patients in their catchment areas. Coordination of these two streams of public mental health care must be greatly increased. Further, since nursing and boarding homes usually fall under public health department regulation, a significant amount of coordination between public health and mental health departments is required. Additionally, welfare departments are responsible for Medicaid reimbursable programs, and therefore must be included in planning. Such cooperation is ideal, but often unlikely, given historical conflicts between various state departments. The best solution would be to create a new single agency which would have authority over all aspects of community care, as well as the financial resources to provide those services by itself. Otherwise we will more likely see an increase in the already out of control system of states contracting out for mental health services.

This has certainly been true in Massachusetts, which spent $185 million in fiscal year 1979 in contracting out human services to private providers (Massachusetts Taxpayers Foundation, 1980). In the words of a recent Massachusetts Commissioner of Mental Health, 'the role of the state mental health authority must shift from one of direct services to one of planning, integrating, sanctioning, monitoring, priority setting, and funding' (Okin, 1978). A former Kentucky commissioner likewise proposed an 'advocacy/broker system' whereby state-controlled CMHCs provide a minimal level of services themselves and contract out for the bulk (Farabee and Press, 1977). In Rhode Island, the Senate commission which oversees the state mental health department not only wants to expand utilization of private institutions, but also has proposed turning over the single state hospital to a private concern (Edwards, 1981). Contracting out perpetuates poor coordination, despite the fact that it is centrally implemented by a state mental health department. Such methods are essentially an abdication of public responsibility in favor of the private sector, a transfer of care in the arena of responsibility and accountability.

In the long run, the best approach to solving many of these problems is a comprehensive mental health component of a national health system. Within the capitalist world, Britain's National Health Service is a likely model. In socialist society, Cuba's health system is perhaps the best example. A national health care system is by definition far broader than national health insurance in that it seeks to provide direct services to all citizens, rather than merely financing a private medical sector to augment the public sector. National health coverage would have to incorporate the other social and human services which are so integral to care of the seriously mentally ill. Although a national health service will be difficult to attain in this country, mental health professionals and advocates need to begin teaming up with health professionals and citizens groups in working for such a program.

As a shorter term corrective, mental health services should be coordinated and provided by comprehensive state government agencies. These agencies would need to eliminate the fragmentation and duplication of current practices. This would entail providing a comprehensive set of psychiatric services, in tandem with the related social services. Thus, for example, patients could receive inpatient care and then be transferred (if able) to a less intensive community location where they could obtain rehabilitation, medical, and social support services. This would all be under the aegis of one agency, as opposed to the current multiplicity of bodies. Such an arrangement would require changes in state-level practices as well as in federal financing and regulatory mechanisms. Federal support would be necessary through a large new program. As with the CMHC program, there would be problems between federal planners and states' varied needs and resources. Precautions would be necessary to avoid a repetition of past problems, such as the frequently inappropriate federal demand that all CMHCs provide all the mandated services.

This shorter-term approach can be seen as a basis for pursuing the longer range national health service, though even this short-term model will face great opposition under the current national leadership. In the process of working towards larger-scale programs, there are many shorter-term reforms which would aid mental health care. Medicaid and Medicare reimbursement restrictions, targeted by many as a major obstacle, must be removed, so that these federal programs can pay for outpatient services, nonpsychiatric services for ex-patients, important functions such as case management, and services in CMHCs and other public facilities which are now nonreimbursable. Independent living needs to be strongly emphasized so that people's own living environment and social relations are as open, flexible, and under their own control as much as possible. Independent living should not be discouraged by reducing state Supplemental Security Income supplements to persons living outside of boarding homes. Housing programs are critically needed for ex-patients who do not require full-time care, thus freeing them from the custodialism of the nursing and boarding home industry. As Baxter and Hopper (1980) and Rose (1982) argue, these housing requirements are among the most central, yet most visibly unprovided of needs. Lerman (1982: 183) suggests dealing with SSI and housing together, by federalizing all SSI payments. States would be required to use this windfall — they spent $1.9 billion in fiscal year 1980 on SSI supplements — to finance mortgages for construction or rehabilitation of housing in the least restrictive environment. Such facilities, Lerman continues, should be eligible for federal rental subsidies.

To the extent that existing nursing and boarding homes retain their prominence in community care, state and federal inspection, regulation, and sanctions must have more teeth, rather than the deregulatory emphasis currently at work. In order to protect clients from exploitation by nursing home operators and group apartment landlords, more public congregate care facilities need to be provided. In order to prevent abuses in such public locations, rigorous monitoring will be required. Wages and operating budgets ought to be adequate so that high quality staff and facilities are available. Clients in both public and private care require independent advocacy programs to represent them against abuses and oversights. Community involvement can also make a difference. An exemplary effort is witnessed in the attempt by a neighborhood group in Manhattan's Upper West Side to buy a rundown single-room occupancy hotel. The organization was started by a block association, and attracted religious, civic, and business groups. In early 1983 the group put down an option to buy the 230-unit building, 37 per cent of whose residents are ex-patients. Already, the block association had brought in nurses, psychiatric social workers, and alcoholism counselors, organized recreation programs, and started a hot-lunch program (Wald, 1983). This is a rare form of community advocacy, but one which provides a potent model.

Extending the advocacy issue to a broader level, patients' rights reforms need to be protected from current erosions, as outlined in Chapter 9. Patients' rights represent a significant corrective to abuses in the custodial past. Even the right to refuse treatment can be worked into existing facility operations, given its low extent of application.

REFORM AND CHANGE IN ALTERNATIVE INSTITUTIONS

Some of the above reforms can lead to extension of desirable reform in alternative services. Reimbursement bias removals could prompt further reliance on home care, now rarely covered. The GAO report on boarding homes suggests federal-state cost sharing for home care. Lerman stresses the need to provide such services through Medicare rather than through an indigency-based program such as Medicaid. Other countries have far higher levels of home care through non-indigency programs: Sweden has thirty-two times as high a rate of home helpers per 100,000 population as the U.S. (Lerman, 1982: 193,202).

Home care by oneself or with family is beneficial, as demonstrated by Stein and Test's (1980) well-known study of sixty-five control (mental hospital) and sixty-five (independent living) patients. In the year of treatment the experimental group was provided with a wide range of intensive support for all life areas. They spent far less time in psychiatric institutions as a result; this was not accomplished at the cost of stays in medical or penal facilities. Members of the experimental group spent more time employed, though this was due to more sheltered workshop services rather than competitive employment. The experimental group had less symptomatology and greater medical compliance. They were more satisfied with life, had more contact with trusted friends, and belonged to more social groups, though they did not differ from controls on quality of life and social relations measures. After the experimental year, follow-up showed rapid deterioration for the nonhospitalized group who no longer received special services. They spent twice as much time in hospitals as during the study year, while the control group remained stable in days of hospitalization. Most of the other areas where the home care group exceeded the control group also disappeared.

Stein and Test note that it can not be ascertained if the experimental group's success in the treatment year was primarily due to their higher drug compliance. What is clear, they argue, is that it is possible to treat an unselected group of patients in the community. These findings are similar to other studies, such as Fenton et al.'s (1979) Montreal study and Pasamanick et al.'s (1967) Baltimore study. While costs for such programs may be higher, they are not so much greater. Weisbrod et al. (1980) calculated program costs and total benefits for the Stein and Test study, coming up with a 5 per cent higher cost for the experimental group ($399 per patient), not a huge amount for the improved living conditions. Further, as Test and Stein (1980) document, the experimental group did not yield any greater burden to their families in terms of disruption of life, suicide gestures, arrests, and emergency room use.

Kiesler (1982) reviewed ten randomized studies of various forms of alternative care, including home care, halfway houses, day treatment, and hostel care. The most impressive effects he noted were that alternative care modes reduce hospitalization. Also noticeable were improvements in employment and school attendance. On all measures, outcomes are as good or better for alternative care than for mental hospital treatment. In Kiesler's review, this included costs, although as discussed in Chapter 4 there is mixed opinion on this factor.

In addressing the widespread opposition to alternative care, Kiesler covers some of the points made already about personnel, facility, and funding shortages, and lack of coordination. To this he adds the important issues of family and staff resistance. Families often desire a separation from a mentally ill member. This may appear contrary to Test and Stein's (1980) findings that home care patients produce no measurably greater burdens on families, but personal perception, experience, and expectation no doubt carry more weight than do the results of controlled experiments.

Staff often believe they can learn more from patients, and that they can treat them more intensively, on an inpatient basis. Even when there is little conscious opposition to alternative care, there is much institutional inertia, one of the main themes of this book. Quite simply, public mental health care has developed as an institutional phenomenon, with archaic and rigid structures, beliefs, habits, and funding. Professionals who may have felt a burst of community psychology enthusiasm in the 1960s now fear the uncertainty of innovative treatment modes for which soft money support may easily dry up and in which noninstitutional involvement distances the professionals from many of their peers.

In pursuing a variety of nonhospital alternatives, it is critical to understand that mental health, like other fields, often produces a *routinization of alternatives*. What starts out as radical, innovative, and exciting may be applied in a formulaic manner without renewing the model or taking into account the different locations where the alternative is applied. Or, a good idea may be formulated, yet be difficult to implement; still, the proponents may assert that it is being carried out in practice. Directions such as these have been common throughout the course of U.S. mental health policy — nineteenth-century moral treatment is perhaps the best example. In the mid-to-late twentieth century, an interesting example is the 'therapeutic community.' What Maxwell Jones originated as a bold innovation rapidly lost its psychiatric radicalism and political radicalism, as virtually everything done in mental hospitals became termed 'therapeutic' by virtue of being a component of a self-proclaimed therapeutic milieu. Halfway houses are another example of an innovation which became part of the institutional fabric. These programs originated as somewhat independent of hospital structures but have often become very attached to the hospital.

This dilution of alternatives is akin to the issues raised in Chapter 3 concerning community mental health ideology: mental health activities were relabeled 'community' by reason of their nonhospital (or even in-hospital) location. The key issue here is not that planners and clinicians deceptively applied such labels — though that sometimes occurred — but that the recasting of mental health care was more commonly seen in terms of theory and intention rather than in concrete activities. In light of the difficulties in implementing the contemporary 'third psychiatric revolution,' professionals protected their personal esteem and professional power by dogmatically routinizing the alternative models. In cases where professionals sought to pursue innovative paths, they were faced with mental health bureaucracies which routinized the alternatives.

Because of the likelihood of co-optation and routinization, self-help alternatives are very promising. Self-help mental health programs generally are independent of regular institutions and agencies, even though some self-help groups adhere to a medical model and/or rely on professional guidance. As in the areas of health, disability, and social welfare, mental health self-help groups use their members' personal experiences as curative, supportive, and rehabilitative resources. There are a wide variety of self-help groups: peer counseling, suicide prevention, hotlines, ex-patient groups (with a wide range in their relationships to professionals), rape crisis centers, battered women's shelters. Although some self-help groups receive assistance from professionals, the mental health system has not often enough utilized these groups for referrals. The President's Commission on Mental Health (1978) considered this to be a waste of valuable resources, and urged a greater use of self-help groups. Riessman (1978) supports the increased support and use of self-help groups by mainstream providers, but cautions that the groups may become too dependent on government funds and diverted from their grassroots goals. Self-help groups also offer useful models for change in traditional services. These consumer-run groups can teach more professional providers about democratizing and show them how to benefit from the 'experimental knowledge' of self-help groups (Borkman, 1976).

Fear of job loss is very understandable in the human services field. Aides and nurses have not been the only staff displaced by deinstitutionalization. Social workers and psychologists have also been affected, even if not so powerfully. Future policy directions must provide for job security, including significant retraining for active alternative care.

Building on the preceding material on mainstream and alternative reform, we now examine important — but often underrated — long-term effects of deinstitutionalization. From this we will move to the concluding section on reconceptualizing deinstitutionalization and general mental health policy.

LONG-TERM RESULTS OF DEINSTITUTIONALIZATION

Public mental health policy does not always produce what it sets out to do. For reasons discussed throughout the book, goals are often stymied, and at the same time unintended consequences occur. The centrality of nursing homes, boarding homes, and SROs is becoming more widely understood as the largest and most detrimental of such outcomes. And, as detailed in Chapter 6, the growth of the public-private allied sector is another important development. Whereas the nursing home transfer of care is almost universally negative in consequences, the transfer to the public-private allied sector is mixed. It benefits some poorer patients whose treatment in public-funded private facilities brings better care than they might otherwise receive. Yet such developments also increase the medicalized view of mental illness, as well as removing much care from public inspection and control.

New adult chronic patients

Of recent importance is the category of persons termed 'new adult chronics,' a grouping whose growth and persistence in the community reflects both deinstitutionalization practices and shortcomings of community care. This population has been referred to in earlier material. They are generally male psychotic persons in their twenties and thirties who have no prior long-term hospitalization and who may or may not have a history of repeated short-term hospitalizations. The prevalence of the new chronics is a result of deinstitutionalization, since in the past, these persons would have been placed in state hospitals. The shortcomings of community care also play their role, since non-hospital programs have not provided enough services for the new chronics. For example, many of these patients are denied eligibility for New York State's Community Support Services merely because they are not long-term state hospital veterans (Bachrach, 1982).

Policy questions and service provision are not the sole factors in the creation of a new adult chronic population. Demographic factors are also involved. Baby boom children, who are now between twenty-one and thirty-six, represent one-third of the U.S. population. Their overrepresentation in the population creates a higher number of persons at risk. Further, these age groups are more geographically mobile, and their instability adds them to the ranks of the homeless. Actually, these new adult chronics are not a homogeneous group, but can be seen as comprising three sub-populations: 1) those with complete dependence on the mental health system; 2) those who cope satisfactorily in remission but are seriously disabled by recurrent psychotic episodes; and 3) aggressive, non-compliant persons. The three sub-populations are grouped together due to their impact on psychiatric and medical service: many move rapidly between facilities, many are criminally-involved, and many become emergency room regulars (Bachrach, 1982).

That demographic changes have been at work in producing this new population does not excuse the mental health system from failing to provide new services. After all, one of the tenets of community mental health in the 1960s was the need to tailor services to existing populations rather than to continue to provide only the traditional range of services. Part of the reason for lack of sufficient attention to these new adult chronics is that they appear as part of the growing homeless population, a group which is diverse in problems but includes a large number of emotionally disturbed people.

The homeless persons problem

As mentioned at the end of Chapter 5, the growing ranks of the homeless include many ex-patients — as many as 50 per cent of New York City's estimated 36,000 homeless people are ex-patients, and many others are mentally ill. Homelessness is an expanding problem due to continued severe economic recession and acute housing shortages. But prior to that was the legacy of state hospital dumping and sparse community care programs. In 1982 the Coalition for the Homeless entered a class action suit against state mental health and social service chiefs on behalf of the approximately 6,000 state hospital discharges now living in the open in New York City. Interestingly, the city government warmly welcomed the suit against the state, having itself been the target of a successful 1979 suit requiring city shelters for all homeless people (Shipp, 1982). In the state's 1981 five-year mental health plan, the homeless population was written off as falling under welfare jurisdiction (Baxter and Hopper, 1982). This clearly denies mental health officials' original responsibility, though there is no doubt some public support for this denial. After all, it seems to some people that it is less sensible to spend scarce mental health dollars on such marginal persons than on specific facilities. Also, mental health departments usually have very incomplete records on where clients are located; this makes it hard to demonstrate that specific homeless people are in fact ex-state hospital patients.

The situation of homeless mentally ill persons clearly demonstrates the transfer of care in financial and responsibility terms. Advocates and sympathetic professionals may file class action suits and press governments for services, but many of the public may be content to ignore these people since they appear as yet another component of an amorphous underclass. In this fashion, many deviant populations are indiscriminately grouped by a process of *deviant-lumping* into a shapeless mass of social outcasts.

The new marginality

This deviant-lumping process is facilitated by the blurring of distinctions between criminal behavior and psychopathological behavior, as evidenced in the earlier discussion of ex-patient crime and mental illness among prisoners. It is also blurred by the monolithic conception of community residences and halfway houses, whereby neighbors and the wider public may cease to distinguish between facilities for ex-convicts, ex-patients, substance abusers, and juvenile delinquents. An additional blurring factor is that due to the peculiarities of mental health policy, most mentally ill persons in the community are supported by Medicaid and SSI, which makes it easy to consider these recipients as part of the ideologically important, yet essentially formless category of 'welfare chiselers.'

In fact it is difficult to distinguish among many of the new marginal population. These people, variously termed 'social junk' (Spitzer, 1975) and 'socially terminal people' (Siegal, 1978), are incapacitated in overlapping forms. The majority of psychiatrically impaired persons in the community, as well as a good many ex-offenders, are alcohol-impaired. Many are drug abusers, and, ironically, psychoactive drugs are themselves now part of the growing pharmacopia of street drugs. The past and present environment of severely disturbed persons makes them prone to criminality, and the destructive elements of criminal life make its members prone to mental illness.

Occurring in a period of supposed enlightenment about mental illness, such deviant-lumping is reminiscent of early modern Europe when psychiatry and other social institutions were barely beginning to learn to differentiate between various deviant populations (Rosen, 1968; Foucault, 1971). But if the present appears to mirror the archaic past, this is only partly the case. In terms of the profitability of care, current marginal populations are often lucrative. Following Parry-Jones on the eighteenth- and nineteenth-century 'trade in lunacy' of private entrepreneurial madhouses, Scull (1981b) considers that a 'new trade in lunacy' is taking root as mental patients are being 'recommodified' in the private sector. In this process, Warren (1981) points out, the distinction between non-profit and for-profit facilities is becoming less clear in long-term care facilities, as some facilities change their status to secure changing forms of government funding.

Beyond this blurred distinction is the point made in Chapter 5 that non-profit facilities function to produce entrepreneurial forms of profit for their own professional staff as well as to generate profit within the larger medical-industrial complex. Sometimes the opportunities for such recommodification take place through mental health funding practices and other times through welfare and medical structures, especially nursing and boarding home payments. The growing attention to the new homeless may also generate opportunities for opportunistic entrepreneurs who will capitalize on the hard fought advocacy battles of the present. To the extent that this trend is accelerating, and in light of the various aspects of the transfer of care in the mental health system, it is imperative to reconceptualize deinstitutionalization and the overall framework of mental health policy.

RECONCEPTUALIZING DEINSTITUTIONALIZATION AND MENTAL HEALTH POLICY

Such a reconceptualization requires a brief reminder of what were the dominant conceptions which guided recent mental health reform. Restructuring of the psychiatric system, beginning in the 1950s, was predicated on a belief that new community mental health facilities should largely supplant state hospitals. The hospitals themselves were to be depopulated, and as much as possible, to be closed. Although the new efforts were spearheaded by a unique federal coordination, little effort was made to connect the old hospital system and the new CMHC program. Nor was sufficient planning made for the financial future of psychiatric care after initial federal support ended. With their pervasive optimism about new methods and facilities, professionals put forth a dramatic expansion of psychiatric approaches to a wide array of social problems. This optimism also affected politicians, who joined with professionals in believing that the 'third psychiatric revolution' would succeed on its own merits, even in the absence of having provided a thorough break with past practices.

A reconceptualization of deinstitutionalization and of mental health policy therefore involves the deeper, structural issues discussed throughout this book. This viewpoint grounds mental health practices within the even larger social organization underlying that network. This new approach assumes that correctives to systemic problems lie only partly within the mental health system, and largely outside it.

In Chapter I, I noted Kiesler's (1982a) formulation of policy, which conceives of *de jure* policy as the planned, legislative programs, and *de facto* policy as the actual practices which often undercut *de jure* approaches. Kiesler's perspective holds that unintended consequences of policy are responsible for this discrepancy. Rothman (1980) adds to this approach by demonstrating that mental health reformers entered into new programs without adequate preparations, without knowledge of possible outcomes, and with a blind faith in the benevolently neutral state apparatus. Morrissey et al. (1980) provide a further necessary emphasis by noting that mental health policy makers engage in 'cycles of institutional reform' which repeat prior errors since they cannot see the practical limits of their idealistic goals.

I have sought to expand these useful approaches by arguing that mental health policy in the era of deinstitutionalization — and in prior eras as well — can be reconceptualized by examining three structural forces: political-economy, institutional inertia, and professionalism. Past work has not often enough addressed professionalism, alone and in interaction with the other two forces. More generally, there has been no structural argument to link these three forces in a comprehensive fashion. This has been the central concern of this book. Through this study we can understand that the directions of mental health policy have not stemmed from a basically humanitarian and well thought-out plan of action. Rather, key policies have often occurred as a result of startlingly rising state hospital costs. To the extent that patients' rights concerns have played a role in conscious planning, they too have been largely a response to financial pressures. Further, many changes in the caregiving system have had shortcomings in the professional construction of what was needed, and have been stymied by the economic processes which have made custodial nursing and boarding homes so central to psychiatric maintenance. And, institutional inertia has proven a conservative obstacle to many needed reforms.

Thus, the same structural forces which produced problems in the field have remained barriers to adequate restructuring. For this reason, it has been necessary for the system to be confronted by many outside sources of pressure for change. This is why patients' rights concerns usually entered into conscious planning only when they would benefit the caregiving system, as in the right to treatment. The impact of patients' rights has been greater in the advocacy-type challenge it has presented to the mental health establishment. The lesson here is not solely for the reconceptualization of mental health policy. Rather, it can be extended to the entire range of health concerns. Social movements in health care have increasingly been prominent social change mechanisms which were necessary given the entrenched, conservative structures of most of the health care system. As in many other areas of social organization, external change agents are often necessary since internal structures prevent meaningful change processes from arising internally. Some of the reform suggestions described earlier in this chapter may come partly from within the system, but they will require outside pressures so that they do not repeat the problem of the routinization of alternatives. One method for avoiding such routinization is to provide federal and state funding to programs which are less geared to traditional types of professional hierarchies and which are more self-help oriented. These types of programs may be less amenable to co-optation or routinization, though not completely free of such potential.

By taking into account the above matters we can ask if policy is a guiding hand, or an explanation and justification for what exists. Policy has been both, in varying degrees. Early mental health planning, especially the CMHC program, was a guiding hand, but one largely flawed in ways that have been addressed in earlier chapters. Deinstitutionalization, however, has been too much of an explanation for what exists. To correct the many problems addressed in this book, it is clear that a restructuring of existing services is insufficient. A coherent, new policy is required. The Mental Health Systems Act was one such attempt, but its own drawbacks have been noted earlier. The Act's positive features might have aided mental health care, but were derailed by the Reagan Administration's assault on social services. As proposed earlier in this chapter, structural mental health reform will have more potential if it is linked with structural health care reform and social service expansion in general. National health service is one clear direction for such reform. But this would need to be placed in a larger framework of expanded social services overall. Such shifts in governmental policy require a drastic reduction of military spending for threats of intervention, covert counterinsurgency, and invasions of foreign nations. Large-scale political organizing will be the most likely vehicle for beginning to move actively in such a direction.

But given the political-economic parameters of our society, structural reform in any public policy area is thwarted by the general characteristics of profiteering, militarism, anti-environmentalism, and a basic disregard for human survival. Following the politically and psychiatrically radical deinstitutionalization actions of the Italian psychiatrist Franco Basaglia, Scheper-Hughes (1981) suggests that 'we need to ground deinstitutionalization within a deeper and far more radical movement that explores the social, cultural, and political nature of psychiatric disorder, consequent exclusion, and social control.' She continues:

> *As Franco Basaglia has stated, 'Health needs to be redefined as something other than mere availability for work' or, I might add, more than a social contract to remain mute and invisible within a potentially hostile and rejecting community.*

Recent Italian psychiatric reforms offer very useful lessons for reform in the United States. Italy's Law 180, passed in 1978, stopped the admission of patients to state hospitals and limited to fifteen the number of general hospital psychiatric unit beds in a catchment area (100,000 to 120,000 population). A national health insurance program was passed in the same year, which does not discriminate against psychiatric coverage. Further, medical and social welfare funds are distributed on a per capita basis in each region, thus equalizing funding for all citizens. Community programs are to be made widely available for psychiatric, medical, and social services. Job guarantees were given to all mental hospital staff. In the first year of the radical new law the inpatient population decreased by 18 per cent and compulsory admissions by 60 per cent; localized reforms leading up to the national program had already diminished the inpatient census by nearly 40 per cent in the prior decade. There was little evidence of 'dumping,' and no significant difference in admissions to private hospitals (Mosher, 1982).

Such radical alterations as occurred in Italy do not occur instantaneously. They resulted from a turbulent period of psychiatric and political reform which was pushed along by the 1968 rebellions. Five years earlier, however, Franco Basaglia had led the psychiatric reformers with his restructuring of the Gorizia hospital. Lobotomy, electroshock, and restraints were abolished, close ties were forged with local residents, patients were given more power over treatment, and professionalist hierarchies were altered. In Trieste, where Basaglia later implemented his reform methods, rapid intervention by home visits became a typical form of care, thus eliminating the difficulties of convincing or forcing people to come to a psychiatric facility. Integration with the community was concretely practiced, including work cooperatives involving both hospital patients and unemployed local residents (Lovell, 1978; Mosher, 1982; Ramon, 1983). Thus, community care is a real form of treatment in Italy.

Basaglia and his colleagues in the Psichiatria Democratica organization pursued these transformations in a number of other hospitals, and eventually garnered enough support to bring the national legislation to fruition. Of critical importance was the politicizing of psychiatric issues, an easier task in Italy than in the United States. The reform organizers considered the democratization of patient and staff life as part of a general social democratization. They joined with leftist political parties and trade unions to criticize the traditional practices and ideologies of the conservative medical model. Social roots of psychiatric problems were emphasized, for instance by organizing a women's group at a mental hospital to deal with sexism, and by attacking nationwide unemployment as part of preventive practices (Lovell, 1978; Mosher, 1982).

Of interest are the obstacles which have hindered fuller application of Law 180. Some regions and cities have not implemented the law very widely. Despite job guarantees, hospital staff have been reluctant to give up the old institutional framework. Community placements are still in short supply, partly due to the incredible transformations involved, and partly due to Italy's critical housing shortage; cities with the most firmly established community alternatives are the places where Psichiatria Democratica activists pursued local reforms prior to the new law. Also, university psychiatric departments have not cooperated with the public sector, preferring their selective, private clientele (Mosher, 1982).

Chinese psychiatric reforms bear some resemblance to Italian efforts, though both the general culture and the psychiatric legacy are less similar to American traditions than are the Italian. The socialist system and the relative cohesiveness of Chinese society allow for more comprehensive planning and service delivery. China's 'serve the people' ideology brings with it an egalitarian approach to health services and human services. Integration into the patient's community is important; workmates and neighbors are involved in the treatment process in the hospital and after release. Mental health care is more politically oriented than in Italy, since patients are often encouraged to view their emotional problems in terms of Chinese socialist conceptions. Chinese psychiatry has attempted to break down staff elitism as part of a general social leveling, though the post-Cultural Revolution period has reversed some of these trends.

One clear difference between Italy and China is that Italy's psychiatric restructuring came out of a grassroots upsurge, whereas China's stemmed from the widespread social changes wrought by a revolutionary government (Lu, 1978).

Both Chinese and Italian psychiatric reforms need to be studied more in the United States, since they offer a variety of positive directions which can be implemented at varying degrees of overall social reorganization. There are valuable lessons here in terms of community treatment concepts, institutional structures, professional issues, connection with other human services, and relation to basic concepts of social organization. These lessons can be applied to both the Type II liberal approach and Type III radical approach discussed at the beginning of the chapter. However, the ultimate impact of such lessons is mainly a question of radical reform efforts.

In light of these far-reaching directions for change, one is forced to ask: can planning or reconceptualizing mental health alone accomplish most of the changes suggested here? In the broadest sense, the answer is no; better mental health and better mental health services will be largely a function of structural social change. In a narrower sense, though, planning and reconceptualization can accomplish some changes. As in all forms of social change, the more radical innovations are but the leading edge of a long stream of changes throughout the social system. There are lessons to be learned by those of various persuasions, which can move us to better serving the mental health needs of the population.

But will the current generation of planners and providers be less myopic than in the past? This question is more difficult. The very visible failures of the last three decades of policy and practice should make professionals more aware of the flaws in psychiatric service delivery. So too should the social and psychiatric critique of antipsychiatry forces lead to greater awareness. Yet countering this are two main considerations. First, as has been discussed throughout this book, mental health officials and providers have long engaged in cyclical reform, forgetting earlier lessons. Second, the current government's opposition to social programs makes planners and providers shrink from large-scale reform and expansion, and spend most of their energy on maintaining services in the face of drastic cutbacks. In short, it is a bad time for innovation. That is why I have continually argued that an evaluation of the past, present, and future mental health policy and practice requires a deep analysis of political-economy, professionalism, and institutional structure. This will lead to both a better knowledge of psychiatric issues and to an understanding of how they interact with the overall social fabric.

The sociology of health and illness has outpaced psychiatric sociology in recognizing the inseparability of the health care system from the overall social system. Psychiatric sociology will have to catch up in this area. As pointed out in Chapter 6, these lessons are essential to a fruitful reordering of our thinking about mental health care. As with medical care, mental health care faces the difficulty of aiding people, many of whose problems are extensions of the social system itself. To fail to reconceptualize mental health policy in such a light is to perpetuate that problem.

References

Abramson, Marc P.
1972 'The criminalization of mentally disordered behavior: Possible side effect of a new mental health law.' Hospital & Community Psychiatry 23:101-105.
Affleck, Glenn C., Michael A. Peszke, and Ronald M. Wintrob
1978 'Psychiatrists' familiarity with legal statutes governing emergency involuntary hospitalization.' American Journal of Psychiatry 135:205-209.
Albee, George W.
1959 Mental Health Manpower Trends. New York: Basic.
1979 'Psychiatry's human resources: 20 years later.' Hospital and Community Psychiatry 30:783-786.
American Federation of State, County, and Municipal Employees
1977a 'Current status of AFSCME efforts regarding national developments in mental health, developmental disabilities, and juvenile justice'. Mimeo.
1977b 'Statement of the A.F.S.C.M.E., AFL-CIO, to the President's Commission on Mental Health.' Mimeo, Sept. 26, 1977.
American Psychological Association Monitor
1976 'Supreme Court strikes patient wage standard.' APA Monitor Vol. 7 No. 9-10:16.
1978a 'Changing of the guard: Brown forced out, Klerman in charge.' APA Monitor Vol. 9 No.2:1-7.
1978b 'Parity for mental health.' APA Monitor Vol. 9 No. 6:2.
Anspach, Renée
1979 'From stigma to identity politics: Political activism among the physically disabled and former mental patients.' Social Science and Medicine 13(A):765-771.
Appelbaum, Paul S. and Thomas G. Gutheil
1980a 'Drug refusal: A study of psychiatric inpatients.' American Journal of Psychiatry 137:340-345.
1980b 'The Boston State Hospital case: 'Involuntary mind control,' the Constitution, and the 'right to rot.'' American Journal of Psychiatry 137:720-723.

Appelbaum, Paul S. and Robert M. Hamm
1982 'Decision to seek commitment: Psychiatric decision making in a legal context.' Archives of General Psychiatry 39:447-451.
Appelbaum, Paul S., Anthony H. Jackson and Richard I. Shader
1983 'Psychiatrists' responses to violence: Pharmacologic management of psychiatric inpatients.' American Journal of Psychiatry 140:301-304.
Armstrong, Barbara
1980 'The mental health lobby and how it grew.' Hospital and Community Psychiatry 9:599-605.
Asnis, Gregory M., Michael A. Leopold, Roger C. Duvoisin, and Arthur H. Schwartz
1977 'A survey of tardive dyskinesia in psychiatric outpatients.' American Journal of Psychiatry 134:12 Dec. 1977, pp. 1367-1370.
Asnis, Gregory M., Max Fink, and Sue Saferstein
1978 'ECT in metropolitan New York hospitals: A survey of practice, 1975-1976.' American Journal of Psychiatry 135:479-482.
Associated Press
1977 'Nursing-homes lambasted in AFL-CIO study.' Boston Globe Feb. 27, 1977.
Aviram, Uri, and Steven Segal
1977 'From hospital to community care: The change in the mental health treatment system in California.' CMHJ 13:158-167.
Bachrach, Leona L.
1974 'Patients at Federally Funded Rural Community Mental Health Centers in 1971.' NIMH Statistical Note No. 102, Rockville, MD: NIMH.
1981 'The effects of deinstitutionalization on general hospital psychiatry.' Hospital and Community Psychiatry 32:786-790.
1982 'Young adult chronic patients: An analytical review of the literature.' Hospital and Community Psychiatry 33:189-197.
Baker, Frank and Herbert C. Schulberg
1967 'The development of a custodial mental health scale.' Community Mental Health Journal 3:216-225.
Bardach, Eugene
1972 The Skill Factor in Politics: Repealing the Mental Commitment Laws in California. Berkeley: University of California Press.
Bassuk, Ellen L.
1980 'The impact of deinstitutionalization on the general hospital psychiatric emergency ward,' Hospital and Community Psychiatry 31:623-627.
Bassuk, Ellen L. and Samuel Gerson
1978 'Deinstitutionalization and mental health services.' Scientific American Vol. 238, No. 2:46-53.
Bathen, Sigrid
1976 'Brown Boosts State Hospital Staffs by 1,000.' Sacramento Bee, Dec. 5.

Baxter, Ellen and Kim Hopper
1980 'Pathologies of place and disorders of mind.' Health/PAC Bulletin 11:1-22.
1982 'The new mendicancy: Homeless in New York City.' American Journal of Orthopsychiatry 52:393-408.
Bean, John F., Michael M. Makowiecki, and Mark R. Yessian
1979 'A service delivery assessment of community mental health centers.' ADAMHA: mimeo.
Becker, Alvin, and Herbert C. Schulberg
1976 'Phasing out state hospitals — a psychiatric dilemma.' New England Journal of Medicine Vol. 294: 255-261, Jan. 29.
Belknap, Ivan
1956 Human Problems of a State Mental Hospital. New York: McGraw-Hill.
Berke, Joe and Mary Barnes
1972 Mary Barnes: Two Accounts of a Journey Through Madness. New York: Harcourt.
Bernard, J.L.
1977 'The significance for psychology of O'Connor v. Donaldson.' American Psychologist 32:1085-1088.
Bettelheim, Bruno
1969 'Student revolt: The hard core.' Testimony presented to the House Special Subcommittee on Education, March 20, 1969. Vital Speeches of the Day. Vol. 35, No.1: 405-410.
Binswanger, Ludwig
1963 Being-in-the-World. New York: Harper & Row.
Blain, Daniel
1975 'Twenty-five years of Hospital and Community Psychiatry:1945-1970.' Hospital and Community Psychiatry 26:605-609.
Bleyer, Bill
1982 'Cuts seen in aid for disabled.' Newsday March 11, 1982.
Bloom, Bernard L.
1975 Community Mental Health: A General Introduction. Monterey, CA: Brooks/Cole.
Bloom, Bernard L. and Shirley J. Asher
1982 'Patient rights and patient advocacy: A historical and conceptual appreciation,' pp. 19-56 Bernard Bloom and Shirley Asher, eds. Psychiatric Patient Rights and Patient Advocacy: Issues and Evidence. New York: Human Sciences Press.
Bonovitz, Jennifer Caldwell and Jay S. Bonovitz
1981 'Diversion of the mentally ill into the criminal justice system: The police intervention perspective.' American Journal of Psychiatry 138:973-976.
Booth, Carol
1979a 'Brewster v. Dukakis: Part One.' Mass Psych. Wards Vol. 1, No. 3, May 1979:6-11.

1979b 'Brewster v. Dukakis: Part two.' Mass Psych. Wards Vol. 1, No. 4, June 1979:1-4.

Borkman, Thomasina

1976 'Experiential knowledge: A new concept for the analysis of self-help groups.' Social Service Review 50:445-457.

Braginsky, Benjamin M., Dorothea D. Braginsky, and Kenneth Ring

1969 Methods of Madness: The Mental Hospital as a Last Resort. New York: Holt.

Bramel, Dana and Ronald Friend

1982 'The theory and practice of psychology in the U.S.' In Bertell Ollman, ed., The Left Academy: Marxist Scholars on American Campuses New York: McGraw-Hill.

Brand, Jeanne L.

1965 'The National Mental Health Act of 1946: A retrospect.' Bulletin of the History of Medicine 39:231-245.

Breggin, Peter R.

1973 'Followup study of Thomas R.' Rough Times, Vol.3, No. 6 November-December:50-8.

1977 'If psychosurgery is wrong in principle...?' Psychiatric Opinion, Vol. 14, No. 6:23-27.

1979 Electroshock: Its Brain-Disabling Effects. New York: Springer.

Brenner, M. Harvey

1973 Mental Illness and the Economy. Cambridge: Harvard University Press.

Brill, H. and B. Malzberg

1962 'Statistical report based on the arrest records of 5,354 male expatients released from New York State mental hospitals during the period 1946-1948.' Albany, New York: Department of Mental Hygiene.

Brooks, Alexander D.

1977 'Hospitalization of the mentally ill: The legislative role.' State Government, Autumn:198-202.

Brown, Bertram

1977 'Draft remarks: The NIMH manpower training program.' National Advisory Mental Health Council, Rockville, MD., Jan. 24, 1977: mimeo.

Brown, Bertram, Louis A. Wienckowski, and Lyle W. Bivens

1973 Psychosurgery: Perspective on a Current Issue. HEW Pub. ADM 74-76.

Brown, E. Richard

1980 'Public hospitals in crisis: Their problems and their options.' Health Activists Digest, Vol. 2, No. 3, Fall 1980:3-13.

Brown, Phil

1972a 'Alabama federal court rules for patients' rights.' Rough Times Vol. 2, No. 5, June:8.

1972b 'Social change at Harrowdale State Hospital.' Rough Times Vol. 2, No. 6, April:4.

1977 'Protests hit government approval of lobotomies.' Guardian. April 27.

1981 'The mental patients' rights movement and mental health institutional change.' International Journal of Health Services 11:523-540.

1982a 'Public policy and the rights of mental patients.' Mental Disability Law Reporter 6:55-58.

1982b 'Attitudes towards the rights of mental patients: A national survey in the United States.' Social Science and Medicine 16:2025-2039.

1983 'Mental patients as victims and victimizers.' in Andrew Karmen and Donal Macnamara, eds. Deviance and Victimology. Beverly Hills, CA: Sage.

1984 'Marxism, social psychology, and the sociology of mental health.' International Journal of Health Services 14:237-264.

Brown, Phil and Steven Funk

1984 'Tardive dyskinesia: A case in the social construction and recognition of disease.' Unpublished manuscript.

Bruzelius, Nils J.

1978 'New policy restricts restraints, seclusion.' Boston Globe January 8.

California State Employees Association

1972 'Where have all the patients gone?' Sacramento: California State Employees Association.

Castel, Robert, Françoise Castel and Anne Lovell

1982 The Psychiatric Society. New York: Columbia University Press.

CSEA Newspaper

1977 'Hospital staffing bill moving.' CSEA Newspaper February 23, 1977.

Chamberlin, Judi

1978 On Our Own: Patient-Controlled Alternatives to the Mental Health System. New York: Hawthorn.

Chase, Janet

1973 'Where have all the patients gone?' Human Behavior. Oct. 1973, Pp. 14-21.

Chavkin, Samuel

1978 The Mind Stealers: Psychosurgery and Mind Control. Boston: Houghton-Mifflin.

Chesler, Phyllis

1973 Women & Madness. New York: Avon Books.

Chorover, Stephan L.

1979 From Genesis to Genocide: The Meaning of Human Nature and the Power of Behavior Control. Cambridge: MIT Press.

Chu, Franklin D., & Sharland Trotter

1974 The Madness Establishment: Ralph Nader's Study Group Report on the National Institute of Mental Health. New York: Grossman.

Cocozza, Joseph J., and Henry J. Steadman

1978 'Prediction in psychiatry: An example of misplaced confidence in experts.' Social Problems 25:265-76.

Cohen, Carl I.
1980 'Crime among mental patients — a critical analysis.' Psychiatric Quarterly 52:100-07
Cohen, Jacob and Elmer L. Struening
1962 'Opinions about mental illness in the personnel of two large mental hospitals' Journal of Abnormal and Social Psychology. 64:111-124.
Coles, Gerald S.
1977 Psychosurgery — too much thinking can cause emotional distress.' State and Mind Vol. 5, No. 5, March-April 1977:13-8.
Comptroller General
1974 Need for More Effective Management of Community Mental Health Centers Program. Washington, D.C.: Government Printing Office.
1977 Returning the Mentally Disabled to the Community: Government Need to do More. Washington, D.C.: Government Printing Office.
1979 Entering a Nursing Home: Costly Implications for Medicaid and the Elderly. Washington, D.C.: Government Printing Office.
Connery, Robert H. and contributors
1968 The Politics of Mental Health: Organizing Community Mental Health in Metropolitan Areas. New York: Columbia University Press.
Conrad, Peter, and Joseph W. Schneider
1980 Deviance and Medicalization: From Badness to Sickness. St. Louis: Mosby.
Cooper, David
1967 Psychiatry and Antipsychiatry. New York: Ballantine.
Cooperstock, Ruth and Henry L. Lennard
1979 'Some social meanings of tranquilizer use.' Sociology of Health and Illness 1:331:347.
Crane, George E.
1973 'Clinical psychopharmacology in its 20th year.' Science Vol. 181, July 13:124-8.
Crawford, Robert
1979 'Individual responsibility and health politics in the 1970s,' pp. 247-68 in Susan Reverby and David Rosner, eds., Health Care in America: Essays in Social History. Philadelphia: Temple University Press.
Cumming, Elaine and John Cumming
1957 Closed Ranks. Cambridge: Harvard University Press.
Cumming, John and Elizabeth Markson
1975 'The impact of mass transfer on patient release.' Archives of General Psychiatry 32:804-809.
Dain, Norman
1980 Clifford W. Beers: Advocate for the Insane. Pittsburgh: University of Pittsburgh Press.

Daley, Suzanne
1982 'At summer's end, city is sheltering as many homeless as last winter.' New York Times September 23.
D'Arcy, Carl and Joan Brockman
1977 'Public rejection of the ex-mental patient: Are attitudes changing?' Canadian Review of Sociology and Anthropology 14:68-80.
Daugherty, Lynn B.
1978 'Assessing the attitudes of psychiatric aids toward patients' rights.' Hospital and Community Psychiatry 29:225-226.
Davis, Kingsley
1938 'Mental hygiene and the class structure.' Psychiatry 1:55-65.
Dear, Michael
1977 'Impact of mental health facilities on property values.' Community Mental Health Journal 13:150-157.
Deutsch, Albert
1948 The Shame of the States. New York: Harcourt, Brace & Co.
1949 The Mentally Ill in America: A History of Their Care and Treatment from Colonial Times. 2nd ed. New York: Columbia University Press.
Diamond, Ronald J., Robert K. Booner, Donald Lowe, and Charles Savage
1981 'The use of minor tranquilizers with jail inmates.' Hospital and Community Psychiatry 31:40-43.
Dietz, Jean
1975 'Study shows many mental patients now in nursing homes.' Boston Globe July 20.
1979a 'Deinstitutionalization debate.' Boston Globe, November 22.
1979b 'Hospital in Somerville to pioneer mental plan.' Boston Globe December 19.
1981a 'Hospital phaseout still high priority.' Boston Globe January 29.
1981b 'Mental health class suit.' Boston Globe February 4.
1982 'Hospital wards: New law may shut new mental wing.' Boston Globe November 11.
DiNitto, Diana M. and Thomas R. Dye
1983 Social Welfare: Politics and Public Policy. Englewood Cliffs, NJ: Prentice-Hall.
Doherty, William F.
1981 'Court funding order for hospital halted.' Boston Globe November 17.
Dohrenwend, Bruce P., Barbara Snell Dohrenwend, Madelyn Schwartz Gould, Bruce Link, Richard Neugebauer, and Robin Wunsch-Hitzig
1982 Mental Illness in the United States: Epidemiological Estimates. New York: Praeger.
Donnelly, John
1978 'The incidence of psychosurgery in the United States, 1971-1973.' American Journal of Psychiatry 135:1476-1480.

Donner, Al
1976 'State hospital cutbacks.' Sacramento Union. March 11.
Donovan, Virginia K. and Ronnie Littenberg
1982 'Psychology of women: Feminist therapy'. Pp. 211-235 in Barbara Haber, ed., The Women's Annual: 1981. Boston: Hall.
Doyall, Lesley
1981 The Political Economy of Health. Boston: South End Press.
Dreifus, Claudia, ed.
1977 Seizing Our Bodies. New York: Random House.
Durbin, Jeffrey, R., Richard A. Pasewark, and Dale Albers
1977 'Criminality and mental illness: A study of arrest rates in a rural state.' American Journal of Psychiatry 134:80-83.
Dye, Thomas R.
1972 Understanding Public Policy. Englewood Cliffs, NJ: Prentice-Hall.
Edwards, Jeanne
1981 'Inglesby backs plan to move patients from IMH to private centers.' Providence Journal February 25.
Ehrenreich, Barbara and John Ehrenreich
1970 The American Health Empire: Power, Profits, and Politics. New York: Vintage.
Ehrenreich, Barbara and Deirdre English
1973 Witches, Midwives, and Nurses: A History of Women Healers. Old Westbury, NY: Feminist Press.
Ennis, Bruce
1975 'The impact of litigation on the future of state hospitals.' Pp. 83-89 in Jack Zusman and Elmer Bertsch, eds., The Future Role of the State Hospital. Lexington, MA: Lexington Books.
Epstein, Leon and Paul Lowinger
1975 'Do mental patients want legal counsel? — a survey.' American Journal of Orthopsychiatry 45:88-92.
Esterson, Aaron
1970 The Leaves of Spring. London: Tavistock.
Fanning, Virginia Lee, Grace L. Weist Deloughery, and Kristine M. Gebbie
1972 'Patients involvement in planning own care: Staff and patient attitudes.' Journal of Psychiatric Nursing and Mental Health Services, Jan.-Feb. 1972 :5-8.
Farabee, Dale H. and Lillian Press
1977 'Legislative perspective on public mental health programs.' State Government Autumn: 203-208.
Feldman, Saul
1974 'CMHCs: A decade later.' International Journal of Mental Health Vol. 3, No.2-3:19-34.

Felicetti, Daniel A.

1975 Mental Health & Retardation Politics: The Mind Lobbies in Congress. New York: Praeger.

Fenton, Fred R., Lise Tessier, and Elmer J. Struening

1979 'A comparative trial of home and hospital psychiatric care: One year follow-up.' Archives of General Psychiatry 36:1073-1079.

Ferleger, David

1975 'A patients' rights organization: Advocacy and collective action by and for inmates of mental institutions.' The Clearinghouse Review 8:597-604.

Flamm, Gerald H.

1981 'General hospital psychiatry: Structure or concept?' General Hospital Psychiatry 3:315-319.

Flaschner, Franklin N.

1975 'Constitutional requirements in commitment of the mentally ill: Rights to liberty and therapy.' Pp. 65-81 in Jack Zusman and Elmer Bertsch, eds., The Future Role of the State Hospital. Lexington, MA: Lexington Books.

Flores-Ortiz, Yvette Gissle

1982 'Indigenious paraprofessionals in mental health: An analysis and critique.' Pp. 259-280 in Lonnie R. Snowden, ed., Reaching the Underserved: Mental Health Needs of Neglected Populations. Beverly Hills, CA: Sage.

Foley, Henry A.

1974 'National trends in the financing of mental health programs.' Pp. 75-87 in Dorothy Evans & William L. Clairborn, eds., Mental Health Issues and the Urban Poor.' New York: Pergamon Press.

1975 Community Mental Health Legislation: The Formative Process. Lexington, MA: Lexington Books.

Ford, Maurice D.

1980 'The psychiatrist's double bind: The right to refuse medication.' American Journal of Psychiatry 137:332-339.

Forstenzer, Hyman M. and Alan D. Miller

1975 'Unified services in New York State.' Pp. 281-300 in Jack Zusman and Elmer Bertsch, eds., The Future Role of the State Hospital. Lexington, MA: Lexington Books.

Foucault, Michel

1971 Madness and Civilization: A History of Insanity in the Age of Reason. New York: Plume Books.

Frank, Richard G. and W.P. Welch

1982 'Contracting state mental hospital systems.' Journal of Health Politics, Policy and Law 6:676-683.

Freddolino, Paul P.
1982 'Attitudes toward patient rights: Data from two state hospital studies.' Pp. 246-259 in Bloom, Bernard L. & Shirley J. Asher, eds., Psychiatric Patient Rights and Patient Advocacy: Issues and Evidence. New York: Human Sciences Press.
1983 'Findings from the National Mental Health Advocacy Survey.' Mental Disability Law Reporter 7:416-435.
Freidson, Eliot
1970 Profession of Medicine: A Study of the Sociology of Applied Knowledge. New York: Dodd, Mead.
Friedenberg, Eleanor
1980 'Care of the mentally ill in nursing homes.' Rockville, MD: NIMH, mimeo.
Gil, David G.
1976 Unravelling Social Policy. Cambridge: Schenkman.
Gilbert, Doris C. and Daniel J. Levinson
1957a ' 'Custodialism' and 'humanism' in mental hospital structure and in staff ideology.' Pp. 20-35 in Milton Greenblatt, Daniel Levinson, and Richard H. Williams, eds., The Patient and the Mental Hospital. Glencoe, IL: Free Press.
1957b 'Role performance, ideology, and personality in mental hospital aides.' Pp. 197-208 in Milton Greenblatt, Daniel Levinson, and Richard H. Williams, eds., The Patient and the Mental Hospital. Glencoe, IL: Free Press.
Gilbert, Gustav
1969 Lecture, Department of Psychology, Long Island University, Brooklyn, New York.
Giovannoni, Jeanne M. and Lee Gurel
1967 'Socially disruptive behavior of ex-mental patients.' Archives of General Psychiatry 17:146-153.
Glasscote, Raymond M. and Associates
1976 Old Folks at Homes: A Field Study of Nursing and Board-and-Care Homes. Washington, D.C.: Joint Information Service of the American Psychiatric Association and the National Association for Mental Health.
Goffman, Erving
1961 Asylums: Essays on the Social Situation of Mental Patients and Other Inmates. Garden City, New York: Doubleday.
Goldman, Howard H., Antoinette A. Gattozzi, and Carl A. Taube
1981 'Defining and counting the chronically mentally ill.' Hospital and Community Psychiatry 32:21-27.
Goldman, Howard H., Carl A. Taube, Darrel A. Regier and Michael Witkin
1983 'The multiple functions of the state hospital.' American Journal of Psychiatry 140:296-300.

Goldman, Howard H., Neal H. Adams, and Carl A. Taube
1983 'Deinstitutionalization: The data demythologized.' Hospital and Community Psychiatry 34: 129-134.
Gordon, Barbara
1979 I'm Dancing as Fast as I Can. New York: Bantam.
Gorman, Mike
1956 Every Other Bed. Cleveland: World Publishing.
Gottlieb, Richard M., Theodore Nappi and James J. Strain
1978 'The physician's knowledge of psychotropic drugs: Preliminary results.' American Journal of Psychiatry 135: 29-32.
Gove, Walter R.
1970 'Who is hospitalized: A critical review of some sociological studies of mental illness.' Journal of Health and Social Behavior 11:294-303.
Greenberg, Paul L., Paul P. Freddolino, and Gregory L. Leckltlitner
1982 National Directory of Mental Health Advocacy Programs. Los Angeles: Human Research Institute.
Greenblatt, Milton, Richard York, and Esther Lucille Brown
1955 From Custodial to Therapeutic Patient Care in Mental Hospitals: Explorations in Social Treatment. New York: Russell Sage Foundation.
Greenblatt, Milton
1976 'The evolution of state mental hospital models of treatment.' Pp. 29-42 in Berton H. Kaplan, Robert N. Wilson, and Alexander H. Leighton, eds., Further Explorations in Social Psychiatry. New York: Basic.
Greenblatt, Milton, and Elizabeth Glazier
1975 'The phasing out of mental hospitals in the United States.' American Journal of Psychiatry 132:1135-1140.
Greenhouse, Linda
1981 'Justices restrict a 'bill of rights' for the retarded.' New York Times April 21.
Greenley, James R. and Stuart A. Kirk
1973 'Organizational characteristics of agencies and the distribution of services to applicants.' Journal of Health and Social Behavior 14:70-79.
Greider, William
1975 'After nearly 20 years, an ex-mental patient is indicated.' Washington Post June 27.
Grinker, Roy R. and John P. Spiegel
1945 Men Under Stress. New York: Blakiston.
Grob, Gerald N.
1966 The State and the Mentally Ill: A History of Worcester State Hospital in Massachusetts, 1830-1920. Chapel Hill, NC: University of North Carolina Press.
1973 Mental Institutions in America: Social Policy to 1875. New York: Free Press.

Grosser, G., D. Pearsall, C. Fisher, and L. Geremante
1975 'The regulation of electroconvulsive treatment in Massachusetts: A follow-up.' Massachusetts Journal of Mental Health 5:12-25.
Grossman, Lisa and Frank Summers
1980 'A study of the capacity of schizophrenic patients to give informed consent.' Hospital and Community Psychiatry 31:205-206.
Gruenberg, Ernest
1982 'The deinstitutionalization movement.' Pp. 264-287 in Morton O. Wagenfeld, Paul V. Lemkau, and Blair Justice, eds., Public Mental Health: Perspectives and Prospects. Beverly Hills: Sage.
Gunderson, John G.
1977 'Drugs and psychosocial treatment of schizophrenic revisited.' Journal of Continuing Education in Psychiatry, Dec: 25-40.
Gutheil, Thomas G.
1980 'Restraint versus treatment: Seclusion as discussed in the Boston State Hospital case.' American Journal of Psychiatry 137:718-719.
Health Policy Advisory Center
1972 Evaluation of Community Involvement in Community Mental Health Services. Contract HSM 42-70-106 NTIS: PB-211 267.
Heiman, Elliott M.
1980 'CMHC inpatient unit: Private hospital for the poor?' Hospital and Community Psychiatry 31:476-479.
Herbert, Wray
1978a 'Klerman reaches for control of initial peer review.' APA Monitor Vol. 9, No. 4, April:12.
1978b 'Mental health panel calls for new initiatives, much fine tuning.' APA Monitor Vol. 9, No. 5, May:1,5.
1978c 'Kentucky CMHC bankruptcy draws federal attention.' APA Monitor Vol. 9, No. 6, June:1,9.
Hesse, Alice
1976 'Legislative history of the Community Mental Health Centers Act.' Memorandum June 10, 1976, Legislative Services Unit, NIMH.
Hiday, Virginia A.
1977 'The role of counsel in civil commitment: Changes, effects and determinants.' Journal of Psychiatry and Law 5:551-569.
Holland, Thomas P., Andrew Konick, William Buffum, Mieko Kotake Smith, and Marcia Petchers
1981 'Institutional structure and resident outcomes.' Journal of Health and Social Behavior 22:433-444.
Hollingshead, August B. and Frederick C. Redlich
1958 Social Class and Mental Illness. New York: John Wiley & sons.

Holton, Wilfred E., Peter K. New, and Richard M. Hessler
1973 'Citizen participation and conflict.' Administration in Mental Health Fall: 96-103.
Hutson, Ron
1976 'Bridgewater report: Many are wrongly held.' Boston Globe September 6.
Hynes, Charles J.
1977 Private Propriatry Homes for Adults: Their Administration, Management, Control, Operation, Supervision, Funding, and Quality. New York: Deputy Attorney General's Office.
1978 Third Annual Report. New York: Deputy Attorney General's Office.
Illich, Ivan
1976 Medical Nemesis: The Expropriation of Health. New York: Pantheon.
Interstate Clearing House on Mental Health
1956 State Action in Mental Health, 1955. Chicago: Council of State Governments.
1958 State Action in Mental Health, 1956-1957. Chicago: Council of State Governments.
1960 State Action in Mental Health, 1958-1959. Chicago: Council of State Governments.
Isaacs, Mareasa R.
1982 The Use of Nursing Homes as Long-term Care Facilities for the Chronically Mentally Ill. Bethesda, MD: Alpha Center for Health Planning.
Jacobs, Phillip E.
1974 'Whither community mental health?' International Journal of Mental Health Vol. 3, No. 2-3:35-43.
Jansen, David S.
1974 'Personality characteristics of state hospital patients' rights office visitors.' Journal of Clinical Psychology 30:347-349.
Jeste, Dilip V. and Richard J. Wyatt
1981 'Changing epidemiology of tardive dyskinesia: An overview.' American Journal of Psychiatry 138:297-309.
Joint Commission on Mental Illness and Health
1961 Action for Mental Health: Final Report of the Joint Commission on Mental Illness and Health. New York: Basic Books.
Jones, L. Ralph, Richard R. Parlour, and Lee W. Badger
1982 'The inappropriate commitment of the aged.' American Academy of Psychiatry and Law Bulletin 10:
Kahle, Lynn R., Bruce Dennis Sales, and Stuart Nagel
1978 'On unicorns blocking commitment law reform.' Journal of Psychiatry and Law 6:89-105.
Kahle, Lynn R. and Bruce Dennis Sales
1980 'Due process of law and the attitudes of professionals toward involuntary civil commitment.' Pp. 265-292 in Paul D. Lipsitt and Bruce Dennis

Sales, eds., New Directions in Psycholegal Research. New York: Van Nostrand.

Keill, Stuart L.

1981 'The general hospital as the core of the mental health services system.' Hospital and Community Psychiatry 32:776-778.

Kemp, Donna

1978 Civil Liberties of Institutionalized Mentally Retarded: Development and Implementation. Unpublished dissertation, University of Idaho.

Kennedy, J.F.

1963 'Message on mental illness and mental retardation.' Feb. 5, 1963, Congressional Record Vol. 88, No. 1, CIX, Part 2, 1744-1749.

Kennedy, Louanne

1981 'Voluntary compulsions: The transformation of American health institutions, part II.' Health-PAC Bulletin Vol. 12, No. 8, Nov/Dec: 11-18.

Kenniston, Kenneth

1968 'How community mental health stamped out the riots, 1968-78.' Transaction, July-August: 21-29.

Kenniston, Kenneth and Michael Lerner

1970 'The unholy alliance against the campus.' New York Times November 8.

Kiesler, Charles A.

1982a 'Psychology and mental health policy,' in M. Hersen, A.E. Kazdin, and A.S. Bellak, eds., The Clinical Psychology Handbook. New York: Pergamon.

1982b 'Mental hospitals and alternative care: Noninstitutionalization as potential public policy for mental patients.' American Psychologist 37:349-360.

1982c 'Public and professional myths about mental hospitalization: An empirical reassessment of policy-related beliefs.' American Psychologist 37:1329-1339.

Kiesler, Charles, A. and Amy E. Sibulkin

1982 'Episodic length of hospital stay for mental disorders,' in G.M. Stephenson and J.H. Davis, eds., Progress in Applied Social Psychology, Vol. 2.

Kihss, Peter

1982 'Disabled seek welfare after cutoff of U.S. aid.' New York Times May 19.

Kirk, Stuart A. and Mark E. Therrien

1975 'Community mental health myths and the fate of former hospitalized patients.' Psychiatry 38:209-217.

Klein, Dorothy

1974 'A 'think tank' for psychosurgeons: California center awaits go-ahead.' Rough Times January-February 1974.

Koenig, Peter

1978 'The problem that can't be tranquilized.' New York Times Magazine May 21.

Kopolow, Louis E., Alvira Brands, John L. Burton and Frank M. Ochberg
1975 'Litigation and Mental Health Services.' Rockville, MD: NIMH, Mimeo.
Kotelchuck David, ed.
1976 Prognosis Negative: Crisis in the Health Care System. New York: Vintage.
Koumjian, Kevin
1981 'The use of Valium as a form of social control.' Social Science and Medicine 15E:245-249.
Kramer, Kenneth
1974 'The subtle subversion of patients' rights by hospital staff members.' Hospital and Community Psychiatry 25:475-476.
Kramer, Marcia
1977 'The mental home exodus: 50,232 since '68.' New York Daily News July 5.
Kumasaka, Y. and J. Stokes
1972 'Involuntary hospitalization: Opinions and attitudes of psychiatrists and lawyers.' Comprehensive Psychiatry 13:201-208.
Kunnes, Rick
1972 'Radicalism and community mental health.' Pp. 35-49 in Harry Gottesfeld, ed. The Critical Issues of Community Mental Health. New York: Behavioral Publications.
Kupers, Terry
1982 Public Psychiatry. New York: Free Press.
Kurucz, Janos and John Fallon
1980 'Dose reduction and discontinuation of antipsychotic medication.' Hospital and Community Psychiatry 31:117-119.
Lagos, J.M., K. Perlmutter and H. Saexinger
1977 'Fear of the mentally ill: Empirical support for the common man's response.' American Journal of Psychiatry 134:1134-1137.
Laing, R.D.
1959 The Divided Self: An Existential Study in Sanity and Madness. London: Tavistock.
1963 The Self and Others. New York: Pantheon.
1967 The Politics of Experience. New York: Pantheon.
1976 The Facts of Life. New York: Pantheon.
Laing, R.D. and Aaron Esterson
1965 Sanity, Madness, and the Family. New York: Basic.
Lamb, H. Richard
1981a 'What did we really expect from deinstitutionalization?' Hospital and Community Psychiatry 32:105-109.
1981b 'Securing patients' rights — responsibly.' Hospital and Community Psychiatry 32:393-397.
Lamb, H. Richard and Robert W. Grant
1982 'The mentally ill in an urban county jail.' Archives of General Psychiatry 39:17-22.

Lander, Louise
1975 'The mental health con game.' Health/PAC Bulletin No. 65, July/Aug: 1-25.
Landsberg, G. and R. Hammer
1977 'Possible programmatic consequences of community mental health center funding arrangements: Illustrations based on inpatient utilization data.' Community Mental Health Journal 13:63-67.
Lang, Clare
1975 Professional Stratification & Psychiatric Ideology in a Community Mental Health Unit. Unpublished doctoral dissertation, Brandeis University, Waltham, MA.
Laves, Rona and Alan Cohen
1973 'A preliminary investigation into the knowledge of and attitudes toward the legal rights of mental patients.' Journal of Psychiatry and Law 1:49-78.
Leeman, Gavin P.
1980 'Involuntary admissions to general hospitals: Progress or threat?' Hospital and Community Psychiatry 31:315-318.
Leifer, Ronald
1969 In the Name of Mental Health: The Social Functions of Psychiatry. New York: Science House.
Lerman, Paul
1982 Deinstitutionalization and the Welfare State. New Brunswick, NJ: Rutgers University Press.
Levine, Daniel S. and Dianne R. Levine
1975 'The cost of mental illness — 1971.' NIMH Report Series on Mental Health Statistics — Series B No. 7.
Levine, Daniel S. and Shirley G. Willner
1976 'The cost of mental illness — 1974.' NIMH Statistical Note No. 125, Rockville, MD: NIMH.
Levine, Murray
1980 From State Hospital to Psychiatric Center. Lexington MA: Lexington Books.
Liberation News Service
1972a 'Vacaville: Lobotomies, shock therapy, and torture for 'violent' California prisoners.' Rough Times Vol. 2 No. 5, February.
1972b 'Lobotomies and prison revolts.' Rough Times Vol. 2 No. 6, April: 6.
1973a 'Not a prison nor a mental institution.' Rough Times Vol. 3 No. 4, Feb.-Mar: 4.
Light, Donald
1980 Becoming Psychiatrists: The Professional Transformation of Self. New York: Norton.

Lovell, Anne
1978 'From confinement to community: The radical transformation of an Italian mental hospital.' State and Mind Vol. 6, No. 3:7-11.
Lu, Li-chuang
1978 'The collective approach to psychiatric practice in the People's Republic of China.' Social Problems 26:2-14.
Lubove, Roy
1965 The Professional Altruist: The Emergence of Social Work as a Career, 1880-1930. Cambridge: Harvard University Press.
McGuire, Thomas A.
1981 'Financing and demand for mental health services.' Journal of Human Resources XVI:501-522.
MacKenzie, John P.
1975 'Right to liberty proclaimed for thousands of mentally ill.' Washington Post June 27.
Marcos, Luis R. and Rosa M. Gil
1983 'Muddling through mental health policies.' American Journal of Psychiatry 140:853-856.
Marder, Stephen R., Andrew Mebane, Ching-piao Chien, William J. Winslade, Elizabeth Swann, and Theodore Van Putten
1983 'A comparison of patients who refuse and consent to neuroleptic treatment.' American Journal of Psychiatry 140:47-472.
Markoff, Richard A., Brian S. Yano, Jing Hsu, and Debra Hordan Wright
1981 'The mixed medical-psychiatric unit: An alternative approach to inpatient psychiatric care.' Hospital and Community Psychiatry 32:561-564.
Markowitz, Gerald E. and David Karl Rosner
1973 'Doctors in crisis: A study of the use of medical education reform to establish modern professional elitism in medicine.' American Quarterly XXV:83-107.
Markson, Elizabeth and John Cumming
1976 'The posttransfer fate of relocated patients,' Pp. 97-110 in Paul I. Ahmed and Stanley C. Plog (eds.) State Mental Hospitals: What Happens When They Close. New York: Plenum.
Mass. Psych. Wards
1979 'The Boston state suit.' Mass. Psych. Wards Vol. 1, No. 8, November: 1-10.
Massachusetts Department of Mental Health
Annual Reports, Various Years.
1977 'State hospitals budgets FY 1977.' Boston: Massachusetts Department of Mental Health.
Massachusetts Mental Health Planning Project
1974 Community Mental Health and the Mental Hospital. Boston: United Community Planning Services.

Massachusetts Taxpayers Foundation
1980 Purchase of Services: Can State Government Gain Control? Boston: Massachusetts Taxpayers Foundation.
Mazade, Noel A. and John L. Sheets
1975 'Changing roles and structures of mental health boards.' Pp. 123-129 in Jack Zusman and Elmer F. Bertsch, eds., The Future Role of the State Hospital. Lexington, MA: Lexington Books.
Meislin, Richard J.
1977 'New York state panel urges shift of mental health care to counties.' New York Times January 23.
Melick, Mary Evans
1982 'Factors affecting the continued employment of nurses in a state-supported mental health system.' Presented at the Fourth Southeastern Regional Conference of Clincial Specialists in Psychiatric-Mental Health Nursing, Birmingham, Alabama, October 15, 1982.
Mendelson, Mary Adelaide
1975 Tender Loving Greed. New York: Vintage.
Mental Disability Law Reporter
1983a 'Summary and analysis: A discussion of the Reagan administration's budget proposals.' Mental Disability Law Reporter 5:75-78.
1983b 'HHS alters disability review process.' Mental Disability Law Reporter 7:241.
Meyer, Nessa G.
1976 'Provisional patient movement and administrative data: State and county psychiatric inpatient services, July 1, 1974 — June 30, 1975.' NIMH Statistical Note No. 132. Rockville, MD: NIMH.
Mills, Mark J., Jerome A. Yesavage, and Thomas G. Gutheil
1983 'Continuing case law development in the right to refuse treatment.' American Journal of Psychiatry 140:715-719.
Mintz, Morton
1967 By Prescription Only. Boston: Beacon Press.
Monahan, John and Henry J. Steadman
1983 'Crime and mental disorder: An epidemiological approach.' In Nowall Morris and Michael Tonry, eds., Annual Review of Crime and Justice Vol. 4. Chicago, IL: University of Chicago Press.
Moore, Gary A.
1981 'Mental health deinstitutionalization and the regional economy: A model and case study.' Social Science and Medicine 15C:175-189.
Morrissey, Joseph P.
1982 'Deinstitutionalizing the mentally ill: Processes, outcomes, and new directions.' Pp. 147-176 in Walter Gove, ed. Deviance and Mental Illness. Beverly Hills: Sage Publications.

Morrissey, Joseph P., Nancy M. Burton, and Henry J. Steadman

1979 'Developing an empirical base for psycholegal policy analysis of ECT: A New York State survey.' International Journal of Law and Psychiatry 2:99-111.

Morrissey, Joseph P. and Howard Goldman

1980a 'The ambiguous legacy: 1856-1968.' Pp. 45-95 in Joseph P. Morrissey, Howard Goldman and Lorraine V. Klerman, eds., The Enduring Asylum: Cycles of Institutional Reform at Worcester State Hospital. New York: Grune & Stratton.

1980b 'The paradox of institutional reform: Administrative transition with functional stability.' Pp. 247-278 in Joseph P. Morrissey, Howard Goldman and Lorraine V. Klerman, eds., The Enduring Asylum: Cycles of Institutional Reform at Worcester State Hospital. New York: Grune & Stratton.

Morrissey, Joseph P., Howard Goldman, and Lorraine V. Klerman, eds.

1980 The Enduring Asylum: Cycles of Institutional Reform at Worcester State Hospital. New York: Grune & Stratton.

Mosher, Loren R.

1982 'Italy's revolutionary mental health law: An assessment.' American Journal of Psychiatry 139:199-203.

Musto, David

1975 'Whatever happened to 'community mental health'?' The Public Interest No. 39, Spring: 53-79.

Nassi, Alberta J.

1978 'Community control or control of the community? The case of the community mental health center.' Journal of Community Psychology 6:3-15.

National Institute of Mental Health

1972 Psychiatric Services in General Hospitals. NIMH Mental Health Facilities Report Series A, No. 11. Rockville, MD: NIMH.

1975 Research in the Service of Mental Health. DHEW Publication No. 75-237. Rockville, MD: NIMH.

1976 'The financing, utilization and quality of mental health care in the United States — draft report.' Office of Program Development and Analysis, April 1976. Rockville, MD: NIMH.

1977a 'Implementation plans for the community support program.' April 11, 1977, unpublished memo. Rockville, MD: NIMH.

1977b '1973 survey of 15,737 nursing care homes and personal care homes with nursing.' Memo. Rockville, MD: NIMH.

1977c March 1977 revision of 'The CMHC Program.' Rockville, MD: NIMH.

1977d 'Provisional data on federally funded community mental health centers 1975-1976.' Mimeo. Rockville, MD: NIMH.

1978 'Provisional data on federally funded community mental health centers, 1976-1977.' Rockville, MD: NIMH.

1980 Toward a National Plan for the Chronically Mentally Ill Washington, D.C.: Government Printing Office.

1982a 'Total expenditures in constant dollars (1969), percent distribution, and rate per capita by type of mental health facility: United States, selected years 1969-1979.' Unpublished data. Rockville, MD: NIMH.

1982b 'Number and percent distribution of mental health facilities by type of facility: United States, selected years 1970-1980.' Unpublished data: Rockville, MD:NIMH.

1982c 'Number of inpatients additions, percent distribution, and rate per 100,000 civilian population, by type of mental health facility; United States, selected years 1969-1979.' Unpublished data. Rockville, MD: NIMH.

1982d 'Number of resident patients, total admissions, net releases, and deaths, in state and county mental hospitals: United States, 1950-1980.' Unpublished data: Rockville, MD: NIMH.

Navarro, Vicente

1976 Medicine Under Capitalism. New York: Prodist.

Newsday

1982 'Disability cutbacks criticized.' Newsday January 22.

New York Times

1980 'Drugged man's release is laid to overcrowding.' New York Times. December 8.

1982 'Judge orders benefits restored to mentally ill.' New York Times December 25.

Nunnally, Jum

1961 Popular Conceptions of Mental Health. New York: Holt, Rinehart and Winston.

Okin, Robert L.

1978 'The future of state mental health programs for the chronic psychiatric patients in the community.' American Journal of Psychiatry 135:1355-1358.

Paige, Constance

1972a 'Shock therapy: Pacification program. Boston Phoenix December 5.

1972b 'Board up Bournewood, Mr. Kaplan.' Boston Phoenix December 19.

Pasamanick, Benjamin, Frank Scarpitti, and Simon Dinitz

1967 Schizophrenics in the Community. New York: Appleton-Century Crofts.

Paschall, Nancy and Anita Eichler

1982 'Rights promotion in the 1980's.' Mental Disability Law Reporter 6:116-121.

Paschall, Nancy, Andrew J. Konick, and Susan Ostrander

1983 'Institutional advocacy: Impact one year after legislative change.' Administration in Mental Health.

Pear, Robert

1982a 'Fairness of Reagan's cutoffs of disability aid questioned.' New York Times May 9.

1982b 'Nursing home plan draws opposition.' New York Times June 13.

1982c 'U.S. fund cuts reduce nursing home checkups.' New York Times March 5.

Perrow, Charles

1963 'Goals and power structures: A historical case study,' Pp. 112-146 in Eliot Freidson, ed., The Hospital in Modern Society. New York: Free Press.

1965 'Hospitals: Technology, structure, and goals.' Pp. 910-971 in James March, ed., Handbook of Organizations. Chicago: Rand-McNally.

1979 Complex Organizations: A Critical Essay. Glenview, IL: Scott, Foresman.

Perrucci, Robert

1974 Circle of Madness: On Being Insane and Institutionalized in America. Englewood Cliffs, NJ: Prentice-Hall.

Perry, Steven R.

1982 'The measurement of attitudes toward the rights of psychiatric patients.' Pp. 227-245 in Bernard L. Bloom and Shirley J. Asher, eds., Psychiatric Patient Rights and Patient Advocacy: Issues and Evidence. New York: Human Sciences Press.

Peszke, Michael A. and Ronald M. Wintrob

1974 'Emergency commitment — a transcultural study.' American Journal of Psychiatry 131:36-40.

Pinto, Rodger and Alan Fiester

1979 'Governing board and management staff attitudes toward community mental health center participation.' Community Mental Health Journal 15:259-266.

Piven, Frances Fox and Richard A. Cloward

1971 Regulating the Poor: The Functions of Public Welfare. New York: Random House.

President's Commission on Mental Health

1978 Report to the President. Washington, D.C.: U.S. Government Printing Office.

Price, Trevor, R.P. and Robert Levin

1978 'The effects of electroconvulsive therapy on tardive dyskinesia.' American Journal of Psychiatry 135:991-993.

Public Works Administration

1939 America Builds: The Record of PWA. Washington, D.C.: Government Printing Office.

Rabkin, Judith G.

1980 'Determinants of public attitudes about mental illness: summary of the research literature'. Pp. 15-26 in Judith G. Rabkin, Lenore Gelb, and Joyce B. Lazar eds. Attitudes Toward the Mentally Ill: Research Prespectives. Rockville, MD: National Institute of Mental Health.

Rabkin, Judith G. and Arthur Zitrin
1982 'Antisocial behavior of discharged mental patients: Research findings and policy implications.' Pp. 148-170 in Bernard L. Bloom and Shirley J. Asher, eds. Psychiatric Patient Rights and Patient Advocacy: Issues and Evidence. New York: Human Sciences Press.
Rachlin, Stephen, Alvin Pam, and Janet Milton
1975 'Civil liberties versus involuntary hospitalization.' American Journal of Psychiatry 132:189-191.
Ramon, Shulamit
1983 'Psichiatria Democratica: A case study of an Italian community mental health service.' International Journal of Health Services 13: 307-324.
Rappeport, Jonas R. and George Lassen
1965 'Dangerousness — arrest rate comparisons of discharged patients and the general population.' American Journal of Psychiatry 121:776-783.
1966 'The dangerousness of female patients: a comparison of the arrest rate of discharged psychiatric patients and the general population.' American Journal of Psychiatry 123 4:413-419.
Ray, Wayne A., Charles Federspiel, and William Schaffner
1980 'A study of antipsychotic drug use in nursing homes: Epidemiological evidence suggesting misuse.' American Journal of Public Health 70:485-491.
Redlich, Fritz and Stephen R. Kellert
1978 'Trends in American mental health.' American Journal of Psychiatry 135:22-28.
Regier, Darrel A., Irving D. Goldberg, and Carl A. Taube
1978 'The de facto U.S. mental health services system.' Archives of General Psychiatry 35:685-693.
Rich, Spencer
1976 'Minks, art, hi-fi billed to Medicaid.' Washington Post December 18.
Rickels, Darl, W. George Case, Robert W. Downing, and Andrew Winokur
1983 'Long-term diazepam therapy and clinical outcome.' Journal of the American Medical Association 250:767-771.
Ridenour, Nina
1961 Mental Health in the United States: A Fifty-year History. Cambridge, MA: Harvard University Press.
Rieman, Dwight W.
1982 'Changing practices in personnel preparation and usage,' Pp. 162-194 in Morton O. Wagenfeld, Paul V. Lemkau, and Blair Justice, eds., Public Mental Health: Perspectives and Prospects. Beverly Hills, CA: Sage.
Riessman, Frank
1978 'The President's Commission on Mental Health: The self-help prospect.' Social Policy 9 (1):28-31.

Roberts, Barbara
1972 'Psychosurgery: The final solution to the 'woman problems'.' The Second Wave Vol. 2, No. 1.
Roche Laboratories
1982 'Letter to Doctors' March 1. Nutley, New Jersey.

Rose, Stephen M.
1982 'Deinstitutionalization: Problems and suggestions.' Testimony prepared for the U.S. House of Representatives, Committee on the District of Columbia.
Rosen, George
1968 Madness in Society: Chapters in the Historical Sociology of Mental Illness. New York: Harper.
Rosenblatt, Aaron and John E. Mayer
1974 'The recidivism of mental patients: A review of past studies.' American Journal of Orthopsychiatry 44: 697-706.
Rosenhan, David L.
1973 'On being sane in insane places.' Science 179: 250-258.
Rotegard, Gail
1979 'Mental health needs of those in nursing homes: An assessment in one state.' May 1979, HHS Region I, mimeo. Boston: HHS.
Rothman, David
1971 The Discovery of the Asylum: Social Order and Disorder in the New Republic. Boston: Little-Brown.
1980 Conscience and Convenience: The Asylum and its Alternatives in Progressive America. Boston: Little-Brown.
Rough Times
1973a 'Wisconsin federal district court rules on patients rights.' Rough Times Vol. 3 No. 3, Feb-Mar: 14.
1973b 'Prisoners describe mind control programs.' Rough Times Vol. 3 No. 6 Nov-Dec: 4.
Rubin, Jeffrey
1978 Economics, Mental Health, and the Law. Lexington, MA: D.C. Heath.
Rumer, Richard
1978 'Community mental health centers: Politics and therapy.' Journal of Health Policy, Politics, and Law 2:531-559.
Ruzek, Cheryl
1978 The Women's Health Movement: Feminist Alternatives to Medical Control. New York: Praeger.
Ryan, William
1972 Blaming the Victim. New York: Vintage.
Sacramento Bee
1976 'Veto of hospital staff bill called tragic.' Sacramento Bee, Sept. 30.

Santiestevan, Henry
1976 'Deinstitutionalization: Out of their beds and into the streets.' Washington, D.C.: American Federation of State, County & Municipal Employees.

Schatzman, Morton
1973 Soul Murder: Persecution in the Family. New York: Random House.

Scheff, Thomas J.
1966 Being Mentally Ill: A Sociological Theory. Chicago: Aldine.
1975 ed. Labeling Madness. Englewood Cliffs, NJ: Prentice-Hall.
1976 'Medical dominance: Psychoactive drugs and mental health policy.' American Behavioral Scientist 19:299-317.

Scheper-Hughes, Nancy
1981 'Dilemmas in deinstitutionalization: A view from inner city Boston.' Journal of Operational Psychiatry 12:90-99.

Schlesinger, Herbert J., Emily Mumford, Gene V. Glass, Cathleen Patrick, and Steven Sharfstein
1983 'Mental health treatment and medical care utilization in a fee-for-service system: Outpatient mental health treatment following the onset of a chronic disease.' American Journal of Public Health 73:422-429.

Schmidt, Leonard T., Adina M. Reinhardt, Robert L. Kane, and Donna M. Olsen
1977 'The mentally ill in nursing homes: New back wards in the community.' Archives of General Psychiatry 34:6.

Schulberg, Herbert C. and Frank Baker
1975 The Mental Hospital and Human Services. New York: Behavioral Publications.

Schwartz, Stephen
1981 Comments at 1981 conference of Massachusetts Mental Health Association. Boston, MA.

Scull, Andrew T.
1976 'The decarceration of the mentally ill: A critical view.' Politics & Society 6: 173-212.
1977a 'Madness and segregative control: The rise of the insane asylum.' Social Problems 24:337-351.
1977b Decarceration — Community Treatment and the Deviant: A Radical View. Englewood Cliffs, NJ: Prentice-Hall.
1981a ed., Madhouses, Mad-doctors, and Madmen: The Social History of Psychiatry in the Victoria Era. Philadelphia: University of Pennsylvania Press.
1981b 'A new trade in lunacy: The recommodification of the mental patient.' American Behavioral Scientist 24:741-754.

Segal, Steven P. and Uri Aviram
1978 The Mentally Ill in Community-Based Sheltered Care: A Study of Community Care and Social Integration. New York: Wiley.

Sehdev, Harcharan S.
1976 'Patients' rights or patients' neglect: The impact of the patients' rights movement on delivery systems.' American Journal of Orthopsychiatry 46:660-668.

Shadish, William R., and Richard R. Bootzin
1981 'Nursing homes and chronic mental patients.' Schizophrenia Bulletin 7:488-498.

Shadish, William R. Jr., Robert B. Straw, A. John McSweeny, Dianne L. Koller, and Richard R. Bootzin
1981 'Nursing home care for mental patients: Descriptive data and some propositions.' American Journal of Community Psychology 9:617-632.

Sharfstein, Steven S.
1978 'Third-party payers: To pay or not to pay.' American Journal of Psychiatry 135:1185-1188.

Shipp, E.R.
1982 'Suit on homeless mental patients asks New York State for housing.' New York Times May 21.

Short, C.W. and R. Stanley Brown
1939 Public Buildings: A Survey of Architecture of Projects Constructed by Federal and Other Governmental Bodies Between the Years 1933 and 1939 with the Assistance of the Public Works Administration. Washington, D.C.: Government Printing Office.

Shwed, Harvey
1980 'Social policy and the rights of the mentally ill: Time for re-examination.' Journal of Health Politics, Policy, and Law 2:193-198.

Sidel, Victor W. and Ruth Sidel
1974 Serve the People: Observations on Medicine in the People's Republic of China. Boston: Beacon.

Siegal, Harvey
1978 Outposts of the Forgotten: Socially Terminal People in Slum Hotels and Single-Room Occupancies. New Brunswick, N.J.: Transaction Books.

Smith, Christopher J. and Robert Q. Hanham
1981 'Deinstitutionalization of the mentally ill: A time path analysis of the American states, 1955-1975.' Social Science and Medicine 150:361-381.

Smith, M., L. Kucharski, and C. Eblen
1979 'Tardive dyskinesia in schizophrenic outpatients.' Psychopharmacology 64:99-104.

Sosowsky, Larry
1978 'Crime and violence among mental patients reconsidered in view of the new legal relationship between the state and the mentally ill.' American Journal of Psychiatry 135:33-42.

Spiegelman, Richard
1977 'Prison psychiatrists and drugs: A case study.' Crime and Social Justice Spring-Summer 7:23-39.
Spitzer, Stephen
1975 'Toward a Marxian theory of deviance.' Social Problems 22:638-651.
Srole, Leo, Thomas S. Langner, Stanley T. Michael, Price Kirkpatrick, Marvin K. Opler, and Thomas A.C. Rennie
1962 Mental Health in the Metropolis. New York: McGraw-Hill.
Stanton, Alfred H. and Morris S. Schwartz
1954 The Mental Hospital. New York: Basic Books.
Starr, Paul
1983 The Social Transformation of American Medicine. New York: Basic Books.
Steadman, Henry J.
1980 'The right not to be a false positive: Problems in the application of the dangerousness standard.' Psychiatric Quarterly 52:84-99.
1981 'Critically reassessing the accuracy of public perceptions of the dangerousness of the mentally ill.' Journal of Health and Social Behavior 22:310-316.
Steadman, Henry J. and Alexander Brooks
1977 A Program for Mental Health Advocacy Services for Pennsylvania. Albany, New York: New York State Department of Mental Hygiene.
Steadman, Henry J., Joseph J. Cocozza, and Mary Evans Melick
1978 'Explaining the increased arrest rate among mental patients: The changing clientele of state hospitals.' American Journal of Psychiatry 135:816-820.
Steadman, Henry J., Donna Vanderwyst, and Stephen Ribner
1978 'Comparing arrest rates of mental patients and criminal offenders.' American Journal of Psychiatry 135:1218-1220.
Steadman, Henry J. and Stephen A. Ribner
1980 'Changing perceptions of the mental health needs of inmates in local jails.' American Journal of Psychiatry 137:1115-1116.
1982 'Life stress and violence among ex-mental patients.' Social Science and Medicine 16:1641-1647.
Steadman, Henry J., John Monahan, Barbara Duffee, Eliot Hartstone, and Pamela Clark Robbins
1983 'The impact of mental hospital deinstitutionalization on United States prison populations, 1968-1978.' Psychiatric Opinion Quarterly, forthcoming.
Stein, Leonard I. and Mary Ann Test
1980 'Alternatives to mental hospital treatment: I. Conceptual model, treatment program, and clinical evaluation.' Archives of General Psychiatry 37:392-405.

Sterling, Peter
1976 'Comments on ECT. Prepared as testimony for the plaintiff in Rice v. Nardini.' Philadelphia: University of Pennsylvania School of Medicine.
Stone, Alan A.
1975 'Overview: The right to treatment — comments on the law and its impact.' American Journal of Psychiatry 132:1125-1134.
Stotsky, Bernard A.
1969 Psychiatric Patients in Nursing Homes. Rockville, MD: NIMH report.
Strauss, Anselm, Leonard Schatzman, Rue Bucher, Danuta Ehrlich, and Melvin Sabshin
1963 'The hospital and its negotiated order,' Pp. 147-169 in Eliot Freidson, ed., The Hospital in Modern Society. New York: Free Press.
1964 Psychiatric Ideologies and Institutions. New York: Free Press.
Suchotliff, Leonard C., George J. Steinfeld, & Gerald Tolchin
1970 'The struggle for patients' rights in a state hospital.' Mental Hygiene 54:230-240.
Sullivan, Ronald
1977 'Hospitals to change mental-care policy.' New York Times November 15.
Swank, Glenn E. and Darryl Winer
1976 'Occurence of psychiatric disorder in a county jail population.' American Journal of Psychiatry 133:1331-1333.
Swenson, Norma, Phyllis Cater, Val D. MacMurray, Perry Cunningham, and Seymour Bellin
1975 'Technology of evaluation by outsiders.' Presentation at American Psychological Association Meeting, Chicago.
Szasz, Thomas
1961 The Myth of Mental Illness. New York: Hoeber.
1970 The Manufacture of Madness: A Comparative Study of the Inquisition and the Mental Health Movement. New York: Dell.
Talbott, John A.
1979 'Why psychiatrists leave the public sector.' Hospital and Community Psychiatry 30:778-782.
Tancredi, Laurence R.
1980 'The rights of mental patients: Weighing the interests.' Journal of Health Politics, Policy, and Law 5:199-204.
Tancredi, Laurence R. and David Clark
1972 'Psychiatry and the legal rights of patients.' American Journal of Psychiatry 129:328-330.
Task Force on Community Mental Health Program Components
1975 Developing Community Mental Health Programs: A Resource Manual. Boston: United Community Planning Corporation.

Taube, Carl A.
1974 'Readmissions to inpatients services of state & county mental hospitals 1972.' NIMH Statistical Note No. 110. Rockville, MD: NIMH.
Taube, Carl A., and Richard W. Redick
1975 'Recent trends in the utilization of mental health facilities.' Pp. 319-354 in Jack Zusman and Elmer F. Bertsch, eds., The Future Role of the State Hospital. Lexington, MA: Lexington Books.
Temerlin, Maurice K.
1968 'Suggestion effects in psychiatric diagnosis.' Journal of Nervous and Mental Disease 147:349-358.
Test, Mary Ann and Leonard I. Stein
1980 'Alternative to mental hospital treatment: III. Social cost.' Archives of General Psychiatry 37:409-412.
This Month in Mental Health
1982 'SSI Cuts.' This Month in Mental Health September Vol. 5 No. 5:1.
Thomas, Alexander and Samuel Sillen
1972 Racism and Psychiatry. New York: Brunner/Mazel.
Thompson, James W., Armand Checker, Michael J. Witkin, Morton M. Silverman, and Howard Goldman
1983 'The decline of state mental hospitals as training sites for psychiatric residents.' American Journal of Psychiatry 140:704-707.
Tringo, J.
1970 'The hierarchy of preference toward disability groups.' Journal of Special Education 4:295-306.
United Press International
1977 'HEW to probe spending frauds.' Boston Globe, February 27.
United States Senate Subcommittee on Long-Term Care
1975 Drugs in Nursing Homes: Misuse, High Costs, and Kickbacks. Supporting Paper No. 2 of series 'Nursing home care in the United States: Failure in public policy.' Washington D.C.: Government Printing Office.
1976 The Role of Nursing Homes in Caring for Discharged Mental Patients (And the Birth of a For-Profit Boarding Home Industry). Supporting Paper No. 7 of series 'Nursing home care in the United States: Failure in public policy.' Washington, D.C.: Government Printing Office.
United States Senate Committe on Labor and Human Resources
1980 Report on the Mental Health Systems Act. Washington, D.C.: Government Printing Office.
Vladek, Bruce C.
1980 Unloving Care: The Nursing Home Tragedy. New York: Basic Books.
Wagenfeld, Morton O. and Judith H. Jacobs
1982 'The community mental health movement: Its origins and growth.' Pp. 46-48 in Morton O. Wagenfeld, Paul V. Lemkau and Blair Justice, eds., Public Mental Health Perspectives and Prospects. Beverly Hills: Sage.

Wald, Matthew, L.
1983 'West Side neighbors try to save S.R.O. hotel.' New York Times January 13.
Wald, Patricia M. and Paul R. Friedman
1979 'The politics of mental health advocacy in the United States,' in Paul R. Friedman, ed., Legal Rights of Mentally Disabled Persons. New York: Practicing Law Institute.
Waldron, Ingrid
1977 'Increased prescribing of Valium, Librium, and other drugs — an example of the influence of economic and social factors in the practice of medicine.' International Journal of Health Services 7:37-61.
Warren, Carol A.B.
1981 'New forms of social control: The myth of deinstitutionalization.' American Behavioral Scientist 24:724-740.
Weiner, Samuel, Barbara J. Bird and Arthur Bolton Associates
1973 Process and Impacts of the Closing of De Witt State Hospital. Menlo Park: Stanford Research Institute.
Weiner, Barbara A.
1982 'Supreme court decisions on mental health: A review.' Hospital and Community Psychiatry 33:461-464.
Weinstein, Abbott S.
1983 'The mythical readmission explosion.' American Journal of Psychiatry 140:332-335.
Weinstein, Raymond M.
1981 'Attitudes toward psychiatric treatment among hospitalized patients: a review of quantitative research.' Social Science and Medicine 15E:301-314.
Weisbrod, Burton A., Mary Ann Test, and Leonard I. Stein
1980 'Alternative to mental hospital treatment: II. Economic benefit-cost analysis.' Archives of General Psychiatry 37:400-405.
Weisstein, Naomi
1972 'Psychology constructs the female,' Pp. 390-420 in Phil Brown, ed., Radical Psychology. New York: Harper & Row.
Wenger, D.L. and C.R. Fletcher
1969 'The effects of legal counsel on admissions to a state mental hospital: A confrontation of professions.' Journal of Health and Social Behavior 10:66-72.
Wertz, Richard W. and Dorothy C. Wertz
1977 Lying-In: A History of Childbirth in America. New York: Schocken.
Wilson, Glenn, Cecil G. Sheps, and Thomas R. Oliver
1982 'Effects of hospital revenue bonds on hospital planning and operations.' New England Journal of Medicine, Dec. 2. 507:1426 1430.
Windle, Charles, Rosalyn D. Bass, and Carl A. Taube
1974 'PR aside: Initial results from NIMH's service program evaluation studies.' American Journal of Community Psychology 2:311-327.

Witkin, Michael J.
1977 'Psychiatric service modes in non-federal general hospitals, United States 1973-74.' NIMH Mental Health Facility Reports Service A, No. 19. Rockville, MD: NIMH.
1980 'Trends in patient care episodes in mental health facilities, 1955-1977.' NIMH Statistical Note No. 154. Rockville, MD: NIMH.
1981a 'Provisional patient movement & selective administrative data, state and county mental hospitals, by state: United States, 1977'. NIMH Statistical Note No. 156. Rockville, MD: NIMH.
1981b 'Changes in numbers of additions to mental health facilities, by modality, United States, 1971, 1975, and 1977'. NIMH Statistical Note No. 157. Rockville, MD: NIMH.
1981c 'State and Regional Distribution of Psychiatric Beds in 1978.' NIMH Statistical Note No. 155, Rockville, MD: NIMH.

Woolhandler, Stephanie, David U. Himmelstein, Ralph Silber, Martha Harnly, Michael Bader, and Alice A. Jones
1984 'Public money, private control: A case study of hospital financing in Oakland and Berkeley, California.' American Journal of Public Health, forthcoming.

Yett, Donald E. and Daniel S. Levine
1972 'The cost of mental illness 1969, 1975, 1980, & 1985.' Draft final report under contract to NIMH, HSM 42-71-91. Los Angles — University of Southern California.

Yolles, Stanley F.
1975 'Community Psychiatry:1963-1974.' Paper presented April 25, 1975 at Missouri Institute of Psychiatry Research Seminar, University of Missouri School of Medicine, St. Louis, 24pp.

Zitrin, Arthur, Anne S. Hardesty, Eugene I. Burdock, and Ann K. Drossman
1976 'Crime and violence among mental patients.' American Journal of Psychiatry 133:142-149.

Zola, Irving K.
1972 'Medicine as an institution of social control.' Sociological Review 20:487-504.

Zusman, Jack
1972 'The catchment area concept.' Pp. 2032 in Allen Beigel and Alan I. Levenson, eds., The Community Mental Health Center. New York: Basic.

Zusman, Jack and Elmer F. Bertsch, eds.
1975 The Future Role of the State Hospital. Lexington, MA: Lexington Books.

Name Index

Subject Index